Two-Way

Two-Way Mirror Power

Selected Writings by Dan Graham on His Art

edited by Alexander Alberro

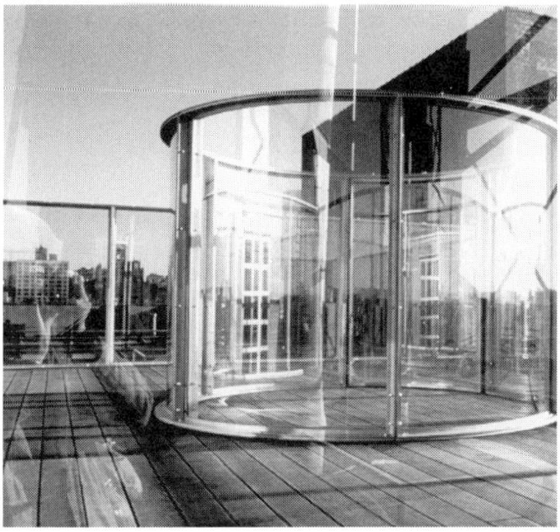

The MIT Press
Cambridge, Massachusetts
London, England
Published in association with the Marian Goodman Gallery, New York

This book was set in Didot and Univers by Graphic Composition, Inc. and was printed and bound in the United States of America.

Library of Congress Cataloging-in-Publication Data

Graham, Dan, 1942–
Two-way mirror power : selected writings by Dan Graham on his art / edited by Alexander Alberro.
p. cm.
Includes bibliographical references.
ISBN 0-262-07197-5 (hc : alk. paper); 0-262-57130-7 (pbk. : alk. paper)
1. Graham, Dan, 1942– —Themes, motives. I. Alberro, Alexander. II. Title.
NX512.Z9G73 1999
700—dc21 99-25413
CIP

Contents

List of Illustrations vii

Preface ix

Introduction: Partially Reflective Mirror Writing x
Jeff Wall

I. Dan Graham 1
1 The Artist as Producer (1978–1988)

II. Magazine Pages 10
10 My Works for Magazine Pages: "A History of Conceptual Art" (1985)
18 Legacies of Critical Practice in the 1980s: Dan Graham (1986)
21 Legacies of Critical Practice in the 1980s: Discussion (1986)

III. Video/Television/Architecture 38
38 Two Consciousness Projection(s) (1972)
39 Present Continuous Past(s) (1974)
42 Yesterday/Today (1975)
42 Notes on *Yesterday/Today* (1975)
46 Video Piece for Two Glass Office Buildings (1976)
47 Video Piece for Showcase Windows in a Shopping Arcade (1976)
48 Notes on *Video Piece for Showcase Windows in a Shopping Arcade* (1976)
49 Production/Reception (Piece for Two Cable TV Channels) (1976)
52 Essay on Video, Architecture, and Television (1979)
62 Dan Graham Interviewed by Ludger Gerdes (1991)

IV. Films 84
84 Film and Performance/Six Films, 1969–1974 (1976)
94 Cinema (1981)
96 Dan Graham Interviewed by Eric de Bruyn (1997)

V. Performance 121

121 Lax/Relax (1969)
122 Past Future/Split Attention (1972)
124 Performer/Audience/Mirror (1977)
135 Musical Performance and Stage-Set Utilizing Two-Way Mirror and Time-Delay (1983)
136 Stage-Set for *Guaire* (1985)
137 Theater-Cinema (1986)
142 Performance: End of the '60s (1989)
144 Dan Graham in Conversation with Brian Hatton (1992)

VI. Pavilion Sculptures 155

155 Notes on *Public Space/Two Audiences* (1978)
159 Alteration to a Suburban House (1978)
163 Pavilion/Sculpture for Argonne (1978–1981)
165 Two-Way Mirror Cylinder Inside Cube and Video Salon: Rooftop Park for Dia Center for the Arts (1991)
167 A Guide to *The Children's Pavilion,* a Collaborative Project by Jeff Wall and Dan Graham (1989)
172 Heart Pavilion (1991)
174 Two-Way Mirror Power (1996)
176 Two-Way Mirror Bridge and Triangular Pavilion to Existing Mill House for Domaine de Kerguehennec (1987)
178 Three Linked Cubes/Interior Design for Space for Showing Videos (1986)
179 Two-Way Mirror and Hedge Labyrinth (1989–1991)
179 Skateboard Pavilion (1989)
180 "Star of David" Glass Pavilion for Schloss Buchburg (1996)
182 Yin/Yang (1998)
183 Dan Graham Interviewed by Mike Metz (1994)

List of Illustrations

1.
Dan Graham
Side Effects/Common Drugs, 1966
page xx

2.
Dan Graham
Schema (March 1966) 1966
page 14

3.
Dan Graham
Schema (March 1966),
1966 (variant 1967)
page 15

4.
Dan Graham
Schema (March 1966),
1966 (variant 1969)
page 16

5.
Dan Graham
Schema (March 1966),
1966 (variant 1972)
page 17

6.
Dan Graham
Two Consciousness Projections, 1972
page 38

7.
Dan Graham
Present Continuous Past(s), 1974
page 39

8.
Dan Graham
Present Continuous Past(s), 1974
page 40

9.
Dan Graham
Opposing Mirrors and Video Monitors on Time Delay, 1974
page 41

10.
Dan Graham
Yesterday/Today, 1975
page 43

11.
Dan Graham
Video Piece for Two Glass Office Buildings,
1974–1976
page 46

12.
Dan Graham
Video Piece for Two Glass Office Buildings, 1974
page 46

13.
Dan Graham
Video Piece for Showcase Windows in a Shopping Arcade, 1976
page 48

14.
Dan Graham
Projection/Reception, 1976
page 51

15.
Dan Graham
Projection/Reception, 1976
page 51

16.
Dan Graham
Projection/Reception, 1976
page 51

17.
Dan Graham
Two Correlated Relations, 1969
page 86

18.
Dan Graham
Roll, 1970
page 88

19.
Dan Graham
Roll, 1970
page 88

20.
Dan Graham
Body Press, 1970–1972
page 90

21.
Dan Graham
Binocular Zoom, 1969
page 91

22.
Dan Graham
Helix/Spiral, 1973
page 92

23.
Dan Graham
Cinema, 1981
page 94

24.
Dan Graham
Cinema, 1981
page 94

25.
Dan Graham
Past Future/Split Attention, 1972
page 123

26.
Dan Graham
Performer/Audience/Mirror, 1977
page 124

27.
Glenn Branca and Dan Graham,
Musical Performance and Stage-Set, 1985
page 136

28.
James Coleman and Dan Graham
Guaire, 1986
page 137

29.
Dan Graham
Design for *Theater-Cinema,* 1986
page 141

30.
Dan Graham
Theater-Cinema, 1986
page 141

31.
Dan Graham
Public Space/Two Audiences, 1976
page 155

32.
Dan Graham
Public Space/Two Audiences, 1976
page 156

33.
Dan Graham
Alteration to a Suburban House, 1978
page 159

34.
Dan Graham
Alteration to a Suburban House, 1978
page 160

35.
Dan Graham
Pavilion/Sculpture for Argonne, 1978–1981
page 163

36.
Dan Graham
Two-Way Mirror Cylinder Inside Cube, 1989
page 165

37.
Jeff Wall and Dan Graham
The Children's Pavilion, 1989
page 167

38.
Jeff Wall and Dan Graham
The Children's Pavilion, 1989
page 168

39.
Dan Graham
Heart Pavilion, 1991
page 173

40.
Dan Graham
Two Adjacent Pavilions, 1978–1981
page 174

41.
Dan Graham
Two Adjacent Pavilions, 1978–1981
page 175

42.
Dan Graham
Two-Way Mirror Bridge and Triangular Pavilion to Existing Mill House for Domaine de Kerguehennec, 1987
page 176

43.
Dan Graham
Three Linked Cubes/Interior Design for Space for Showing Videos, 1986
page 178

44.
Dan Graham
Two-Way Mirror and Hedge Labyrinth, 1989–1991
page 179

45.
Dan Graham
Skateboard Pavilion, 1989
page 180

46.
Dan Graham
"Star of David" Glass Pavilion for Schloss Buchburg, 1988–1996
page 181

47.
Dan Graham
Yin/Yang, 1997–1998
page 182

48.
Dan Graham
Yin/Yang, 1997–1998
page 182

Preface

A word of explanation about this second volume of critical writings by Dan Graham published by the MIT Press: six of the texts included here have already been published in *Rock My Religion: Writings and Art Projects 1965–1990/Dan Graham,* edited by Brian Wallis (1993). However, four of them were published there as extracts; we present them here in their entirety. To omit them from this collection would be to distort its structure, particularly with regard to part V, "Performance." The absence of the second and third texts in that group—"Past Future/Split Attention" and "Performer/Audience/Mirror"—would be troublesome, for they articulate a method of working that governs Graham's subsequent writings. And "My Works for Magazine Pages: 'A History of Conceptual Art'" is indubitably one of Graham's most important writings, informing the reader of the conditions that led to the emergence of his activities in the art world.

I want to thank Jeff Wall for writing an introduction at once informative and provocative. Thanks as well are due to the four writers whose interviews with Graham are reprinted here: Ludger Gerdes, Eric de Bruyn, Brian Hatton, and Mike Metz; and to Lora Rempel, Matthew Abbate, and Carolyn Anderson for copyediting the bulk of the manuscript. Finally, I would like to thank the MIT Press (and more specifically Roger Conover) and Marian Goodman, whose belief in this project made it a real possibility.

Alexander Alberro

Introduction: Partially Reflective Mirror Writing

Jeff Wall

Dan Graham is or has been a sculptor and a photographer, an essayist and a performer, an architect, a curator, a gallerist, a teacher, and an archivist. In the early 1960s, he came into the visual arts from an interest in writing, and, as is by now well known, fell in with a group of young artists who were also involved in making some new alliances between word and image, word and thing: Sol LeWitt, Lawrence Weiner, Robert Smithson, among others. He began writing and taking photographs and, in the spirit of conceptual art, proposed that at least some of the writing be considered works of art. He has never gone so far as to claim that his photographs are works of art.

The idea that a written essay or commentary could be validly considered as an art object the way a painting or a sculpture had been is now part of the lore of the sixties. This idea has been ignored, dismissed, studied, and researched, and has become a kind of falsehood that will not disappear. The claim thus constitutes a moment of unknowability, in which the logic of art appears to reinvert itself. We think we know, without really having to prove it, that a written essay cannot, as Art & Language termed it, "come up for the count" as a work of art, even a work of art like a readymade. Essays are about art objects; therefore, they cannot be art objects. But an art object can be "about" its own status as an art object, so why can we not accept the fact that the written text as art object just makes all that perfectly explicit?

And so the argument goes on. The experimental claim made in conceptual art can neither be proved nor disproved. Rather, it has the status of a vanishing point in the logic of aesthetics, a vanishing point that may have, in fact, vanished, since it is hardly taken seriously anymore, but nevertheless informs the whole spectrum of contemporary practices in which virtually anything—any thing, gesture, event, or action—can be and is considered to be an art object (for example, Vanessa Beecroft's performances or Damien Hirst's shark in a tank of formaldehyde).

There is a relationship between the conceptual "degree zero" of the essay-about-its-own-status-as-an-art-object-as-art-object and the juggernaut of total artistic liberty that has characterized the past thirty years. Duchamp invented this liberty, of course, but, because he did not care to explain himself, left implicit the logical problem he raised. The movement from implicitness to explicitness was therefore placed on the historical agenda, and the generation that made conceptual art confronted the question, giving what seems to be a definitive answer. The content of that answer, that there is no logical or theoretical barrier to making the claim that a written text on the subject here at hand can and even must be considered an art object, showed that Duchamp's readymades were not special readymades. Indeed, in the words of the French artist-group Readymades Belong to Everyone, readymades could be made and remade by any artist because there was no means to invalidate the repetition of the practice of making something that evoked, more or less explicitly, art's dubious, unprovable logical status. This "could," this implicit liberty, has become a "should," a "must," a kind of categorical imperative, one that it seems less and less easy for any artist to avoid.

In the thirty years since Donald Judd championed art that had the "look of non-art," almost all new art has taken on that appearance, so much so that the "look of art"—lush oil paintings or bronze sculptures—now almost has the look of non-art. Dan Graham is one of those who took most seriously the look-of-non-art approach. This was, in part, natural for him, since what he was making was, in the terms of the time, not art, but journalism, poetry, criticism, or photography. He was therefore one of those who abandoned the older aesthetics of representation and the slightly less old one of expression. Along with Bruce Nauman, Gordon Matta-Clark, Weiner, Smithson, Mel Bochner, Joseph Kosuth, and others, he experienced and helped to instigate the freedom from the aesthetic that opened so many doors in the sixties.

This freedom—to make things as art that did not resemble art—was animated by the desire to have art draw itself closer to everyday experience. The contradiction here was that everyday experience had, for centuries, included the experience of works of art as they had been. The young artists of the sixties protested that too few people in modern societies were able to have that experience, being barred from it by social and political strictures. Art as it had been was irrelevant to the great majority and, if that was the case, irrelevant to the artists, too. It had been for some time, they—or we—argued, but now that this was being recognized radical action was being taken. And so, in the wake of Pop art, experimental conceptual art moved toward its engagement with new cultural forms.

Although some of the new forms were familiar in the context of popular culture, they were unfamiliar in the guise of works of art. This unfamiliarity was interpreted, correctly, as a new version of the "defamiliarization" process to which earlier avant-garde movements, like constructivism and surrealism, were so committed. The look of non-art was the new version of modernist "difficulty."

A difficult work cannot be experienced as a work without some insight into the historical conditions to which it responds and which, in that sense, have brought it into being. The new look-of-non-art art succeeded in forcing new patterns of perception, but these were not spontaneously available. Explication was required. Such works, not being familiar, demanded a new social role for commentary, primarily written commentary.

The legitimation of an art requiring, and therefore including, a moment or process of explication was one of the achievements of the sixties and seventies. It might be a dubious achievement. The idea that a work of art required some kind of explanation—as part of the experience of the work—was and is hotly contested, since it appears to violate one of the canonical aesthetic rules: that a work of art is self-sufficient and need be experienced but not necessarily understood. The fact that it can be experienced successfully without really being understood has always been considered a mark of its self-sufficiency, its distinctness from other kinds of practice, like science or philosophy. The new art, deriving as it did from an intellectual apprehension of the historical, logical, and structural problems of the notion of art—the Duchampian strain—was driven to challenge this criterion.

The new argument, imbued with aspects of structuralist and post-structuralist theory, claimed that all works exist in a constant atmosphere of commentary and evaluation, and indeed would have no meaning outside that. The meanings we appreciate in art appear to us in the necessary form of commentary. Necessity becomes a virtue, no apology is made for the commentary required to legitimate the new forms. Instead, the new idea of commentary is woven into a concept of the socially necessary process of experiencing art; commentaries that were always outside the experience of the work became, since Derrida, recognized as an interior, even an anterior, condition of experience and perception. The idea that an unfamiliar experience came equipped with the explanation it would in any case provoke a viewer to call for emerges from the same dynamic in which an essay could itself be seen as an art object.

Over the past twenty or twenty-five years, Graham, of all his generation, has been perhaps the most consistently involved with this problematic of the commentary. Only Victor Burgin, who in 1973 published a book titled *Work and Commentary,* can be said to have taken the problem as seriously. Although during the sixties and early seventies Graham made a number of significant purely conceptual works in language form, his writing soon moved in a different, even opposite direction, into the genre of the commentary.

Graham's transition from linguistic conceptual work to commentary was rather gradual, emerging from both pragmatic production conditions, and philosophical questions about the autonomy of the work of art and the ways in which its content could be experienced in the absence of a commitment to representation or expression. Graham's commentaries were written during and then after the establishment of the legitimacy of the essay-as-a-work-of-art, and they continually respond to that problematic legitimacy. Once a written text could be accepted, or rendered acceptable, in these terms, a new question emerged, one, again, that probably could not be answered: under what conditions, now, could an essay *not* be considered an art object?

This question seems absurd, since almost no essays achieved such status; but the absurdity doesn't really affect the fact that for an artist like Graham, there had to be a means to either establish definitively the identity of every text as now an art object akin to a drawing, or to withdraw a text, a group of texts, or even a class of texts, from that condition without necessarily returning them to the status or the identity they held previously—that is, as writings simply outside the work of art. Since most of the world never accepted, or even took seriously, the text as an art object, there was no social or institutional problem in continuing with an external relationship. But, for those whose artistic direction had been, at least to a degree, defined by experiments of this kind, a return to the social or cultural status quo was not an acceptable option. For Graham, as for the others, there was never any question of being a writer. What artists wrote was not literature, not even art criticism; somehow it was art, or at least it had an internal and maybe a historically new relation to art.

Graham and his fellow conceptual artists understood that a text could be an art object only under certain very specific conditions, conditions he helped to define with early pieces like *Schema (March 1966).* The first condition was that the text refer exclusively to its own status as both text and as proposal for an art object. Only if this condition were met was it possible for the work as text to take its place in a historical development that originated with the readymade, and included the other extremist formulations of art's boundaries—the monochrome and the unrealized work that may not aim to be realized, like Tatlin's tower. Joseph Kosuth and the authors in Art & Language wrote this kind of text, published it, and attempted to formulate ways the ideas presented in their texts-as-art-objects could be developed in other texts, and whether the subsequent texts would also be art objects, or have to be art objects. A new situation emerged, in which it was conceivable that texts could be written that could not be withdrawn from the condition of being art objects.

To follow the argument, if an essay that met the conditions under which an essay could be legitimated as an art object should actually achieve such status, to the extent not only of being presented as such but actually accepted as such, by being exhibited by reputable institutions and acquired in art collections, then could another essay on the same topic, even if written from a somewhat different point of view, be excluded from such status? Several possibilities appeared, each comparable to other accepted artistic practices. For example, could the same artist rewrite essentially the same text, with maybe a few minor textual variations, and present it as another work of art, related to but distinct from the first essay?

At the same moment, On Kawara was making paintings bearing only the date on which they were painted, producing a series of very similar paintings of sequential dates. Each of these paintings was accepted as a discrete work, related to but independent of each other regardless of the repetition involved. In this context, how could a slightly different essay be ruled out as an art object if a previous one was accepted? There are obviously other possibilities, each as dizzying as the previous; all of them resemble the model of the extremist, experimental art object or gesture which, once established as an expression of the boundaries of art, can and even must be repeated in order for the seriousness of the reflection on the logical problem of art to be conveyed. Daniel Buren's stripes, Kawara's, Roman Opalka's, and Alan Charlton's canvases, or Niele Toroni's brush marks, gain rather than lose aesthetic luster by their having been repeated over what are now long periods of time. Nothing like this has ever happened, explicitly at least, in art before now. I say "explicitly" because repetition has always been present in art, but not as a mark of art's legitimacy. The repetition of stereotypical formulae by mediocre artists is just as consistent and relentless as Buren's repetition of his motif, but Buren has taken on that negative energy in art and worked dialectically with it, turning it into something else. In the post-Buren, post-Kawara, post-Ryman, post-Toroni, post-Art & Language period, repetition tends toward the inescapable, and most artists have included it in their practice in one way or another.

The critical literature on Graham has established that his work is ambivalent about these strategies of repetition in an exemplary way. As time passes and we witness the continuation of projects like Buren's or Toroni's, we understand that, regardless of the apparently unbreakable legitimacy they have achieved, they are nonetheless limited. After some decades it is now the insistent, even resigned theater of repetition that we accept in these works. The fact that they have abjured, apparently for good, any involvement with the world outside the methodological possibilities established thirty years ago, is both a mark of achievement and a reason for now looking elsewhere for seriousness in art. Graham articulated this kind of discontent at the very beginning of the process, in the sixties and seventies. Yet, unlike most critics and opponents of conceptual art, he did so from a position almost indistinguishable from those from which he was seemingly taking his leave.

Graham's aim was to remain involved with the wider world as a subject and occasion for art, but to structure that involvement in the rigorously self-reflexive terms made mandatory by the intellectual achievements of conceptual art. *Schema (March 1966)* was made at the same time he was writing articles for art magazines on his own and other artists' work, as well as what used in the magazine world to be called "think pieces"—discursive essays on phenomena or epiphenomena of culture, pieces like "Eisenhower and the Hippies" (1968), "Dean Martin/Entertainment as Theater" (1969), and "Homes for America" (1966–1967). The think pieces were actual essays on actual topics and at the same time glosses on the art works or photographs Graham was then making or preparing to make. He has consistently referred to these writings as "journalism." And they are journalism, except they are also not quite journalism, in the sense that, with them, the category "journalism" is rearticulated and relegitimated in terms established by the self-reflexivity of the category essay-as-a-work-of-art. This implies that a work of art is to be made through the principle of "the look of non-art" in the sphere of the written. Just as Dan Flavin made sculptures by repositioning common lighting equipment, Graham moved toward making textual art works or "magazine pieces," as he calls them, by writing about various subjects as if he were writing the essay about its possible status as a work of art. This process of mimesis, of constructing journalism in the "as if" mode, was a way of testing the new category of the essay-as-a-work-of-art. It is clear, maybe only in hindsight, that the outcome of the test was known in advance. To reiterate, the essay-as-a-work-of-art can only be an essay about the proposal of that essay as a work of art; it can't be about any other subject. Graham seems to have wondered, If an artist could write an essay about another subject, but write it "as if" it were an essay about the proposal of itself as a work of art, would the resulting essay then be able to be experienced as a work of art the way the accepted essay-as-a-work-of-art is experienced? The answer seems clearly to be no, but it is a complex "no," especially if we imagine the resonance of that "no" around 1969 or 1970.

Let us follow this unlikely argument further. Graham might have thought, Okay, the essay-as-a-work-of-art is definitely limited to the one subject. He might then have thought about the possibility of writing a second such essay, with a few minor textual changes, and he would have concluded that that essay, too, would obviously be an essay-as-a-work-of-art, for the reasons we have already outlined. A certain perspective and logic necessarily appear to the mind at this point. It would be clear that what has been created is a unique and transformed version of the methodology of artists like Buren or Toroni, but in written form, that is, in a form that will always remain liminal and problematic as visual art or as an art object.

Graham might have thought that this liminal space was both absolutely determined in the terms we have established, but that, at the same time, by being a liminal and problematic category, it contained unknown possibilities. The most immediate way to experiment with those possibilities was to breach the apparently fundamental rule by introducing another subject matter, while still attempting to write, or make, a "magazine piece" rather than a magazine article, strictly speaking. It's clear that this was a failure, and that the essays have become magazine articles or critical essays, and, generally speaking, this has been the case with Graham's writings. Previous collections, like *Articles* (Van Abbe Museum, 1978), *Video-Architecture-Television* (Nova Scotia College of Art and Design, 1979), and *Rock My Religion* (1993), have treated them that way. We make no argument against this categorization except one.

Graham, like a few other artists of his generation, has appeared to accept the idea that he could do more than one thing, and that he could be an artist and an essayist, journalist, or critic. The world has also accepted this in him, as it has done with Donald Judd, Robert Smithson, and, more recently, Peter Halley. Nevertheless, we understand that none of these essays would have been written, no critiques composed, unless somehow the content of the essay was connected to the inner aspects of the artist's work. This is what distinguishes these artists from others who have had far more public and distinguished careers as art critics, like Patrick Ireland, Peter Plagens, Thomas Lawson, or, among the younger generation, Collier Schorr. Their critical writing must have some relation to their artistic work, but it has been occasioned by the institution of criticism and essayism in a way that Graham's has never been. With Graham, as with Smithson and one or two others, there has always been a resistance against writing on any occasion except one provided by the evolution of the artistic work as a whole. Although we can determine that Graham's essays emerge from various specific contexts, we can see that they are not created in response to a summons from the institution of criticism. They may function as criticism, even cultural criticism, but this function can be compared to the function of an intervention by Buren as criticism. That intervention might be critical of something—for example, the institution in which it is exhibited—but that criticism is not made directly, as actual criticism, that is, as writing within the institution of criticism. It is made incidentally, in the process of making a certain kind of work of art, and that art is made within the institution of art. This work of art might be called "functionalist," or post-autonomous, as it has been. What that means is that it achieves its functional purposes by means of being a work of art and taking on the form of a work of art, albeit an experimental form. Post-autonomous art achieves its functional aims through the process of being created within the very framework of autonomous art; that is, it responds to no external functional or practical command, it is freely chosen and made by the artist. The artist chooses to make his or her work useful in some way, or even just to pretend it might be useful, to act "as if" it could be useful. This pretense invents possible functions, and presents them to the public, which might not have otherwise ever thought of them. In this light, post-autonomous art is only a liminal type of autonomous art. In saying this, I mean no negative criticism of that art. The borderland of these categories generates experiments that might lead somewhere authentically new.

Graham's essays occupy this borderland. They achieve their discursive and critical aims not through the artist's acceptance of his identity or role as critical writer, but rather through his avoidance of it, his stance as a "writer," in quotes, an artist impersonating a writer in order both to write, freely, and also to work as an artist in the expanded way "artistic practice" became defined in the sixties and seventies. The critical essays and commentaries on his own work are in a permanent state of "category shift," in that they are simultaneously about their various subjects and are yet formulations that emerge from contemporaneous aspects of Graham's practice, whether in his photography, architectural-pavilion work, performance, or video. Graham's writing is not writing about art, of even "art-writing"; rather, Graham's art is an art with writing in it, or, maybe more precisely, an art with the writing it contains glinting in the form of texts.

Two-Way Mirror Power

SIDE EFFECT / COMMON DRUG	Anorexia (Appetite loss)	Blood clot	Blurring of vision	Constipation	Convulsion	Decreased libido	Dermatosis	Depression, torpor	Headache	Hepatic disfunction	Hypertension	Insomnia	Nasal congestion	Nausea, vomiting	Pallor
STIMULANT also APPETITE DEPRESSANT															
Dextroamphetamine (Dexadrine)	●			●	●				●		●	●		●	
Methamphetamine chloride (Desoxyn)	●			●	●				●		●	●		●	
ANTI-DEPRESSANT															
Iproniazid				●					●	●	●				
Trofanil			●				●		●		●				
TRANQUILIZER															
Chorpromazine				●		●	●	●	●						●
Hydroxyzine				●			●	●	●					●	●
Meprobamate					●			●			●				
Promazine			●				●	●	●						
Resperpine	●				●	●	●	●				●	●		
Thiopropazate			●	●	●		●	●	●	●		●		●	
SEDATIVE															
Barbitol			●					●						●	
Phenobaritol			●					●						●	
ANTI-MOTION SICKNESS															
Dimenhydrinate (Dramamine)							●	●						●	
Marezine							●	●							
Meclizine							●	●						●	
CONTRACEPTIVE															
Norethynodrel (Enovid)		●	●						●	●				●	●

1
Dan Graham
Side Effects/Common Drugs, 1966

I. Dan Graham

The Artist as Producer

> Jewish popular tradition credits . . . Rabbi Judah Loew ben Bezalel with the creation of a Golem—a creature produced by the magical power of man and taking on human shape. . . . The Golem was produced by the human mind [as] a reflection of God's power. . . . The Rabbi put a slip of paper with the mystic . . . name of God [and] the lump of clay. . . . Every Sabbath the Rabbi would remove the slip of paper with God's name. Once he forgot to remove the Name [and] . . . the Golem ran amuck. When the Rabbi removed the Name of God from the Golem's mouth it fell to the ground . . . a lifeless mess. It is written that a Golem is but a replica of Adam. As God created Adam from clay and invested him with a spark of intelligence and spiritual life, so the Rabbi had created his Golem.[1]

In the early 1950s, a new category, the "teenager," a class which Karl Marx hadn't predicted, emerged as a force in America. Because of economic changes in America, teens were not required as a work-force immediately after school; they were more vital as a consuming, a new leisure class to be educated as total consumers if the mass production, assembly-line, automated economy was to continue. They didn't inherit the Protestant work-ethic of their parents. Like sci-fi stories of robots created with clearly delineated functions by a dominant human order (which, because of their particular view of the world, develop their own, non-human consciousness, and a more advanced critique of the society created for them for their own purposes), the teenage class was both exploited and given the false consciousness of freedom. However, as the concept of total leisure time turned to boredom, teenagers' understanding of their freedom led to revolt—or at least pseudo-revolt. But adult society must always be tolerant, for the simple fact that teenagers and rock music are helping the economy.

Rock presented a departure from pop music; it was for one "class" alone—the "teenager." On one hand, it appeared to be totally exploitative, a music controlled (at first) by "out for bucks" adults using black urban blues in order to turn their lyrics into vehicles for publicity-created teenage stars like Hollywood players. In fact, this was only half the truth. Ambiguously built into rock music was the teenager's awareness that it is a commercialized form; the music and lyrics are and are not to be taken totally at face value. Rock preceded "Pop art" by 15 years in that the listener could discern in its ironies the nature of its compromised position. Although it exploits adolescents as a vast, new consumer market, whose consciousness it tries to form and manipulate through radio, television and films, the industry doesn't care as long as it can make money out of the music. At the same time, rock expresses the real ideology of adolescent culture.

In 1958 a riot broke out during one of Alan Freed's highly popular stage shows. Observing the police hassling the audience with unnecessary zeal, Freed responded from the stage: "I guess the police don't want you kids to have any fun." Acts like this led to Freed being seen as a dangerous pied piper of youth who, with rock, promoted juvenile delinquency and instigated riot and revolution. Like other radio jockeys, Freed accepted gifts from record companies or artists wishing to promote their act. But although not alone in this practice, Freed was singled out by a Congressional Committee investigating what it called "payola" (plugging records). Because he refused to testify against associates or publicly recant, Freed lost his radio contract. He died of throat cancer a few years later in his late 30s. As parental society repressed their fear of black violence and projected "delinquency" onto their kids, Freed became a scapegoat, accused of exploiting teenagers' maladjustments to society for his own financial gain.

While teens identified with the black music Freed played in his first Cleveland broadcasts, Freed altered his radio personality to the jive style of black musicians—he helped write, produce and promote both black and white groups he discovered. White teens copied the blacks' use of double entendre to covertly communicate sexual and political protest. Parents feared rock 'n' roll because it precipitated lewd dance and aped the mannerisms of blacks in the northern cities and blacks in tribal Africa revolting against the colonial masters. Rock lyrics such as "Be Bop A Lula" and choruses like "Papa Mu Mu Maw," suggested a return to the Stone Age.

Rock ideology of "fun" was born of the futility of deferred pleasure. In a world that seemed doomed as the specter of the A-bomb haunted teenagers, sex was no longer linked to family responsibility or reproduction. And rock is based on sex—it elevates the power of male adolescent sexuality. Anti-Oedipal, it mocks parental belief in sexual sublimation, marriage and work as necessary. Rock heroes are unrepentant sinners; rock groups form a new model for communal, non-nuclear families.

Rock stars, who are both real adolescents and fictions of the entertainment world, become models for a new class that refuses to grow up. Rock and adolescence are eternal states. "Teenagers" re-deploy the Victorian idea of childhood as angelic and innocent; they see teen sexuality as innocent and angelic, relating to the purity and ecstasy of sexual feeling divorced from adult repression and responsibility, family and conventional male/female roles. Sex is androgynous; teenagers are "teen angels."

In the 1960s, rock music merged with "counterculture," resistance to the Vietnam War and various personal liberation movements. Hippies believed that one died symbolically when one reached 30; their slogan was "Don't trust anyone over 30."

Herbert Marcuse's writing, in which American "Counterculture" was joined to the politics of Paris, May 1968, and "Situationism," disputed Freud's insistence on the triumph of the "Death Instinct." This instinct, and the tendency of an organism to seek equilibrium, should be seen more as a Nirvana. Its destructive impulse should be diverted from its use for social control by the liberation of its energies. Along with the Life Energies, in a non-repressive re-sexualization, the genitals used in reproduction would return to the state of "polymorphous perversity" of the child. "Only with the entire body re-eroticized," argued Marcuse in *An Essay on Liberation* (1969), "could alienated labor, grounded in the non-genital areas of the body, be overcome." Aesthetic play would replace the suffering of work. Marcuse was a political anarchist, refusing all established order. His belief was that life could only be lived in the present here and now.

Yippies paralleled the Situationists in France, creating ironic honor and "counter-spectacles" in the heart of corporate America. They distributed free money at the Stock Exchange, washed police cars and scheduled a free concert for police involved in suppressing a race riot in Newark. Abbie Hoffman titled his best-selling book *Steal This Book* (1971). The paradox was that the media saw it as a "con"—P.R. to gain attention as much for Hoffman as for the "Yippie" Movement, a ploy to penetrate the market. It was Hoffman's media "star" quality which, in the first place, guaranteed an interested buying public. Thus, Hoffman and his book were defined in terms of both media stereotypes and the publisher's economic needs (to promote publishing events by temporarily famous personages).

In the 70s, punk rock questioned the notion of the 60s rock star. It saw the rock star entrenched in corporate rock show biz: "Take a band that's good, you bust it up and sell 3 times as many records," noted the Akron, Ohio band, Devo. Punk groups like The Stooges, Pere Ubu, and the Ramones, coming out of the post-Vietnam War disillusionment and urban devastation of American cities, broke with the position rock performers had been placed in. "What do you think rock and roll is in America," asked Devo, "besides propaganda for corporate capitalist life? . . . Since pop music is definitely a vulgar art form connected with consumerism, the position of any artist, in 'pop' entertainment, is really self-contempt."

Andy Warhol's films allude to the Hollywood studio production system (his artist's studio becomes a film studio), which was built on the marketable personality of the star. In the 30s producers discovered that the most economic and investable business approach to create product identification for their films was via the name brand of the stars. The star system rationalized consumer demand for brand name products while, at the same time, establishing an easy way to rate, distribute and promote films. As a by-product, it eliminated all but the major studios which had the cash to invest in promoting a star. By the early 70s, the power of the studios as film producers had waned; rock music becoming their main source of income. While film had become a director's medium (and many stars themselves became directors), television, which was organized differently from cinema, although dominated by the large networks, gave the individual (often independent) producer the creative role held by directors in presenting film. Television as a medium established the independent producer as creative force. Norman Lear, having created and produced *Maude* and *All in the Family,* was given $100,000 by CBS to produce two pilots of what was to become *Mary Hartman, Mary Hartman.* As CBS declined to pick up its option on the idea, Lear eventually sold it to enough local stations to interest advertisers. He packaged the series, hired writers, actors and two directors.

Brian Epstein, the first rock manager/entrepreneur as couturier, constructed the Beatles image in terms of hair style and dress code: he had them substitute leather jackets with velvet collars for their original "Gene Vincent" look. Epstein used fashion to package the Beatles and to express his desires.

By the late 60s in Britain and America, rock culture had merged with "Pop" art (the Beatles influenced by Richard Hamilton, Velvet Underground produced by Andy Warhol) and "Conceptual" art (Yoko Ono influenced John Lennon, Art and Language doing rock records). Epstein's packaging of the Beatles was influenced by "Pop" art's strategies: to avoid the media packaging—appropriating them instead—they packaged themselves first. Andy Warhol is an example of "Pop" art as personality. He avoided packaging by the media by packaging himself first, for the media, becoming in turn the self-referring subject of his art, a self-packaged "star."

The late 60s dreams of arcadian utopia turned, by the 70s, into a bland corporate rock. The MC 5, the Velvet Underground and Patti Smith among other groups turned rock into an urban political weapon. Patti Smith coming from the poetry and art world sees rock as an art form which could encompass poetry, sculpture, painting—as well as its own form of revolutionary politics: "Everybody says art's dead or sculpture is finished. I don't care. Rock 'n' roll is in its pterodactyl state, and it's ours." Rock criticism and the 50s rock revival begins to make rock self-conscious, academicized, a branch of culture with its own aesthetics and history.

Malcolm McLaren, an art student for nine years, was drawn to rock culture in terms of fashion codes. His boutique, Sex, was an experiment to demonstrate how "the incestuousness of English culture ultimately rest[s] upon clothes which conceal a repressed sexuality."[2] McLaren's anthropologically-inspired media art operations were influenced by art history, Brian Epstein's ambivalent example, Situationism, and a left-anarchist take on Andy Warhol's equation of art and business:

> I always found that . . . , when I was managing groups, or running a store, or producing a record, or whatever . . . , it was best for an artist like me to have a cloak, such as a "business-like" custom. This way . . . I could create tremendous chaos under the guise of being business-like and respected.[3]

The Sex Pistols, created from the customers of McLaren's shop, exemplify Warhol's idea that everyone will be famous for one hour. The Sex Pistols were also a vehicle through which the corporate entertainment structure could be attacked with humor and destabilizing ploys. With the Pistols and with Bow Wow Wow, McLaren's strategy was to focus on the economic contradictions within the corporate entity, instead of on the star or the music, and to self-consciously use the media to achieve (media) success, only to expose the machinations of the corporate system. In other words, to use the media to become famous in order to "de-construct" the idea of media-based fame; to show the media for what it really is by forcing its contradictions (and the Pistols' or Bow Wow Wow's contradictions as a rock act) into the open. A side effect was the exposure of the relation of the corporate entertainment structure as an economic entity to both its "product" and the media.

> Present to the public a near incompetent rock band that would sing with unprecedented fervor about the politics of nihilism, whatever that was. . . . He would wipe out the history of rock 'n' roll, making everything that had come before sound effete, compromised and cowardly; start the pop culture story all over again; expose the fragility and repressiveness of welfare state capitalism by eliciting a hail of abuse from those in power.[4]

As with art in the late 70s, it is hard to tell whether McLaren's attitude is cynical or revolutionary. McLaren has been accused of "being a Jewish rag-seller from SoHo," like Alan Freed, Abbie Hoffman, Brian Epstein and Phil Spector, other urban Jews who were producers. All exploited the media for their own purposes and at the same time used this exploitation to carry revolutionary possibilities to the masses. All (but perhaps Epstein) used humor as a liberating weapon. All of these figures had to deal with the media's revenge for their earlier exploitation of it. According to McLaren, the reason he made *The Great Rock and Roll Swindle* was to admit his culpability in the Pistols' "swindle," and thereby avoid these potential problems,

> I've never allowed myself to be upset by my image. . . . That's why I've always been able to survive. . . . The [record company men] all dance to the same tune. You don't have people explaining to you that what you are doing is wrong, because you know at the end of the day they all really would so much want to be doing the same thing. They just can't, that's all; they're just a bit too square.[5]

McLaren is now approaching Hollywood movie companies about projects which he could produce. One of these resembles *The Great Rock and Roll Swindle*—it is the other side of all sentimental documentaries on the history of rock 'n' roll told through clips of the original performers. McLaren's vehicle would be loosely titled "Rock 'n' Roll Godfather," taking 30 years of rock 'n' roll, from 1955 to 1985, and seeing it from the point of view of the entrepreneur and the hustler. Looking at what basically began as a fad that turned into a mega-industry, a sort of Robespierre story, privateer versus the corporation, and using it as a background to make a very tough, hard-core gangster movie:

> Set with that background of 30 years, you trace from one guy's life, from the age of 18 until the age of 50. From the slums of Brooklyn Bel-Aire mansion with a problem . . . you do it almost like *Godfather II.* A being hung out the window—Robert Stickwood . . . with his feet—with "Half-way to Paradise" playing in the background. . . . I sold that to Disney.[6]

McLaren conceived of Bow Wow Wow as a metaphor for Thatcher's Britain, involving corporate giants versus pirates, romance novel and opera soundtrack: "Sunshine and adventure . . . [with] Bluebeard who kidnapped a girl like Annabella. She would be one of those mulatto types . . . a great symbol for this pirate look."[7] Instead of working through the network of independent record companies and distribution systems, a return to craft-based small entrepreneurial or primitive capitalism, McLaren's approach has been to deal with major companies on their own terms in order to expose the contradictions inherent in the system. Piracy is capitalism's nostalgic dream. The sense of the individual marketeer as an anarchic pirate lingers in such vernacular phrases as "Captains of Industry." Bow Wow Wow's first song, "C-30 C-60 C-90 Go!" encouraged kids to "pirate"—tape—records off the radio, from libraries, and from record shops, rather than buying them. Ironically, the LP was released by the biggest corporation in the entertainment field, EMI. At that moment, record prices were high (partly due to the artificially manipulated oil shortage of the mid-1970s), while cheap cassette players and blank audio tapes enabled kids to illegally "pirate" music, instead of buying it. Encouraging teenage delinquency is part of rock 'n' roll tradition—the music industry feels secure that it can continue to translate youth's "rebellion" into profit in mass marketing terms. The next step was for EMI to release a very inexpensive Bow Wow Wow cassette, E.P. length, of eight new Bow Wow Wow songs in a cigarette-style flip-top pack.

> Both Bow Wow Wow and a new project, a children's film based on "Beauty and the Beast," uses the premise of . . . a romantic tale . . . [to look] through clothing [at] how society [defines] its codes . . . and a girl's [simultaneous] awakening to her sexuality.[8]

Bow Wow Wow was conceived when "child nymphets," like the model Brooke Shields, were being used in fashion and advertising to eroticize childhood in order to extend to a much younger audience the consumption of eroticized products. This had a dual appeal, both to adults' prurient interest in young girls (not unlike their appeal a century ago to Lewis Carroll), and to children themselves, who are in touch with "sex" through the magic of the television image.

McLaren used Annabella to produce a Situationist "counter-spectacle." As she is of mixed Burmese and English blood, Annabella could also function as a symbol of Britain's colonial people coming back to threaten the pure English blood through miscegenation, and the class system by their economic enterprise. In short, Annabella played the same role in British rock as the black "race record" singers did in America in the early 50s.

The British album cover for the first Bow Wow Wow release used a nearly-nude photo of Annabella in the modern form of a fashion photograph of Manet's *Luncheon on the Grass.* The photograph shows two male members of the group posed in romantic costumes, reclining next to Annabella, who is nude. A picnic lunch is spread out on the grass next to them. The fourth member of the group is wading in the pond and McLaren is rowing a boat. The way Annabella is pictured in this photograph alludes to a broader iconography of French Romantic painting. Her coy disposition and nudity recall Ingres's odalisques, while her exotically colored (hence "Oriental") skin suggests an oblique relation to another well-known painting, Manet's *Olympia.* In *Olympia,* the girlish prostitute is white and is attended by a black serving maid. Both the naked child prostitute and the exotic black servant (wearing highly fashionable, bourgeois clothes) were unsettling images to the middle-class art public of the mid-nineteenth century. In a Britain subconsciously fearful of the loss of "Britishness" through interracial coupling, Annabella presents a similarly unsettling ambiguity. Is she a normal, British girl, or is she exotic and hence erotically desirable? Or, to put it another way, is she a prostitute, or is she a chaste, middle class virgin? In the iconography of the photograph, according to McLaren's critics, she is represented as a child prostitute.

T. J. Clark writes about *Olympia:* "Like any society, the empire needed a representation of sex. . . . 'Prostitution,' wrote the *Westminster Review* in 1868, 'is as inseparable from our present marriage customs as the shadow from the substance. They are two sides of the same shield.' . . . The sign of class in *Olympia* was nakedness. . . . Nakedness is a strong sign of class. . . . [Critics] were perplexed that Olympia's class was nowhere but in her body."[9]

In the Bow Wow Wow LP, a Margaret Mead-like anthropological critique of patriarchy is wedded to the light opera or musical review. In a ritual war dance in the song "Hello Daddy (I'll sacrifice you)," inspired by musical comedies such as *South Pacific,* young Princess Annabella sings of her impending marriage to her brother. This will necessitate the sacrifice, not of her, but of her father, to ensure the success of her queenly reign. Brother/sister incest triumphs over the sacrifice of maidens.

Comic book "Polynesian" post-modern mythology is the theme of another of the projects McLaren developed in Los Angeles for a film dealing with surfing:

> [To surfers] the beach was their street. . . . The ocean was their roadmap and the ocean was the soul. Surfing was almost a religious experience. . . . I thought one thing you can't do is you can't make California blue; you've got to make it acid rain . . . , gray, . . . and flat with shadows, . . . and you've got to make . . . that whole beach completely privatized, no access, filled up with nuclear power plants, oil rigs, pylons, dilapidated 50s condo, almost falling apart in total decay. The only things that are left . . . standing are the old European-Spanish missions that still linger on with little gardens of odd Indian food that reminds us of people who once inhabited the place. And there, within all of that, I centered it on a girl—I thought you had to have somebody with some power—who could call up a wave. At night those kids who want to surf break through the "No Access" sign. And

> gangs proliferate—be they second generation Vietnamese, Koreans, Pakistanis, or your blond, blue-eyed Aryan, USC, bad-assed surfin' jock. . . . When . . . this girl calls up the wave, she turns blue.[10]

Since Bow Wow Wow, McLaren seems to be moving from the voyeurism of media spectacle to an autobiographical feeling for his subject(s). With Annabella, McLaren oversaw/staged the spectacle of her erotic blossoming, her child sexuality for *us* as spectators—and for *him.* We desired to see, voyeuristically, how female sexuality is produced. In McLaren's first project of 1987, a collaboration with Jeff Beck, he focused on what Freud called the "latency period" before adolescent sexual awareness begins at age thirteen. He intended to "make a very romantic record about courtship, partners, foreplay, being swept off your feet . . . a waltz record [based on Strauss] . . . with prepubescent lyrics. . . . It's the romantic period . . . that everybody seems to have forgotten . . . [but] one always wants to get back to. I've decided to write from that point of view—get my head into being a nine year old—and try to think myself back there."[11]

Notes

1. Gershom Scholem, *On The Kabbalah and Its Symbolism* (New York: Schocken, 1969).
2. Malcolm McLaren, in conversation with the author.
3. Ibid.
4. Greil Marcus, source unknown.
5. Malcolm McLaren, in conversation with the author.
6. Ibid.
7. Ibid.
8. Ibid.
9. T. J. Clark, *The Painting of Modern Life: Paris in the Art of Manet and His Followers* (Princeton: Princeton University Press, 1984).
10. Malcolm McLaren, in conversation with the author.
11. Ibid.

This essay was written between 1978 and 1988, and has been published in various versions. This one is previously unpublished.

II. Magazine Pages

My Works for Magazine Pages: "A History of Conceptual Art"

I became involved with the art system accidentally when friends of mine suggested that we open a gallery. In 1964, Richard Bellamy's Green Gallery was the most important avant-garde gallery and was just beginning to show people such as Judd, Morris and Flavin. Our gallery, John Daniels, gave Sol Lewitt a one-man show, as well as doing several group shows which included all the "proto-Minimalist" artists whether they already showed at Green Gallery or not. We had also plans to have a one-man exhibition of Robert Smithson—then a young "Pop" artist. However, the gallery was forced to close due to bankruptcy at the end of the first season.

If we could have continued for another two years, with the aid of more capital, perhaps we might have succeeded. Nevertheless, the experience of managing a gallery was particularly valuable for me in that it afforded the many conversations I had with Dan Flavin, Donald Judd, Jo Baer, Will Insley, Robert Smithson and others who, if they were not able to give works for thematic exhibitions, supported the gallery by recommending other artists and by dropping by to chat. In addition to a knowledge of current and historical art theory, some of these artists had an even greater interest, which I shared, in intellectual currents of that moment such as serial music, the French "New Novel" (Robbe-Grillet, Butor, Pinget, etc.), and new scientific theories. It was possible to connect the philosophical implications of these ideas with the art that these "proto-Minimal" artists and more established artists such as Warhol, Johns, Stella, Lichtenstein and Oldenburg or dancers such as Yvonne Rainer or Simone Forti were producing.

The fall after the gallery failed I began experimenting myself with art works which could be read as a reaction against the gallery experience, but also as a response to contradictions I discerned in gallery artists. While American "Pop" art of the early 1960s referred to the surrounding media world of cultural information as framework, "Minimal" art of the middle through late 1960s seemed to be referring to the gallery's interior cube as the ultimate contextual frame of reference or support for the work. This reference was only compositional; in place of a compositional reading interior to the work, the gallery would compose the art's formal structure in relation to the gallery's interior architectural structure. That the work was equated with the architectural container tended to literalize it; both the architectural container and the work contained within were meant to be seen as non-illusionistic, neutral and objectively factual—that is, as simply material. The gallery functioned literally as part of the art. One artist's work of this period (although not always his later work) examined how specific, functional architectural elements of the gallery interior prescribed meaning and determined specific readings for the art defined within its architectural frame: Dan Flavin's fluorescent light installations.

Lighting—light fixtures—within the architectural setting of the gallery/museum is normally disregarded, or considered merely functional or minor interior decoration. As gallery space is meant to appear neutral, the lighting, which creates this neutrality as much as the white walls, and at the same time is used to highlight and center attention on the artwork on the wall or floor, is kept inconspicuous. While the background in general makes the artworks visible, the lighting literally makes the works visible.

The lighting system, within which the specific light fixtures of a gallery arrangement function, is both part of the gallery apparatus and part of the larger, existing (non-art) system of electric lighting in general use:

> I believe that the changing standard lighting system should support my idea within it.
>
> —***Dan Flavin, "Some Remarks,"*** **Artforum,** ***1966.***

Flavin's installations make use of this double functioning (inside and outside the gallery/art context) as well as the double connotation of lighting as minor decoration (interior decoration) and anonymously functional creator of the gallery's neutrality.

> I believe that art is shedding its vaunted mystery for a common sense of keenly realized decoration. Symbolizing is dwindling—becoming slight. We are pressing downward toward no art—a mutual sense of psychologically indifferent decoration—a neutral pleasure of seeing known to everyone.
>
> —***Dan Flavin, "Some Other Remarks,"*** **Artforum,** ***1966.***

His arrangements of light fixtures in a gallery space depend for significance, contextually, upon the function of the gallery, and the socially determined architectural use of electric lighting. Use of electric light is related to a specific time in history. Flavin has observed that when the existing system of electric lighting has ceased to exist, his art will no longer function. Being a series of standardized, re-placeable units, which, in Flavin's words, "can be bought in any hardware store," his arrangements of fluorescent tubes within the interior or adjacent exterior architectural frame of the gallery exhibition space function only in situation installation, and upon completion of the exhibition cease to function artistically.

Perhaps I misread the implications of these works by suggesting a conscious intention to examine the relation of the value of art to the question of the gallery in which it was exhibited. I also felt that the "solution" Marcel Duchamp had found to this problem of art's "value" was unsatisfactory.

In his "readymades," Duchamp brought objects which were not considered art when placed outside the gallery, into the gallery to prove dialectically that it is in fact the gallery which gives the object its value and meaning. Instead of reducing gallery objects to the common level of the everyday object, this ironic gesture simply extended the reach of the gallery's exhibition territory. In bringing the "non-art" object into the gallery, Duchamp wished to place in apparent contradiction the conventional function of the gallery to designate certain objects as "art" and to exclude others.

Essentially Duchamp attempted to question the aristocratic function of art and the art gallery as an institution. Because this question was only presented on a logical abstract level, his critique was itself immediately integrated back into the institutional system of gallery or museum art, becoming a kind of "idea" art. A further problem with Duchamp's analysis is the resolution of the contradiction between gallery art and art in relation to its social value based on a historical concept; the condition of art is seen as neither social nor subject to external social change. By contrast, Flavin's fluorescent light pieces are not merely a priori philosophical idealizations, but have concrete relations to specific details of the architectural arrangement of the gallery, details which produce meaning.

In addition, Duchamp saw the problem of value and meaning in art as a simple binary opposition, inside the gallery or outside in the world. He failed to link this opposition of art and so-called "non-art" to more ambiguous phenomena such as the reproduction of the art object by the media, which was mediated upon by the critic Walter Benjamin in the 1930s and was even earlier an important aspect of Constructivist art.

Through the actual experience of running a gallery, I learned that if a work of art wasn't written about and reproduced in a magazine it would have difficulty attaining the status of "art." It seemed that in order to be defined as having value—that is, as "art"—a work had only to be exhibited in a gallery and then to be written about and reproduced as a photograph in an art magazine. Then this record of the no longer extant installation, along with more accretions of information after the fact, became the basis for its fame, and to a large extent, its economic value.

From one perspective, the art object can be analyzed as inseparably connected to the institution of the gallery or museum; but from another perspective it can be seen as having a certain independence, as it belongs also to the general cultural framework which the magazine is a part of. Magazines specialize in a way which replicates other social and economic divisions. Any magazine, no matter how generalized, caters to a certain market or a specific audience in a particular field. All art magazines are directed to people who are involved in the art world professionally in one way or another. Furthermore, the art magazine itself is supported by advertisements which, with one or two exceptions, come from art galleries that are presenting exhibitions. It follows that in some way the advertisers have to be taken care of in that their shows have to be reviewed and made a matter of record in the magazine. Thus these shows and works are guaranteed some kind of value and can be sold on the market as "art." The fact that sales do take place yields enough money for the gallery to purchase more advertisements in art magazines and to sustain the art system in general.

Art magazines ultimately depend upon art galleries for their economic support, just as the work shown in galleries depends on photographic reproduction for its value in the media. Magazines determine a place or are a frame of reference both outside and inside. Magazines specialize in a "field"—for instance, the specialized "world" of art and artists termed the "art" world. *Sports Illustrated* caters to those who are interested in sports, the *American Legion* magazine caters to members of the American Legions. Art magazines cater to artists, dealers, collectors, connoisseurs, and writers who have a professional interest in art. And the art magazine itself is supported by advertisements.

Note

This essay was written in 1985 and published in Gary Dufour, Dan Graham, *exh. cat. (Perth: Art Gallery of Western Australia, 1985), pp. 8–13, from which the present version is drawn. An extract was included in* Rock My Religion: Writings and Art Projects 1965–1990/Dan Graham, *ed. Brian Wallis (Cambridge: MIT Press, 1993), pp. xviii–xx.*

DAN GRAHAM

SCHEMA for a set of pages whose component variants are to be published in various places. In each published instance, it is set in its final form (so it defines itself) by the editor of the particular publication where it is to appear, the exact data used to correspond in each specific instance to the specific fact(s) of the published final appearance. The work defines itself in place only as information with simply the external support of the facts of its external appearance or presence in print in place of the object

(March, 1966)

(number of) adjectives
(number of) adverbs
(percentage of) area not occupied by type
(percentage of) area occupied by type
(number of) columns
(number of) conjunctions
(depth of) depression of type into page surface
(number of) gerunds
(number of) infinitives
(number of) letters of alphabet
(number of) lines
(number of) mathematical symbols
(number of) nouns
(number of) numbers
(number of) participles
(perimeter of) page
(weight of) paper sheet
(type of) paper stock
(number of) prepositions
(number of) pronouns
(number of point) size type
(name of) typeface
(number of) words
(number of) words capitalized
(number of) words italized

2
Dan Graham
Schema (March 1966) 1966

35	adjectives
7	adverbs
35.52%	area not occupied by type
64.48%	area occupied by type
1	column
1	conjunction
0 mms.	depression of type into surface of page
0	gerunds
0	infinitives
247	letters of alphabet
28	lines
6	mathematical symbols
51	nouns
29	numbers
6	participles
8"x 8"	page
80 lb.	paper sheet
dull coated	paper stock
.007" thin	paper stock
3	prepositions
0	pronouns
10	point size type
univers 55	typeface
61	words
3	words capitalized
0	words italicized
58	words not capitalized
61	words not italicized

3
Dan Graham
Schema (March 1966),
1966 (variant 1967)

Offsetplatte Rohpapier

1 Adjektiv
3 Adverbien
1192 1/2 qm unbedruckte Fläche
337 1/2 qm bedruckte Fläche
1 Satzspalte
0 Konjunktionen
kein Eindruck der Drucktype in die Papieroberfläche
0 Gerundien
0 Infinitive
363 Buchstaben aus dem Alphabet
27 Zeilen
2 mathematische Symbole
38 Hauptwörter
52 Zahlen
0 Partizipien
8 1/2 x 5 Satzspiegel
17 1/2 x 22 1/2 Papierformat
Offsettplatte Rohpapier
5 Präpositionen
0 Pronomen
10 Punkt Schriftgrad
Antiqua Schriftart
59 Wörter
2 Wörter versal
0 Wörter kursiv
57 Wörter nicht versal
59 Wörter nicht kursiv

4
Dan Graham
Schema (March 1966),
1966 (variant 1969)

37	adjectives
0	adverbs
87.40%	area not occupied by type
12.60%	area occupied by type
2	columns
0	conjunctions
0 mms.	depression of type into surface of page
0	gerunds
0	infinitives
24	letters of alphabet
28	lines
11	mathematical symbols
36	nouns
49	numbers
7	participles
5⅜″ × 8″	page
Dondell	paper sheet
uncoated offset	paper stock
.0039″	paper stock
6	prepositions
0	pronouns
10 point	size type
Aster	typeface
60	words
2	words capitalized
0	words italicized
58	words not capitalized
60	words not italicized

182

5
Dan Graham
Schema (March 1966),
1966 (variant 1972)

Legacies of Critical Practice in the 1980s: Dan Graham

It is extraordinary to be in this room illuminated by the work of Dan Flavin, always a favorite artist of mine and an inspiration both in his art and in his writing; he was also the first to appreciate my writing.

In the first Dia discussion the question of artist/writers came up. It is from this position of artist/writer that I and the other two panel members speak. Our topic is strategy for the 80s—which, it is assumed, is different from strategy in the 70s or the 60s. My strategy has evolved from the 60s idea of art as a phenomenology of the present-time/presence of things, to an involvement in structuralism; from there to deconstruction, and within the last five years to a rejection of deconstruction in favor of a concern with historical memory. (This evolution is evident in my "Minimal" sculpture/pavilions, for instance, in my *Rock My Religion* video, and in various articles such as "Gordon Matta-Clark" and "Theater, Cinema, Power.") I believe now that the task of the artist is in part to resuscitate the just-past—that period in time made amnesiac by commodity culture—and to apply it as an "anti-aphrodisiac" (Walter Benjamin's phrase). The Rolling Stones's song "Yesterday's Papers"—"Who wants yesterday's papers? Who wants yesterday's girl? No one in the world"—makes this anti-aphrodisiac aspect of the just-past clear.

According to Benjamin, "progress," the 19th-century scientific and ultimately capitalistic myth, is expressed in commodities, fashion goods which "produce a sense of eternal newness."[1] This makes progress a mythical goal, never to be reached, for there is always the new and it is always superseded by the next new. For Benjamin, then, progress is actually a state of stasis.[2] And yet it is this very stasis that makes the recovery of the just-past potentially subversive.

In the plan for his *Passagen-Werk,* the project about 19th-century Paris on which he worked from 1927 to 1942, Benjamin wished to demonstrate that for his generation slightly out-of-date—just-past—objects of mass culture possessed a latent revolutionary power, a notion he developed from surrealism. (The 19th-century consumer arcades and crystal palaces of the universal expositions functioned for Benjamin in a similar way; they were "dream houses" that induced a "time space/time dream.") He wanted his arcades writings to serve as a dialectical "fairy tale": "to reverse the myth of the late 19th century created by constant newness and induced amnesia of the recent past, which undermined the historical meaning of the past in favor of the present and fantasized future of the commodity dream (progress)." Such a fairy tale might effect this, he thought, "by changing what adults saw as newness into the archaic and mythical." As a consequence, each generation of children might see remnants of the just-past not only as archaic but as endowed with a mythical capability to restore the past. For Benjamin this was one way in which "the commodity dream" might be broken.

Benjamin's goal was to restore historical memory in opposition to historicism, or the idea that everything we know about the past is dependent upon the interpretation of the fashion of the present. In historicism there's no real past, only an overlay of interpretations or a simulation of the "past." Benjamin opposed this idea with the notion of an actual though hidden past, mostly eradicated from consciousness but briefly available in moments of dreams, hallucinations, stoppages, etc.

In proposing this idea Benjamin had to dispute Marx's rejection of memory while saving his "theological" premises. In his 19th-century context Marx had wished to shed the ideological shackles of memory for an empirical approach to history:

> The social revolution of the 19th century cannot draw . . . from the past, but only from the future. It cannot begin before it has stripped off all superstition in regard to the past. Earlier revolutions required reminiscences of past world history so as to hide from themselves their own content. In order to achieve its own object the revolution of the 19th century must let the dead bury the dead.[3]

For Benjamin, on the contrary, bourgeois ideology was maintained by the notion of progress, a notion supported by an empirical, "scientific" ideology of "objective," historical progress. In opposition to this ideology of progress, he proposed a recuperation of historical memory. Without a redemption of past oppression, Benjamin felt, Marxism could only fall into the dominant rationalism of capitalist society:

> The past carries with it a temporal index by which it is referred to redemption. There is a secret agreement between past generations and the present one. . . . Like every generation that preceded us, we have been endowed with a weak Messianic power, a power to which the past has a claim. . . . Nothing that has ever happened should be regarded as lost for history. . . . [The oppressed] have retroactive force and [their struggle] will constantly call in question every victory, past and present, of the rulers. . . . To articulate the past historically does not mean to recognize it "the way it really was" (Ranke). It means to seize hold of a memory as it flashes up at a moment of danger. . . . Only that historian will have the gift of fanning the

spark of hope in the past who is firmly convinced that even the dead will not be safe from the enemy if he wins.[4]

The work of Gordon Matta-Clark is a good recent example of how one can cut away and reveal the just-past. "There is a kind of complexity," Gordon once said, "which comes from taking an otherwise completely normal, conventional (albeit anonymous) situation and redefining it, retranslating it into overlapping and multiple readings of conditions past and present." With his cuts into and removals from existing architecture, Matta-Clark intended his work to function as a kind of urban agit-prop—like the 1968 acts of the Paris situationists, who saw their temporary spectacles as public "cuts" in the otherwise seamless urban fabric. "By undoing a building," he argued, "[I open] a state of enclosure which had been preconditioned not only by physical necessity but by the industry that proliferates suburban and urban boxes as a pretext for insuring a passive, isolated consumer."[5]

Paradoxically, Matta-Clark's cuts are still a form of architecture, one that uses "gaps, void places that were not developed" or that were covered over as contradictions in architectural and bureaucratic logic. His work thus exposes the private integration of compartmental living space, revealing how the family copes with the imposed social structure of its container. Matta-Clark's cuts demonstrate this constructional imposition, along with our adaption to its concealed order, in the form of "sculpture." In this way his art works to open up both the unconscious and historical memory.

Notes

1. Walter Benjamin, quoted in Susan Buck-Morss, "Benjamin Passagen-Werk: Redeeming Mass Culture for the Revolution," *New German Critique,* 29 (Spring/Summer 1983), pp. 211–240. Unless otherwise noted, all other Benjamin quotations are from this source.

2. For the relation of this to recent architectural debates, see my "Not Post-Modernism: History As Against Historicism, European Archetypal Vernacular in Relation to American Commercial Vernacular; and the City as Opposed to the Individual Building," *Artforum,* December 1981.

3. Karl Marx, source unknown.

4. Walter Benjamin, "Theses on the Philosophy of History," in *Illuminations,* ed. Hannah Arendt (New York: Schocken Books, 1969), pp. 254–255.

5. Gordon Matta-Clark, *Avalanche,* December 1974. For more on Matta-Clark see my essay in *Parachute,* 43 (June–August 1986), pp. 21–25.

This text was first published in Hal Foster, ed., Dia Art Foundation/Discussions in Contemporary Culture, Number One *(Seattle: Bay Press, 1987), pp. 88–91.*

Legacies of Critical Practice in the 1980s: Discussion

Dan Graham

I'm always struck by how absolutely different the New York art world is from the world of European culture—or from other places in the U.S. In other words, this is a very parochial situation, and despite our talk about artist/writers there are many who have been forgotten and left out. It might be good to keep those others in mind—if only to shake up our own discourse.

Moderator (Hal Foster)

Dan, I wonder if you want to respond to the charge that Silvia made about the construction of the subject in Minimalism and Conceptualism—that this subject is not differentiated.

Graham

Well, my work at the time was about how the phenomenological model that Minimalism took up was a failure, about how the phenomenological "I" had been questioned and eroded elsewhere in culture. In art this goes back at least as far as Jasper Johns, who showed the erosion of his "I" in terms of the subliminal influence of advertising and media images.[1]

Silvia Kolbowski

I wasn't talking about an erosion of the "I"; I was talking about the ways in which the "I" is encoded and inscribed—or the ways in which its inscription is suppressed, and how that suppression affects the construction of both the work and the spectator. My point was that there's a very strong effacement of the position of the "I" both in the production of art and in critical and historical writing.

Graham

I think that's a misreading of Minimalist and Conceptual art. The "I" projected by Minimalism is like Samuel Beckett's "I"—invaded, subliminally disintegrated by mass advertising and corporate cliches. People like Robert Smithson thought this art got rid of anthropocentrism, but that was not my experience. In "Subject Matter" (written in 1969 and included in my Eindhoven exhibition catalogue *Articles*) I saw Minimalism as a crisis in the subjectivity of the spectator—of his or her consciousness in relation to the intention of the artist. That often became the "content" of the work.

Below this content was another ostensive content, of which the relation to the gallery structure was emblematic: the relation of the work to the city and its housing. The work of both Flavin and Judd alludes to architecture and mass architectural containerization, and I read it as both Constructivist and Expressionist in feeling.

Audience

Dan and Aimee, how do you propose memory to be used as a revolutionary force? Aimee, you point to some prelinguistic realm of the real which has the status of an origin and is not affected by difference—but theorists like Derrida would say that's impossible.

Aimee Rankin

Well, it's only impossible once we enter the system of signification, and this process, which Mary Kelly has recorded in her work, is hardly a simple procedure. I'm not arguing for some return to infancy; I'm interested in the schizophrenic aspects of postmodern culture—which Fredric Jameson has seen not only negatively as a breakdown in the signifying chain but also positively as an experience of hallucinatory brilliance, an iridescent flow of images. The mass media, for example, tries to get at a kind of subliminal memory trace, a kind of phantasmatic plenitude that we can only construct after the fact.

Audience

More specifically, my question was: How do you propose that such memories be employed in a political or discursive way?

Rankin

There's no way to apply them directly. As subjects we retain a sense of loss that goes back to those memories and that colors our relationships to discourse with ambivalence.

Kolbowski

Aimee, I'm curious: Would you say that you try to create a phantasmatic plenitude in your own work? Visually?

Rankin

No, I'm dealing with the loss of that plenitude; I don't believe one can recreate it. I'm not trying to get back to the real as such. But I am trying to make a space for reverie, about its loss.

Foster

Aimee, I was struck by a point of contact between your statement and Dan's. You use a Lacanian model; he referred to Benjamin—but you both talked about a strategy that would deploy the imaginary against the symbolic. You gave a few examples of what you meant; maybe your own work is an example. My question is for Dan: In your statement you talked about a recovery of the "just-past," and you refer to dreams and childhood . . .

Graham

My work isn't programmatically about dreams or fairy tales per se; that's what Benjamin's arcades writings were partly about. He attempted to bring the subliminal fixation of the spectator of film, the dream state produced by the newness of the commodity, surrealism, Freud—all this together with his idea of historical memory. I bring in Benjamin instead of Lacan and Baudrillard in order to suggest an historical, maybe contradictory, way to see our crisis; as (post)structuralists Lacan and Baudrillard seem to float academically in an ahistorical limbo. But I too like to juxtapose people or social groups that don't quite fit, whether it is "President Eisenhower and the Hippies" (in my 1967 article of that title) or Julia Kristeva and Ari Up (of the Slits) or Lydia Lunch (as in my article "New Wave/Feminism," commissioned by *Screen* but rejected for my "misuse" of Kristeva's "semiotic chora").[2] I think that's the only way for an artist to work through theory.

Kolbowski

How recent is the just-past?

Graham

Well, for Benjamin it's the last newness before the current newness. In America it seems to come in decades: back to the future, back to the past. For example, when people were drawn to the plenitude of the '50s they jumped over the '60s—jumped over the actual struggle between those periods. I discovered this when I did my videotape *Rock My Religion* and noticed people's interest in the '60s. (My view, by the way, is very negative of the '60s.)

Audience (Barbara Kruger)

I'm not sure this is a question, but I'm interested in these words "plenitude" and "open inquiry." I think of Trinh Minh-ha and her persistence in questioning the notion of conflict, the concept of challenge, the idea of hierarchical address—in really encouraging the idea of plenitude and open inquiry. On the one hand, where are those things found if not in the furtherance of one's own desire and in the tolerance of others? On the other hand, how can we use the discursive space of authoritarian fathers and not be appropriated by their presence? How can we encourage work which is not exemplary but merely different?

Rankin

I'm trying to understand how those spaces or structures come about and what they really mean . . .

Kruger

And not to reenact them.

Rankin

I don't know if we have that choice—but our reenactment can be inflected by an awareness of the stakes of their construction.

Audience (Douglas Crimp)

Silvia, I feel compelled to respond to your paper. It's very complicated to respond because I don't really recognize "the voice of the father" in what I said two weeks ago—certainly not my father. To clarify my position I need to talk about the response to my statement. There was very little response at that time, but what I heard afterward reflected the general feeling that when a gay person speaks from an explicitly gay position it is taken to be a confessional speech. That's always a risk (in fact it's something I wrote about five years ago in an essay about Fassbinder); and that, it seems to me, was turned against me. On the one hand, what I did was considered confessional; on the other hand, it was treated as a polemic—a polemic based on a kind of personal affront that was part of my confessional speech. Now it doesn't seem to me I was doing that at all. I was talking about issues of the gay community. That is why I assumed, at the moment, the position of a subject unified around being gay. In order to claim a political stake I think one has to assume that kind of position at certain moments. Whatever the rhetoric or theory, if I want to claim there are very great stakes in relation, for example, to the oppression of gay people because of AIDS, I have to assume the risk that this will be misread, A) as confessional and B) as polemical.

Kolbowski

I didn't read your presentation as either purely confessional or polemical; as a matter of fact, I'm not sure I would look negatively on either. I think what you said was very important, but you didn't question the discourses you used in making your accusations. I'm not saying one can't speak with conviction or one can't be accusatory. I'm saying one has to take into account the discourses one employs, and there was nothing in your presentation that really acknowledged your position as critic and historian. What I heard throughout the presentation was the voice of the father—not a literal father but academia as the father.

Crimp

I know you don't mean a literal father. But I'm not sure that the voice of the father is called into play in my or any discussion of gay politics.

Kolbowski

One can speak in the voice of the father and say almost anything—or maybe everything.

Crimp

Given your claim that I made certain accusations, can you repeat one?

Kolbowski

Aside from not questioning the discourses you employed, your points weren't raised in the spirit of inquiry or in the questioning of certain givens. For example, you used a lot of quotes to bolster your argument, and you never once questioned what it meant to use such quotes—from artists, filmmakers, academics . . .

Crimp

There were two quotations, both from gay people.

Kolbowski

It was not clear to me as part of the audience that they were solely from gay people; and besides, I'm not sure I agree that being gay completely undermines the positions of authority that many of them also fill. I don't think that being gay is enough to undermine certain constructs of authority.

Crimp

Of course it's not . . . But Pasolini—whom I did quote—devoted his entire life to questioning authority: the authority of the church, of the family, of the Italian state, of the Communist Party. And he was vilified by all of them. He was literally on trial for most of his adult life. So to construct Pasolini in turn as authority is a very strange thing to do.

Kolbowski

I can't recall your exact quotes, but my general feeling was that your argument was not presented in the spirit of an open-ended or self-questioning inquiry—it was presented as a kind of watertight accusation. You did recognize the conflicts within the gay community—it was not watertight in terms of saying, "This is the gay position." Nevertheless, your voice was an unquestioning voice.

Audience (Rosalyn Deutsche)

I disagree. One of the central themes of Douglas's talk was the questioning of the construction of Hans Haacke as an exemplary political artist—which is something Douglas himself was involved in. So there was a questioning.

Kolbowski

What, in his presentation, would make us question Douglas's authority?

Audience (William Olander)

As a matter of fact, I thought his presentation was quite similar to yours, with the exception of the reflection about the "I" at the beginning—that it, too, was in the form of questions.

Kolbowski

Maybe other people can also comment.

Audience (Abigail Solomon-Godeau)

Silvia, given your preconditions, there's a question whether it's possible to speak at all. Your statement problematizes first-person address and acknowledged that this is a position that is assumed. But when the first-person voice is made problematic from one side or the other, it becomes virtually impossible to produce political speech at all, much less to define political stakes.

Kolbowski

I don't think it precludes speaking; it's about producing a different kind of political speech. There are definitely different levels of access to the position of the "I"—that was the point of my talk. I started out with a quote from a woman—a Third World woman—in a position of aphasia, in which there is a recognition of the difficulty of speaking the "I" at all. But I don't think that difficulty precludes political address; I'm just calling for a different kind of political speech.

Solomon-Godeau

Could you be more specific about the nature of this political discourse?

Kolbowski

I don't know for certain, but it's not a self-righteous one. More often than not what is typified as political discourse comes from the myth of a center which is unselfquestioning and unselfconscious.

Crimp

Could you tell us, Silvia, how you viewed the recent series on television about the black civil rights movement in the South in the late '50s and early '60s [*Eyes on the Prize*]? What about this movement as an articulation of political discourse?

Kolbowski

Nothing whatsoever in my talk precluded political activism. I'm not sure why you're interpreting it that way. I'm calling for a difference in the way one articulates such action and for a recognition that one often speaks from a position of power even in challenging power. Without that difference, without that recognition, the spectator or addressee is placed in a passive position.

Audience (Craig Owens)

One of the things I also heard in your talk is the necessity not to accept certain unified "I"s, the necessity to deconstruct notions of identity or the places from which we speak as given to us institutionally. Now the identity of the gay man is an institutionally prescribed position—it is largely constructed by medical and legal discourses. And one has to question that position when one wants to address issues as a gay man—that's what I heard in your talk. Otherwise, it becomes a self-referential discourse: to say who I am before I speak. That's also why it tends to be perceived as "coming out" when one doesn't question that identity.

Crimp

How does one take an action without assuming an identity?

Kolbowski

I wasn't suggesting that one not assume an identity. In my talk I questioned whether the unempowered mustn't sometimes attempt to construct unified positions of power. I'm also not calling for a disintegration of the "I." But I agree with Craig that one can't just say, "I am this." Instead, one could say, "Perhaps I am constructed this way," or "I assume this position" or "This position is created for me—and I have to question that position as I speak."

Audience (Margaret Morgan)

I felt a certain ambivalence, Douglas, when you talked with the assured voice of the gay man, but more so and more to my chagrin, given this privileged audience, when Barbara Kruger two weeks ago held up her working-class credentials. There seem to be certain views about gayness and working-classness that we're not allowed to transgress. It becomes easy to say, "I am like this, so this is what I do."

Kruger

What I said was said not in terms of a class reference but in terms of the structure of the market.

Morgan

I took your point. I just didn't think it was necessary to wear your own badge.

Kruger

Well, variety is the spice of life.

Morgan

I felt foreclosure not variety, and I felt the same foreclosure when Douglas suggested that a particular stake can only be a stake for a particular group. Does that mean I can't speak on his behalf?

Audience (Gregg Bordowitz)

It seems to me that strategies for calling into question idealist presuppositions of the subject—as in Minimalist or Conceptual art—have in turn been called into question. I think of Yvonne Rainer saying she only talks about the personal insofar as it exemplifies social relations—that was one strategy of pointing to the various positions that subjects occupy as social beings. I also think of Martha Rosler's strategies of questioning idealist subjectivity, and her discourse developed counter to Conceptual art.

Audience (Krzysztof Wodiczko)

Why not use all those strategies? When one has a position of power, maybe that's the moment to question that power; when one does not, maybe then one has the right to speak the word "I." Douglas might speak sometimes from the point of view of the academic professor, but he might also speak as a person whose role is to scream or to use, as Derrida says, bad language.

Foster

I wonder, though, what the politics of this plurality of voices would be. In a way this gets us back to the first discussion—the opposition between balkanized audiences and imaginary public.

Olander

Silvia, how can you accuse Douglas of assuming the voice of the father when he is trying to challenge institutionalized structures based on that discourse?

Kolbowski

He is associated with *October;* he has a role that is recognized in the art world . . .

Olander

But to characterize the issues which he addresses as "academic" is extraordinary!

Kolbowski

In no way did I say he was not challenging certain structures. In fact, I acknowledged that he was and that I supported that challenge. My point was that he did not include within that challenge a challenge to his own authority. And I agree with Craig: he was not questioning what constructed him as a gay man. There's a danger in attempting to separate form and content.

Crimp

Would you characterize the gist of my speech as "academic"?

Kolbowski

Yes, in the sense that you didn't question your position except to say, "I am a gay man, this is my identity." I would call that academic to a certain degree. It's aligned with certain philosophical discourses very often employed by academics.

Foster

There's obviously a personal difference here, but there's also an important strategic difference—between, on one hand, a deconstruction of discursive positions in the abstract and, on the other hand, work within institutions in order to change them directly and materially. That opposition is too blunt, too simplistic, if posed in these terms . . .

Owens

It is also the mutual exclusiveness of those two things that is in question.

Foster

Right.

Owens

That's exactly what Silvia's text was about: that one can't speak as an activist without such questioning.

Foster

But it seemed to me that Silvia suggested there was a space outside institutions where one might question discursive "I"s, and I don't know what that space might be.

Kolbowski

I think I inscribed myself within my presentation in several ways.

Crimp

I don't want this to come back to the same thing, but I need to clarify what I said. This motive behind it was that I felt the art world floating on discourse. For example, in the first discussion, I couldn't tell what anyone's stakes were. What are the stakes, for example, of deconstructive discourse? It seems to me that the stakes of deconstruction have largely been lost in its transportation to the United States. That's why I wanted to be concrete—to talk about a specific show, "Home Video" at the New Museum, and a specific audience, the gay community. It was an attempt to make concrete and specific one possible political stake, and that keeps getting lost. What are the real political stakes of people in the art world right now?

Kolbowski

I fully appreciate the fact that you did bring up those stakes in this series. I feel very strongly about that. But I still find problematic that you could bring up those stakes and yet not question the position from which you spoke—as if to identify yourself in a single phrase was enough. For me the stakes of such questioning are as great as any other; so too the stakes of maintaining the fiction of a voice that speaks from a position of authority—outside—are as great as any other.

Graham

In an American context always criticizing one's own position is very puritanical—and self-righteous.

Foster

What is the alternative to this self-questioning?

Graham

I was simply bringing up a cultural reference—we're Americans. There are no European artist/writers up here, though we constantly bring in translated quotes from European theorists (often removed from their historical, cultural contexts). Conceptual art is heir to intellectual puritanism (opposed, in the cultural cliche, to the material and sensuous but corrupt gallery/market art commodity). And one of the forms that an imported deconstruction takes on is puritanical—I mean a self-referential questioning of motives and positions, and endless, tautological examination of self-consciousness and conscience. This idea of the correct "position," politically speaking, of the "correct" I.

Kolbowski

I think you're speaking in different terms than I am. What I have in mind is not puritanical in the least.

Graham

I'm not negative about puritanism. Self-questioning is what we're doing now—not only Silvia, everybody. All the questions are about that. But there's a certain circularity here.

Kruger

To me puritanism is about a desire to pull everything back to one thing: to say, "This is not historically grounded, not politically correct, not properly footnoted . . . but that is exemplary." Puritanism reduces things to a univocal voiceover or dictation of fact. Why not allow for a number of different voices, a number of different positions—a horizontal rather than a vertical, hierarchical structure?

Kolbowski

Voices and positions that might question each other as well.

Kruger

Exactly.

Audience (Jane Weinstock)

Aimee, I was confused by your talk, especially as it relates to the question of some kind of exemplary practice in the real, and how that relates to the imaginary . . .

Rankin

I know of no such practice in the real, but I think a lot of work today gets caught up in its own tactics in a way that has backfired. For me the work in the "Difference" show used Lacanian theory as a kind of master discourse, as a way of authorizing its own investigation. That to me is a problem—the kind of repressive attitude towards the image that came from a late '70s scorched-earth policy in feminist criticism (as in Laura Mulvey's "Visual Pleasure and Narrative Cinema," where she calls for "the destruction of pleasure as a radical weapon"). American practices—Minimalism, Conceptual art—also had this attitude toward the image: to interrupt its seductive qualities or distance the spectator. This is an interesting project, but it often uses language in order to sidestep the question of how images work—by discussing desire at arm's length rather than dealing with it in material terms.

Then there's this work related to Baudrillard that emphasizes the object in a very fetishistic way, that is more about commerce than desire (exchange in Baudrillard's theory takes the place of desire in Lacan's theory). I would like my own work to fall closer to the third group I mentioned in my paper, but I think it's less complex than theirs because it isn't time-based. I'm interested in questioning suspect structures of spectatorship in imagistic representation through a kind of critical play that's not about a distanced form of mastery but rather about a critical immersion—where one is working within a system of representations and yet trying to deal with what flows through the cracks of that system. This is where the time-based work picks up and goes much further.

Weinstock

You're setting up a hierarchy and reducing a multiplicity of single lines. In the "Difference" show there was certainly a lot of different work on the image and work on the text: to reduce all of it to a pleasureless, scorched-earth policy is extreme.

Foster

Also, Aimee, work that you see as simply a replication of theory is often more a questioning of theory—or an extending of theory.

Rankin

I don't mean to question that. Mary Kelly's work is very important for the way it puts the theoretical articulation of the construction of subjectivity in conflict with her own personal narration, with all its different layers and voices. She not only appropriates certain discourses but furthers them in her own practice. I was talking about the tendency in other related work not to question language to the same degree that it questions the image. I don't mean to sound so negative about the work I mentioned.

Audience (Dennis Thomas)

Aimee, in your statement you suggested that the prelinguistic is somehow liberatory. I don't see it.

Rankin

No, not liberatory. But the repression of that prelinguistic state, which occurs in the construction of subjectivity, will always load it with a particular kind of nostalgia or sense of loss. I don't think there's any way to get back to this mythic origin of subjectivity, but one might imagine it as yet unformed in a way that might help one see that subjectivity is constructed at very high cost.

Afterwords

Dan Graham (references)

1. The essential truth about art of the last thirty-five years, continually erased from consciousness by the ideology of internationalist liberalism, is that fascism didn't die with the cessation of World War II, to be replaced by avant-garde progressive art, but remains the repressed collective unconscious of the present. New techniques of mass psychology or product representation (swastika, national flag, corporation logo) replaced traditional forms of representation in Nazi propaganda and spread to postwar corporate advertising . . .

In the Cold War, advertising merged with patriotism; the subjective desires of the consumer were enlisted by the ad, coercing him/her to consume more goods "for a better life." As the product became inseparable from the advertising image, the corporate trademark, like Coca-Cola, functioned as a psychologically all-pervasive archetype. Advertising techniques merged with those of large-format color photography and film, placing the spectator in a new relation to the overpowering voyeuristic image which, as Laura Mulvey observes in "Visual Pleasure and Narrative Cinema," produced "the alienated subject, torn in his imaginary memory by a sense of loss, by the terror of potential lack in phantasy."

The irony is that at the same moment that abstract expressionism was evolving its oversized, abstractly subjective painting, advertising forms also made a shift toward the oversized billboard, use of the color photograph, the wide-screen film and the picture magazine format (*Life, Look*) which plunged the viewer inside the giant images. Like the viewer of an abstract expressionist painting, the viewer of the new publicity form inserted him/herself into a psychologically ambiguous space where the absence of objectively signifying meaning allowed the unconscious self to project a "personal" meaning. . . . Although the artist still believed that the meaning of his work was determined solely by his uncompromised subjective intuition, market and media forces were giving the work a different meaning—one beyond the artist's control.

Jasper Johns was the first American artist to fully understand that the newly subjectivized advertising icon and the gestures of the abstract expressionist painting (which struggled against the cultural domination of these new forms) were virtually identical. Because Johns's work (and psyche) takes a passive position relative to these phenomena (the opposite of abstract expressionism's active struggle), the advertising/propaganda icon which invades the unconscious, private space of the individual is experienced as unmediated. Johns's work directly confronts the loss of an undivided self to the totalitarianism of mechanical reproduction and a publicity form become all-pervasive, determining both popular and fine art forms and meaning. This is the unconscious core "truth" which it is liberalism's ideological task to keep concealed. (Adapted from "The End of Liberalism," *ZG* 2 [1981].)

2. Kristeva equates the prelinguistic realm of primary drives and feelings with the time when the child identifies with the mother—before the fixed, social, "stable" ego necessitated by symbolic language and produced by the castration complex forces conscious denial of these primary drives. The movements of the chora are not between positions of the speaking ego, as in rational discourse, but between the fragmented zones of the body, expressed in heterogeneous gestures and feelings—especially in vocal intonations like "the babbling of a child or musical rhythms." In music the feminine is to be found within the vocal expression more than the overtly comprehensible lyrics and melody. Examples can be found in the songs of the Swiss all-female group Kleenex (e.g., the sibilant insertions in "U"), of the Raincoats (e.g., the polyphonic counterpoint in "In Love"), and especially in the music of Lydia Lunch. . . . As the order of social speech is dependent upon the construction of a singular, unified identity for the individual subject, it must deny the shifting and heterogeneous im-

pulses and feelings of the body reflected in Kristeva's "semiotic chora." An art which is "plurivocal . . . heterogeneous [and] polymorphous" can liberate the level of the chora and "create a place where the social code is destroyed." (Adapted from *Live* magazine.)

Aimee Rankin

I haven't heard so much talk about positions since the last time I played Twister. To speak, as we have seen, is to assume a certain position. If we call for "a number of voices and positions that might question each other," as Barbara and Silvia agree to do, we are still left with the sticky question of the position one assumes in asking questions. It all goes to show how easy it is to get lost in the labyrinth of language. If, as has been suggested and as I truly hope, the system of logic which models our thinking process is showing signs of wear, soon we might be able to assume whatever positions we wish in an exuberant orgy of mental gymnastics that would freely encourage a fluid interchange of meaning. Until that time, we operate within our broken logic in the only way we know: by tracing patterns on an axis of similarity and difference and trying to make sense of the mosaic. For me, coming to terms with the artistic practices that inspire me posed this challenge. To become aware of one's own position one must situate oneself and others in some way. To question positionality can become the most rigid position of all by pointing an accusing finger at the awkwardness of others.

Like everything else, this makes me think of sex. Somebody's got to assume a position sooner or later or nothing will get done. It doesn't matter who's on top as long as it feels good. Sometimes discourse fucks me nicely and I don't begrudge myself this pleasure. Sometimes I like to use it to fuck it back—discourse as a sort of strap-on prosthetic dick. I like being able to play in more than one position.

In the end it all boils down to power. How do we fight the dynamic of power since in fighting it we place ourselves within it? Rather than avoiding confrontation, which would eliminate the pleasurable rubbing of one idea against another to see what sparks fly, I would suggest a refusal of the stakes. This is why we should never take this discursive game or our places within it too seriously. Whatever happened to that old 70s idea, "the revolutionary power of women's laughter"? Who would want a revolution that didn't allow for dancing in the first place? And what could make the overswollen dick of culture shrivel faster than a woman's well-timed laughter? The sadness of our predicament is so absurd that in the end all one can do is laugh, and encourage the illicit copulations of language to be more and more perverse, more fluid and slick and polymorphous. And then the dancing can begin.

Silvia Kolbowski

Access, and fictions of access . . . to an "I." Perhaps the most fictitious is the notion of a directly assumable access. And yet the effacement of the difficulty involved is a commonplace. Do we (I/you/they/who?) not need to question the historical legacies of these fictions, these effacements?

Sometimes needing to enact a fiction as though it were not one . . . as a strategic prop. And at other times questioning whether challenging the transparency of the structures surrounding and producing political address is expendable, deferable . . . in a call for change. Might not certain small-scale audiences be seen as a field on which to attempt to create new ground, on several different levels, even in a period of heightened political conservatism? Or precisely because of such a period?

The creation of political models—their perfection—and the perfecting of them: these are processes needful of institutions. Not just the institutions of critical journal or museum, but the elusive—because too familiar—institutions of philosophical discourses. Discourses that reinforce the role of the model—to deny access, yet generate the desire for perfectibility. Perhaps in response we could question . . . not only what is offered to us, but the very politics of articulation—suppressed—of that offering.

Note

This discussion took place on March 3, 1987, at Dia Art Foundation, 155 Mercer Street, New York. The panel included Dan Graham, Aimee Rankin, and Silvia Kolbowski. It was first published in Hal Foster, ed., Discussions in Contemporary Culture *(Seattle: Bay Press, 1987), pp. 105–118.*

III. Video/Television/Architecture

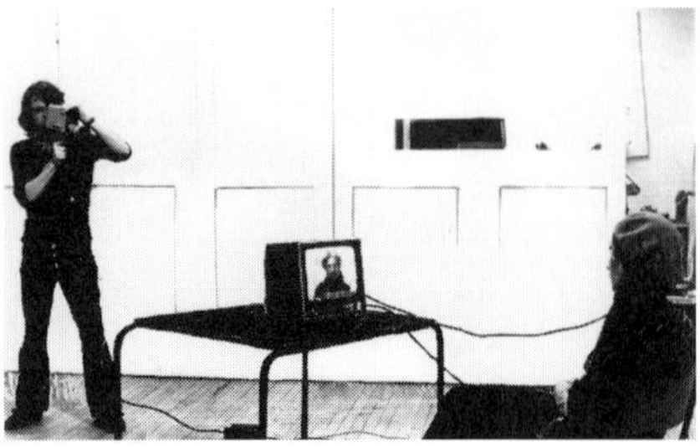

6
Dan Graham
Two Consciousness Projections, 1972

Two Consciousness Projection(s)

The woman focuses consciousness only on a television-monitor-image of herself and must immediately verbalize (as accurately as possible) the content of her consciousness. The man focuses consciousness only outside himself on the woman, observing her objectively through the camera connected to the monitor. He also verbalizes his perceptions. The man's and the woman's self-contained conscious, unconscious, or fantasized intention—consciousness—is projected. The audience sees on the video screen what the man and woman "objectively" are seeing, at the same time that they hear the two performers' interior views.[1] Because of each of the performer's time-process of perception, verbalization and perception-response to the other's verbalization, there is an overlap of consciousness (of the projections of each upon the other). Each's verbal impression, in turn, affects the other's perception: the man's projection on the periphery of the woman's affects her consciousness or behavior. A field is created in which audience and performers place reciprocal controls on each other. The audience's reactions to the man's responses (his projection of the woman) may function for him as a "superego," inhibiting or subtly influencing the course of his behavior or consciousness of the situation. Likewise, the man's responses on the periphery of the woman's consciousness interfere with her self-consciousness so that her behavioral responses, including those of self-perception, may be "subconsciously" affected. Each of the three elements functions mutually as a feedback-device governing behavior—a "superego" or "subconscious" to the consciousness and response of the others.

An abstractly presupposed psychological[2] (or social)[3] model is physically observable in the audience. The specific results of the piece vary according to the context in which it is performed, with changing historical circumstances, locale, or use of different social classes of audience or actors.

Notes

1. While an audience might initially assume that the woman is being "made into an object," it becomes apparent that her position is more powerful than the man's, as her subject and her object are not separated (separable). The more the man (to himself) strives to be objective, the more he appears unconsciously subjective to any observer from the outside (the audience).

2. The Freudian axiom that one person is always projecting himself into his observation of a second person.

3. Imposed behavioral ("psychological") differentiations between men and women.

This text was written in 1972 and first published Dan Graham: Video/Architecture/Television: Writings on Video and Video Works, 1970–1978, *ed. Benjamin H. D. Buchloh (Halifax: The Press of the Nova Scotia College of Art and Design; New York: New York University Press, 1979), p. 4.*

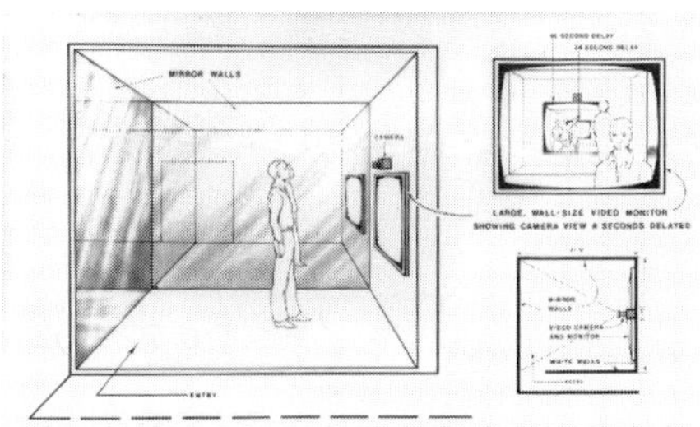

7
Dan Graham
Present Continuous Past(s), 1974

Present Continuous Past(s)

The mirrors reflect present time. The video camera tapes what is immediately in front of it and the entire reflection on the opposite mirrored wall.

The image seen by the camera (reflecting everything in the room) appears eight seconds later on the video monitor (via a tape delay placed between the video recorder which is recording and a second video recorder which is playing the recording back).

If a viewer's body does not directly obscure the lens's view of the facing mirror, the camera tapes the reflection of the room and the reflected image of the monitor (which shows the time recorded eight seconds previously). A person viewing the monitor sees both the image of himself eight seconds ago, and what was reflected on the mirror from the monitor eight seconds ago of himself, which is sixteen seconds in the past (because the camera view of eight seconds prior was playing back on the monitor eight seconds ago, and this was reflected on the mirror along with the then present reflection of the viewer). An infinite regress of time continuums within time continuums (always separated by eight second intervals) within time continuums is created.

The mirror at right angles to the other mirror-wall and to the monitor wall gives a present-time view of the installation as if observed from an "objective" vantage exterior to the viewer's subjective experience and to the mechanism

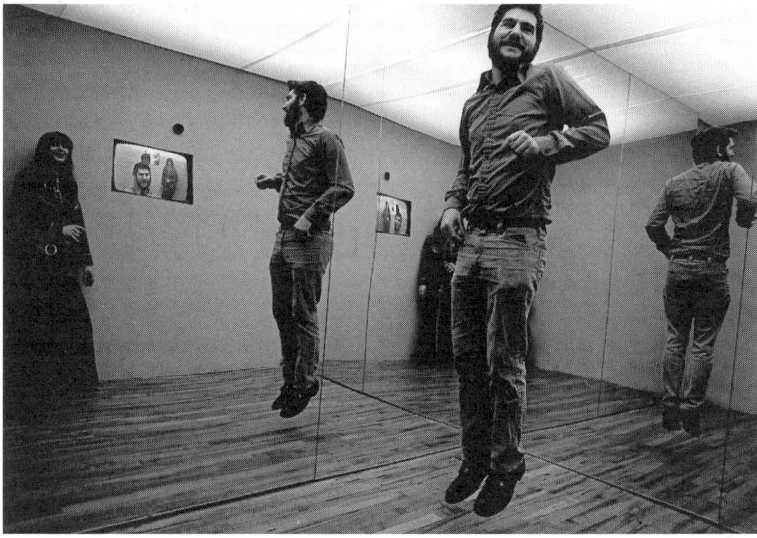

8
Dan Graham
Present Continuous Past(s), 1974

that produces the piece's perceptual effect. It simply reflects (statically) present time.

The length of the mirrors and their distance from the cameras are such that each of the opposing mirrors reflects the opposite side (half) of the enclosing room (and also the reflection of an observer within the area, who is viewing the monitor/mirror image).

Each of the videotaped camera views is continuously displayed five seconds later, appearing on the monitor of the opposite area. Mirror A reflects the present surroundings and the delayed image projected on Monitor A. Monitor A shows Mirror B five seconds ago, the opposite side's view of Area A. Similarly, Mirror A contains the opposite side's view of Area B.

A spectator in Area A (or Area B), looking in the direction of the mirror, sees: 1) a continuous present-time reflection of his surrounding space; 2) himself as observer; 3) on the reflected monitor image, five seconds in the past, his area as seen by the mirror of the opposite area.

A spectator in Area A turned to face Monitor A, will see both the reflection of Area A as it appeared in Mirror B five seconds earlier and, on a reduced scale, Area A reflected in Mirror B now.

Note

This text was written in 1974 and first appeared in Dan Graham: Video/Architecture/Television: Writings on Video and Video Works 1970–1978, *ed. Benjamin H. D. Buchloh (Halifax: The Press of the Nova Scotia College of Art and Design; New York: New York University Press, 1979), p. 7.*

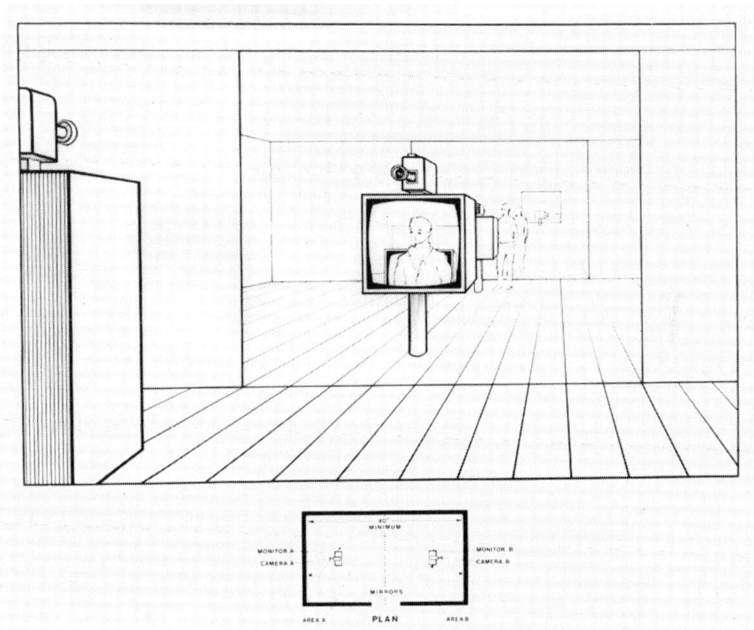

9
Dan Graham
Opposing Mirrors and Video Monitors on Time Delay, 1974

Dan Graham

Yesterday/Today

A video monitor in a public space displays a present-time view of the visual activities of a second, nearby room. In this space, the inhabitants' daily activities follow a defined routine with rhythmic periodicity related to a specific time of day, where people discuss ongoing activities (informing an ongoing chronicle), and which imposes a definite modification in role, or of consciousness, upon someone entering it.

The visual scene on the monitor is accompanied by an audio play-back of sounds, tape-recorded from the second room one day before, but at exactly the same time of the day. Two time continua having presumably the same rate of forward flow, one aural and the other visual, can be observed separately or conjointly. The visual activities and the sounds may more or less phase rhythmically, overlap, or actually coincide. As the room is nearby, the spectator may directly enter its actual space if he desires. The installation may be repeated daily indefinitely.

Note

This text was written in 1975 and originally published Dan Graham: Video/Architecture/Television: Writings on Video and Video Works 1970–1978, *ed. Benjamin H. D. Buchloh (Halifax: The Press of the Nova Scotia College of Art and Design; New York: New York University Press, 1979), p. 42.*

Notes on *Yesterday/Today*

Whereas video by artists tends to emphasize the purely visual aspects of the medium, broadcast television subordinates the visual image to the narration imposed upon the image (expressed in vocal commentary and in the ordering of the visual sequences). In broadcast TV any dissociated or contradictory reading of the relation between the narrative and visual is suppressed, narrative interpretation being always dominant. An example of this is in news stories about Communist China using visual footage supplied by the Chinese, which, when shown, is "put in perspective" by the spoken words of the news commentator. Unlike film, where both sound and visual tracks are of necessity in the past and constructed from discontinuous segments, edited and recorded according to conventional rules of syntax, video (both visual and audio tracks) is assumed to correspond/be congruent to the real, present time-

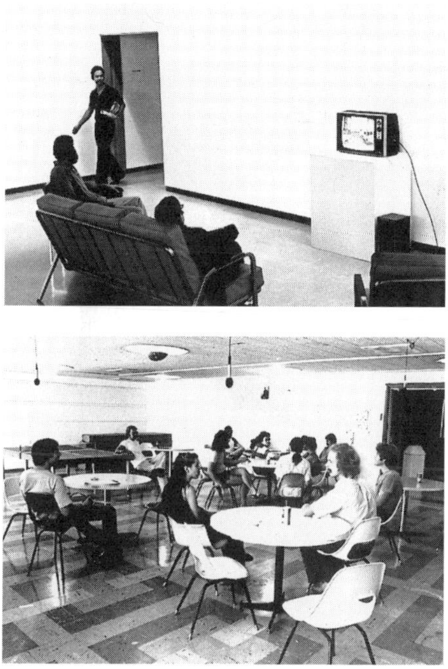

10
Dan Graham
Yesterday/Today, 1975

space continuum, or the identical continuum from an earlier time, shared by both the producers and receivers of the video. In video, unlike film, the sound and visual tracks are presumed to be different perceptual aspects of this space's physical presence.

In *Yesterday/Today,* as the visual image and the audio recording take place 24 hours apart, the formal distinction between the aural and visual representations of a nearby space become evident. Similarly, the distinction between the real space and the representation of that space is made evident. As similar types of activities happen in the depicted space on a daily basis, the aural and the visual representations may nearly coincide; thus, there are two ways to read their close, but not total identity: as due to the one-day time delay in the sound or due to the difference between sound and video tracks as representation. Since the video image, the audio, the spectators, and the real space—documented one day delayed and live—all share the same continuously forward flowing space/time, there is always a historical (real) relation between the present time/space depicted on the monitor and the one-day delayed audio, just as there is a relation between the real space and the monitor image's depiction of it, and between the audio documentation of yesterday's spoken text and events observable in that space today.

Yesterday/Today is representational and narrative. It is better read, not as immediate image, but over an extended time period. It is contextually related to the real (historical, unpredictable) events of the particular space, to the viewer's relation to that space (and to the institution it encloses), and to the real world environment. All these factors have a bearing on the work's "reading." The observer must compare the narrative contained in the work with the actual event/place of the art (the gallery). Being grounded in real space and time, the verbal "soap opera" structure of *Yesterday/Today* contradicts the usually stressed visual, instantaneous and silent comprehension of the visual artwork.

In *Yesterday/Today* the video/audio system historizes the institutional space. This is contrary to the neutral "timeless" quality implied by most architectural spaces. Historical reality depends upon the medium through which it is documented and represented. Video and audio can add a historical and sociological perspective to define the specific function of a space for those who use it. The spectator can follow yesterday's story of a designated space by viewing it on the video monitor from the outside, listen to yesterday's story, and then enter the real space, listening to, participating in the present-moment dialogue (with a mental reference to yesterday's dialogue).

The pattern of the chosen quasi-public/quasi-private space is one which is basically invariant from day to day, although suggesting slight "development" or variation.

A specific architectural space tends to be institutional; it structures the needs, roles and responses of the people who use it (that is, their roles tend to be influenced by the conventions, history and present function of the space). Likewise, the space serves a function in the larger social order. *Yesterday/Today* is best read by those who make up the institution, those who use the spaces it relates. If situated in an art gallery, the characters in its narrative are the art dealer, the art reviewers, the artists, the critics and the various people who service its needs.

In the John Gibson Gallery installation in New York the public exhibition area displayed the monitor and audio recording coming from the immediately adjacent semi-private/semi-public gallery director's office. This outer office, whose door is usually kept open and accessible to the curious gallery visitor, is where real business takes place, as opposed to the purely public exhibition space where the monthly art exhibition is displayed. John and Susan Gibson, the proprietors working in this space (often visited by other people), negotiate with prospective customers, design future exhibitions, talk with artists and critics, view young artists' slides of work, etc. . . . The office space is reacted to somewhat differently by the "regulars" ("people in the business") than by the more easily intimidated members of the general public. What is revealed in this space of the gallery, in distinction to what is hidden in the public gallery space, are the functional, social, and economic relations of the art gallery.

For the Samangallery installation in Genoa, the small single room of the gallery space, serving as both showroom and office, was used to display the monitor and audio recording of activity in a bar directly across a small alley way from the gallery entrance. This bar, like most bars in Italy, had a front entrance to the street and back entrance oriented to the grouping of businesses and residences to its rear (these are usually in a courtyard, but in this instance were dispersed along the small alley way). Such a bar has the dual purpose of servicing both people from the neighboring streets and the businesses to its rear. The bar takes messages for these businesses when they are not open, serves them refreshments and snacks, and becomes a convenient place to meet people during business hours, outside the constricted business interior.

The installation at Galleria Banco in Brescia, recording the immediately adjacent office of Galleria Nuovi Strumenti, connected two ideologically dissimilar galleries. A single wall separated the spaces of the two art galleries. The galleries had wished to conceal their proximity (although members of each gallery were constantly visiting one another through the rear courtyard entrances) and interrelated business dealings. The installation made clear these hidden relationships of each one to the other.

The Art Gallery of Winnipeg installation recorded the activities of a cafe on the top floor. The cafe's clientele were a general cross-section of the users of the museum: museum staff (discussing personal, bureaucratic, political and practical problems usually revolving around the preparation of exhibitions), local businessmen on a coffee or lunch break (discussing business, civic and personal problems), local art lovers (discussing recent music, dance and art events, as well as financial support for cultural institutions) . . . in other words, documenting what is normally not expressed (because of the conventional meditative silence) in front of the art on display in the art museum.

Note

This text was written in 1975 and first appeared in Dan Graham: Video/Architecture/Television: Writings on Video and Video Works 1970–1978, *ed. Benjamin H. D. Buchloh (Halifax: The Press of the Nova Scotia College of Art and Design; New York: New York University Press, 1979), pp. 44–46.*

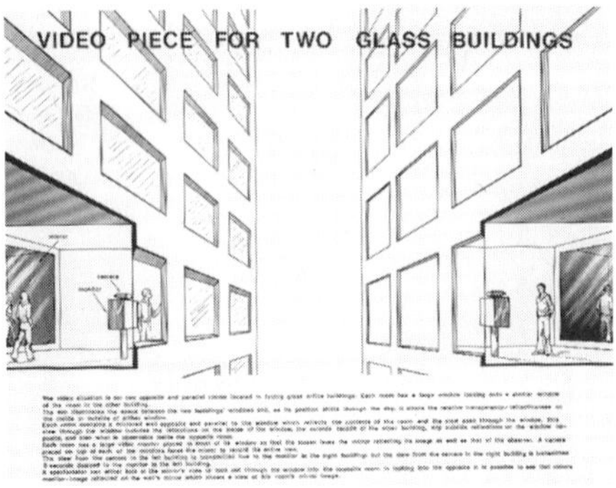

11
Dan Graham
Video Piece for Two Glass Office Buildings, 1974–1976

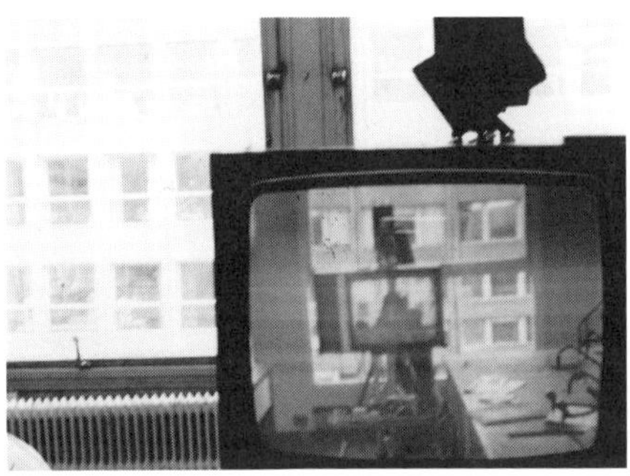

12
Dan Graham
Video Piece for Two Glass Office Buildings, 1974

Video Piece for Two Glass Office Buildings

The video situation is for two opposite and parallel rooms located in facing glass office buildings. Each room has a large window looking into a similar window in the other building.

The sun illuminates the space between the two buildings' windows and, as its position shifts through the day, it alters the relative transparency/reflectiveness on the inside or outside of either window. Each room contains a mirrored wall opposite and parallel to the window which reflects the contents of the room and the view seen through the window. This view through the window includes the reflections on the inside of the window, the outside facade of the other building, any outside reflections on the window opposite, and also what is observable inside the opposite room.

Each room has a large video monitor placed in front of its window so that the screen faces the mirror, which reflects the screen's image as well as that of the observer. A camera placed on top of each of the monitors faces the mirror to record its entire view.

The view from the camera in the left building is transmitted live to the monitor in the right building; but the view from the camera in the right building is transmitted eight seconds delayed to the monitor in the left building.

A spectator can either look at the mirror's view or look out through his window into the opposite room. In looking into the opposite room, it is possible to see that room's monitor-image reflected on the wall's mirror, which shows a view of his room's mirror's reflected image.

Note

This text was written in 1976 and first published in Dan Graham: Video/Architecture/Television: Writings on Video and Video Works 1970–1978, *ed. Benjamin H. D. Buchloh (Halifax: The Press of the Nova Scotia College of Art and Design; New York: New York University Press, 1979), p. 47.*

Video Piece for Showcase Windows in a Shopping Arcade

This video piece takes place in two facing and parallel shop windows, located in a modern shopping arcade where people pass through the arcade between the two windows.

Each shop window contains a mirror on its back wall, opposite and parallel to the window. This mirror reflects both what is inside the showcase and the view through the window. This view through the window includes the reflections on either side of both windows, the interior of the other window, and the spectators (shoppers) passing in the arcade between the two facades.

Both windows have monitors placed in front of them. The monitor within the left window faces outward toward the mirror, whereas the monitor within the right window faces inward toward the mirror. The camera on top of the left monitor faces inward toward the mirror, whereas the camera on top of the right monitor faces outward toward the window.

The view from the camera in the left window is transmitted live to the monitor in the right window; but the view from the camera in the right window is transmitted five seconds delayed to the monitor in the left window.

The show windows can be either empty or contain normal product displays. It may be possible for spectators to enter into the shop window if it is part of a store. These details depend upon the specific situation of the piece's placement.

Note

This text was written in 1976 and originally published in Dan Graham: Video/Architecture/Television: Writings on Video and Video Works 1970–1978, *ed. Benjamin H. D. Buchloh (Halifax: The Press of the Nova Scotia College of Art and Design; New York: New York University Press, 1979), p. 51.*

Notes on *Video Piece for Showcase Windows in a Shopping Arcade*

The conventional showcase display is likely to contain a mirror or mirrored fragments behind the products on view, seductively reflecting fragmented aspects of the spectator's body. The mirror enhances the narcissistic tendencies of the spectator, as well as the alienation of the spectator from his body-image and from the goods. Although its initial effect is to exaggerate these effects, closer inspection of the showcase/video/mirror arrangement proposed here contradicts this initial reading.

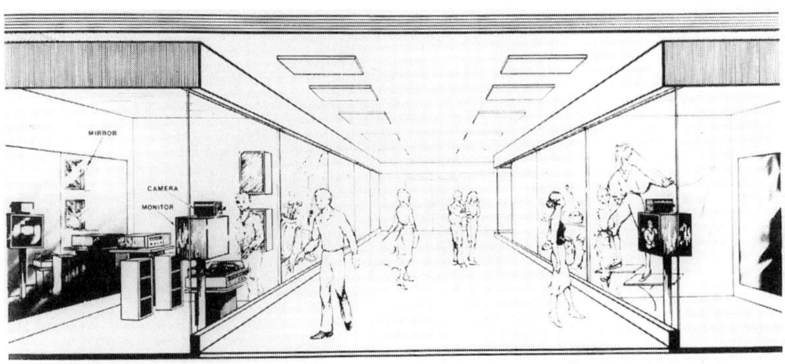

13
Dan Graham
Video Piece for Showcase Windows in a Shopping Arcade, 1976

The conventional showcase has its goods displayed frontally, facing the prospective customer, composed to create a center of visual attention and importance. The front plane of glass of the box corresponds to the Renaissance painting's picture plane, just as the overall, three-dimensional showcase container echoes the contained "three-dimensional space" located "inside" the painting. The view of what is inside the container substitutes for the spectator a view of the real world (behind him); the person looking at the goods is not consciously aware of the corridor space in which he stands, or of other people looking. He sees only a dim reflection of himself and the actual world on the outside surface of the glass. Similarly, the device of the showcase, its framed form, like that of the painting on display, must be inaccessible to consciousness for the image within it to be fully seen.

A "good" shop window, like a "good" advertisement, organizes its selection of goods so that they appear to meet the (psychologically) unique needs of the person who gazes upon them. A spectator standing in front of a show window (like an art viewer standing in front of a painting) feels his perception disturbed if other people are trying to occupy his particular position, or if he becomes too aware of other showcase displays and the people responding to them.

In *Video Piece for Showcase Windows in a Shopping Arcade,* the placement of the mirror parallel to the front glass plane and enlarged to fill the back side of the case, makes fully visible the spectator's look and his body's position in the corridor's real space in relation to the opposite showcase. The video provides views of and from inside the opposite showcase (and also from inside the spectator's own showcase, via the view's reflected image from the opposite showcase's mirror); it provides interior front and back perspectives, front and back views of spectators looking at both showcase displays and of spectators in the "real-world" space in the corridor between the two cases. A spectator can see both sides of his "picture" as well as both sides of the opposite case's picture; and himself and spectators looking at the opposite case from front and back angles simultaneously. The spectator's body is seen in its entirety in relation to the goods; the goods are seen from both sides and in relation to the opposite shop window's display of its goods; the spectator, the showcase, and the goods displayed are seen through the real corridor space in relation to the real world which surrounds (frames) them.

Note

This text was written in 1976 and first appeared in Dan Graham: Video/Architecture/Television: Writings on Video and Video Works 1970–1978, *ed. Benjamin H. D. Buchloh (Halifax: The Press of the Nova Scotia College of Art and Design; New York: New York University Press, 1979), p. 53.*

Production/Reception (Piece for Two Cable TV Channels)

The piece utilizes two cable channels in a local environment in addition to a normal commercial broadcast. Two cable programs are to be broadcast live and at the same time as a commercial program, originating on a local station. Any locally produced commercial program can be used, for instance a local evening news broadcast.

Cable channel A broadcasts a live view originating from a single camera placed inside the control room of the studio producing the local commercial program. A wide-angle lens is used, and the camera, aimed through the glass panel at the stage, shows the entire stage-set, surrounding cameras, cameramen, director, assistants, and the technicians and technical operations necessary to produce the program. Microphones placed in many locations within the stage-set, behind the stage, and in the control booth are mixed together and accompany the visual image. They give a complete sense of *all* relationships occurring within the enclosed space of the commercial TV studio.

Cable channel B broadcasts a live view from a single camera within a typical family house in the community. It shows viewers present observing the local commercial broadcast on their TV set (the view shows both the television image as well as the viewers present). The camera-view is fixed. Occupants of the household may or may not be present in the room watching the TV set at a given time. Sounds from *all* the rooms of the house, documenting all the activities taking place there for the duration of the broadcast, are mixed together and accompany the camera-view.

Anyone in the local community who has cable television in addition to the commercial channels may, by switching from channel to channel, see channel A's view framing the local program in the context of its process of production, or channel B's view showing the program's reception within the frame of a typical family's household; or viewers can turn to the commercial channel and themselves receive the particular local program in their house.[1]

Notes

1. *Production/Reception* was a response to my partial knowledge of an earlier work by my friend Michael Asher, using broadcast television: *The Occurrence of Rolling the Television Program the Tenth of January 1976.* Both works involve a sense of the architectural properties of television. One might compare the differences and the similarities of the two works.

This text was written in 1976 and first published in Dan Graham: Video/Architecture/Television: Writings on Video and Video Works 1970–1978, *ed. Benjamin H. D. Buchloh (Halifax: The Press of the Nova Scotia College of Art and Design; New York: New York University Press, 1979), p. 55.*

14
Dan Graham
Projection/Reception, 1976

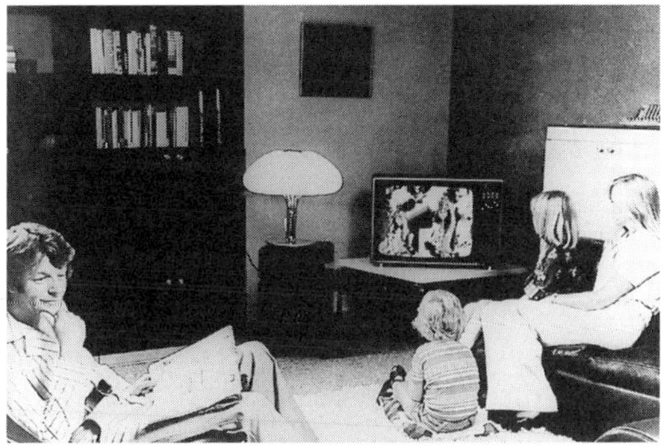

15
Dan Graham
Projection/Reception, 1976

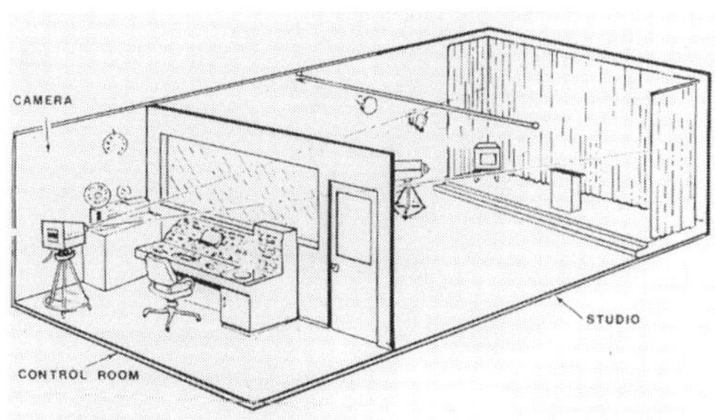

Position of camera in cable channel A broadcast.

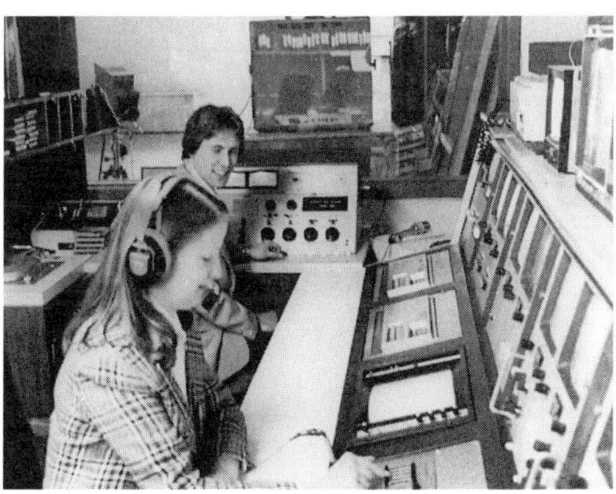

16
Dan Graham
Projection/Reception, 1976

Dan Graham

Essay on Video, Architecture, and Television

Film and Video: Video as Present-Time

Video is a present-time medium. Its image can be simultaneous with its perception by/of its audience (it can be the image of its audience perceiving). The space/time it presents is continuous, unbroken, and congruent with that of the real time which is the shared time of its perceivers and their individual and collective real environments. This is unlike film, which is, necessarily, an edited re-presentation of the past of another reality/an other's reality for separate contemplation by unconnected individuals. Film is discontinuous, its language constructed, in fact, from syntactical and temporal disjunctions (for example, montage). Film is a reflection of a reality external to the spectator's body; the spectator's body is out of the frame. In a live-video-situation, the spectator may be included within the frame at one moment, or be out of the frame at another moment. Film constructs a "reality" separate and incongruent with the viewing situation; video feeds back indigenous data in the immediate, present-time environment or connects parallel time/space continua. Film is contemplative and "distanced"; it detaches the viewer from present reality and makes him a spectator.

Centralization/Decentralization of Information

The distribution of both films and broadcast television represents an asymmetrical imposition of information by capital. Film is a consumption product, as is broadcast television, which, in the interest of advertisers of products, installs a terminal in the home and controls access to information. The concentration of power through capital is also facilitated through the mythology contained in the storylines of programs and advertisements, and through withholding or controlling the availability of information.[1] The centralized production facilities of film or broadcast TV exploit the saleable (product) aspects of culture at the expense of the existential. A cable system, by contrast, presents the possibility of becoming two-way and decentralized. Individuals, families and the local, extant cultural system could be given potential self-determination and control. Local cable television could feed *back* the immediate environment.

Addendum:

TV gains much of its effect from the fact that it appears to depict a world which is immediately and fully present.

The viewer assumes that the TV image is both immediate and contiguous (as to time) with the shared social time and parallel "real world" of its per-

ceivers—even when this may not be the case. This physical immediacy produces in the viewer a sense of psychological intimacy, where people on TV and events appear to directly address him or her.

The Architectural Code/The Video Code

An architectural code both reflects and directs the social order. In the not too distant future one can envisage that this code will be modified and in part supplanted by a new code, that of television. As cable television images displayed on wall-size monitors connect and mediate between rooms, families, social classes, "public"/"private" domains, connecting architecturally (and socially) bounded regions, they take on an architectural (and social) function. Video in architecture will function semiotically speaking as window and as mirror simultaneously, but will subvert the effects and functions of both. Windows in architecture mediate separated spatial units and frame a conventional perspective of one unit's relation to the other; mirrors in architecture define, self-reflectively, spatial enclosure and ego enclosure.

Architecture defines certain cultural and psychological boundaries; video may intercede to replace or rearrange some of these boundaries. Cable television, being reciprocally two-way, can interpenetrate social orders not previously linked; its initial use may tend to deconstruct and redefine existing social hierarchies.

"Public"/"Private" Codes

Public versus private can be dependent upon architectural conventions. By social convention, a window mediates between private (inside) and public (outside) space. The interior seen defines or is defined by the publicly accepted notion of privacy. An architectural division, the "house," separates the "private" person from the "public" person and sanctions certain kinds of behavior for each. The *meaning* of privacy, beyond its mere distinguishability from publicness, is more complexly connected to other social rules. For example: a private home limits access to members of one family; a bathroom within that house is private as it allows usage by only one person at a time (whereas a toilet in a public space is public as it allows multiple access, but is gender restricted); the individual bedroom of a child or adult member of the family may be considered to be private at certain times. Moral sanctions are attached to violation of these codes. There are areas which reflect transitional social change. The taping of private conversations for public law enforcement is one area of unresolved claims between private (including interpretation of the term "private") rights and public rights to justice or knowledge. The widespread use of video surveillance cameras involves similar "moral"/legal issues. The use of video would have social-psychological implications for the family structure: for instance, children being continuously observed through the use of a video camera by their parents "lose" their "right" to be different in private, that is, to have separate "public" and "private" identities.

Conventions of the Glass Window

The glass window, like the Renaissance painting, creates a picture plane that places the world at a measured distance for the viewer on either side. The world, held at a distance, frames a conventional view which is defined by the specific size, shape, and direction of orientation of the opening of the window frame. A view from one space into the other space, by what is allowed to be seen, defines one space's socially (pre-)conceived "view" of the other. What someone on one side of the window can see of the other space, *and* what can be seen of them as part of their space by a viewer on the other side (*and, vice versa,* for someone occupying that other side), is conventionalized by the social/architectural code. A view from one side, as opposed to a view from the other side, may be symmetrical, appear symmetrical but not be, or be clearly asymmetrical. The "picture-window" appears to be symmetrical in the length of time allowed a person on either side to stare, but actually is not. An employer's view of his employees' work space through one-way glass, as opposed to the employees' view of their employer's office, is asymmetrical, expressing inequalities of power.

The Mirror Image/The Video Image

A mirror's image optically responds to a human observer's movements, varying as a function of his position. As the observer approaches, the mirror opens up a wider and deeper view of the room-environment and magnifies the image of the perceiver. By contrast, a video image on a monitor does not shift in perspective with a viewer's shift in position. The mirror's image connects subjectivity with the perceiver's time-space axis. Optically, mirrors are designed to be seen frontally.[2] A video monitor's projected image of a spectator observing it depends on that spectator's relation to the position of the camera, but not on his relation to the monitor. A view of the perceiver can be transmitted from the camera instantaneously or time-delayed over a distance to a monitor which may be near or far from the perceiver's (viewing) position in space or time. Unlike the flat visuality of Renaissance painting, in the video image geometrical surfaces are lost to ambiguously modeled contours and to a translucent depth. Mirrors in enclosures exteriorize all objects within the interior space, so that they appear on the mirror as frontal surface planes. In rectilinear enclosures, mirrors create illusory perspective boxes. The symmetry of mirrors tends to conceal or cancel the passage of time, so that the overall architectural form appears to transcend time, while the interior area of the architecture, inhabited by human movements, process and gradual change, is emptied of significance. As the image in the mirror is perceived as a static instant, place (time and space) becomes illusorily eternal. The world seen on video, by contrast, is in temporal flux and connected subjectively (because it can be identified with) to experienced duration.

Addendum:
The child sees itself formed as an image in the same way as an Other, beside which it identifies. The child's "ego" is formed by an identification with its likeness: that other human being who is in the mirror and the reflection of its body, which is dissimilar to its subjective experience, but is identified with it. In the mirror-image, its "ego" seems to be located in two places simultaneously, outside itself (in the world of other objects and looking back at the child), and within itself (looking out at the image of itself). The child falsely imagines his body image to be a unified and complete entity, identified with the image of Otherness.

Mirrors and "Self"
Mirrors are metaphors for the Western concept of the "self." In his theory of the "mirror phase," Jacques Lacan has posited that a developing child first discovers his "self" by a mirror-like identification with the image of an Other. When the mother holds the child up to the mirror, the child views his body-image reflected in the mirror as an objectified and complete form, at a time when it is subjectively experienced as incomplete and uncoordinated. The child identifies itself with an image of an Other, or an image which is outside its body sensations, but, in terms of social reality, must be taken to be its identity.

Video Feedback
The video feedback of "self"-image, by adding temporality to self-perception, connects "self"-perception to physiological brain processes. This removes self-perception from the viewing of a detached, static image; video feedback contradicts the mirror model of the perceiving "self." Through the use of videotape feedback, the performer and the audience, the perceiver and his process of perception, are linked, or co-identified. Psychological premises of "privacy" (as against publicness) which would derive from the mirror-model, depend on an assumed split between observed behavior and supposedly un-

observable, interior *intention.* However, if a perceiver views his behavior on a five to eight second delay[3] via videotape (so that his responses are part of and influence his perception), "private" mental intention and external behavior are experienced as one. The difference between intention and actual behavior is fed back on the monitor and immediately influences the observer's future intentions and behavior. By linking perception of exterior behavior and its interior, mental perception, an observer's "self," like a topological Möbius strip, can be apparently without "inside" or "outside." Video feedback time is the immediate present, without relation to past and hypothetical future states—a continuous topological or feedback loop forward or backward between just-past or immediate future. Instead of self-perception being a series of fixed "perspectives" for a detached ego, observing past actions with the intent of locating "objective truth" about its essence, video feedback encloses the perceiver in what appears to be (only) what is subjectively present. While the mirror alienates the "self," video encloses the "self" within its perception of its own functioning, giving a person the feeling of a perceptible control over his responses through the feedback mechanism.

The Glass Divider, Light and Social Division

Window glass alienates "subject" from "object." From behind glass, the spectator's view is "objective," while the observed's subject(ivity) is concealed.[4] The observer on the outside of the glass cannot be part of an interior group's "intersubjective" framework. Being mirror-reflective,[5] glass reflects the mirror-image of an observer, as well as the particular inside or outside world behind him, into the image of the space into which he is looking.

Abstractly, this reflectiveness of glass allows it to be a sign signifying, at the same time, the nature of the opposition between the two spaces and their common mediation. The glass in the window through its reflectiveness unites, and by its physical impenetrability separates inside and outside. Due to its reflective qualities, illumination within or without the space that the glass divides, produces either complex reflections, non-reflective transparency, or opacity. Light signifies various distinct spatial or temporal locations. Artificial light is often placed in contrast to natural illumination (defining indoors and outdoors). The pattern of illumination phases with, and marks off, natural and cultural diurnal rhythms of human activities taking place on either side of the glass partition. Illumination is a controller of social behavior. Both glass and light (separately or conjointly) enforce social divisions.

Glass Used in Shop Windows/Commodities in Shop Windows

The glass used for the showcase displaying products, isolates the consumer from the product at the same time as it superimposes the mirror-reflection of his own image onto the goods displayed. This alienation, paradoxically, helps arouse the desire to possess the commodity. The goods are often displayed as part of a human mannequin—an idealized image of the consumer. Glass isolates (draws attention to) the product's surface appeal, "glamour," or superficial appearance alone (attributes of "workmanship" that link craftsmen to a specific product being lost), while denying access to what is tangible or immediately useful. It idealizes the product. Historically, this change in the appearance of the product corresponds to the worker's alienation from the products he produces; to be utilized, the product must be bought on the market in exchange for wages at a market value, with the conditions of its production obscured. Glass is helpful in socially alienating buyer from producer, thereby concealing the product's connection to another's real labor and allowing it to acquire exchange value over and above its use value.

> In a sort of way, it is the same with Man as with commodities . . . man sees himself reflected in other men. Peter only establishes his own identity as a man by first comparing himself with Paul as being of the same kind, and thereby Paul, "in hide and hair," Paul in his Pauline corporality, becomes entirely to Peter the phenomenal form of the genus of Man.[6]

> Capitalistic society makes all personal relations between men take the form of objective relations between things. . . . Social relations are transformed into "qualities of . . . things themselves" (commodities).[7]

Under capitalism, just as the ego is confused with the body image in the mirror, so that ego is confused with the commodity. The individual is made to identify himself (in his feeling for "himself") with the image of the commodity. The commodity object is a substitute (*fetish*) for his lack—the lack his desire expresses. The glass and mirrors of the shop window beckon the potential customer by arousing doubts and desires about his self-image/self-identity. It is as if in looking at the product behind the glass showcase, the consumer is looking at an ideal image of himself (in the mirror). Or he sees in the reflections that he deviates from the ideal (represented by the mannequin), but is given the possibility of acquiring attributes of this ideal if he buys the merchandise. The commodity reflects his desire for a more complete "better self," identified with the alter *ego.*

Inseparable from the goods the consumer desires is the illusion that buying them will "complete" that which is "incomplete" in himself. This desire is never satisfied (as the market system must continue to function), but because the consumer identifies himself with (his projection onto) the commodity, he infuses the commodity with a psychological value which now becomes part of its market value.

In the showcase display the prospective customer's point of view, his sense of "self," is equated not only with the object centered in his view, but with the System (which created the device). The showcase window as a framing or optical device replicates the form of the Renaissance painting's illusionary, three-dimensional "space." Like a painting's perspective, it frames a determined view (determines a view), creating a point of focus—meaning—organized around a central vanishing point. The customer's gaze is focused upon the centered object's external form; focus creates value. The spectator's "self," unseen, projected into the space, is identified with the thing(s) represented. The spectator's gaze, his "self-projection," organizes meaning around the centered object, meeting his centered look.

The material components of the showcase affect the viewer slightly differently from the painting. First, glass becomes a screen upon which a partial mirror-image of the observer himself (accentuated by the use of mirrors in the back of the case facing the front plane) is imposed. By means of strong overhead lighting, the faint reflection of the spectator, as well as that of the outside, real world, is superimposed on the glass in front of the visually highlighted objects seen within. The glass of the showcase is optically halfway between the invisibility (which hides the spectator's and the original painter's self-image) of the Renaissance painting and the reflectivity of the mirror (which shows the spectator himself looking, plus that part of the real space which is normally invisible behind him).[8] Often a rear mirror or smaller fragments of a mirror are positioned behind objects displayed in showcases, to fracture the ideal image of the spectator, partially glimpsed on the glass surface and rear mirror. By these means a viewer's initially desired ideal "self"-image is focused and imposed upon—identified with—the inaccessible, but visually desired, commodity for sale; the object seems imaginarily complete, while the "self" is de-totalized, incomplete, lost, not graspable, except through its visual projection upon the object. The shop window thus captures, focuses, and efficiently employs the latent desires of the casual passerby, to confer a subjective, overdetermined meaning upon the goods it "objectively" places on view.

Glass Buildings: Corporate "Showcases"

At the same time that glass reveals, it conceals. If one looks into a glass showcase, one can have the illusion that the container is neutral, without apparent interest in the content of what it displays; or, conversely, the appearance of what is contained can be seen as a function of the qualities of the container itself.[9] In the ideology of modern functionalist architecture, an architectural form appropriates and merges both of these readings. First, because symbolic form, ornamentation, is eliminated from the building (form and content being merged), there is no distinction between the form and its material structure; that is, the form represents nothing more or less than the material. Second, a form or structure is seen to represent only its contained function, the building's structural and functional efficiency being equated with its real utility for those who use it. Aesthetically, this idea is expressed in the formula: efficient form is beautiful and beautiful form is efficient. This has a "moral" dimension; "efficient" connotes a melioristic, "scientific" approach seemingly uncontaminated by "ideology," which, pragmatically, has (capitalistic) use value. ("Efficiency" is how well a building contributes to the operations of the company housed within it. The look of a building, its cleanness and structural transparency, thus joins the myth of scientific progress to that of the social utility of efficient business practice.)[10] These glass and steel buildings usually house corporations or government agencies. The building's transparent functionalism conceals its less apparent ideological function: justifying the use of technology or bureaucracy by large corporations or government agencies to impart their particular version of order on society. The spectator's view is diverted away from social context by focusing only on the surface material or structural qualities. Glass and steel are used as "pure" materials, for the sake of their materiality. The use of glass gives another illusion: that what is seen is seen exactly as it is. Through the glass one sees the technical workings of the company and the technical engineering of the building's structure. The glass's literal transparency not only falsely objectifies reality, but is a paradoxical camouflage; for while the actual function of a corporation may be to concentrate its self-contained power and control by *secreting* information, its architectural facade gives the illusion of absolute openness. The transparency is visual only; glass separates the visual from the verbal, insulating outsiders from the content of the decision-making processes, and from the invisible, but real, interrelationships linking company operations to society.

The glass building, in attempting to eliminate the disparity between its outside facade (which conventionally mediates its relation to the outside environment where it is sited) and its private, institutional function, pretends to eliminate the distinction between its outer form and its inner content. The self-contained, transparent glass building denies that it has an outside and that it participates as an element in the language of the surrounding buildings with other social functions which make up the surrounding environmental context. Where other buildings are usually decorated with conventional signs of their function for the public to see, the facade of the glass building is virtually eliminated. The aesthetic purity of the glass building, standing apart from the common environment, becomes transformed by its owner into a social alibi for the institution it houses. The building's transparent "openness" to the environment (it incorporates the natural environment) on the one hand, and its claim to aesthetic hegemony over the surrounding environment (its formal self-containment) on the other, efficiently legitimate the corporate institution's claim to autonomy ("The World of General Motors"). A building with glass on four sides gives the illusion of self-containment. While it appears open to visual inspection, in fact, in looking through glass on all sides, one realizes the particular, focused-upon detail, the "interior," is lost (one looks *through* and not *at*) to the architectural generality, to the apparent materialness of the outward form, or to "Nature" (light, sun, sky or the landscape glimpsed through the building on the other side).

Notes

1. One explanation for the form that broadcast television has taken—a centrally originated transmission sent to the passive home viewer on a privately owned TV set—is that television came into being first as a commodity item, mass-produced for the consumer market. When it appeared, the TV set belonged to a new type of inexpensively produced small machines (other examples are automobiles, cameras, electrical appliances, radios) designed to be transportable or provide means to private transportation. The consumer's demand for these goods was a response to the charged work and life conditions of the industrial worker; he was uprooted from his traditional house for a mobile and urbanized pattern. With the aid of these products the newly re-settled worker could plug in quickly to whatever urban social environment he found himself in. At the same time, because of the pressures of a more technically organized work life, the private areas of family and house became retreats for the worker in his "time off." Television programming allowed the person in his private space to feel connected to a larger, public world, but remain free of its demands, sheltered in his private home life.

2. The mirror inverts the position of the spectator seeing a Renaissance painting. There the spectator faces the painting and looks forward into its projected space; in doing this, he reconstructs the exterior (and also the "interior") view of the painter at the point in time and space when he made the painting.

3. Five to eight seconds is the limit of "short-term" memory, or memory which is part of and influences a person's (present) perception.

4. Seen by a second observer on the other side of the glass, the first observer appears as an outsider.

5. There is a physical and a dialectical relation between mirrors and glass, each reflecting, accentuating qualities of the other.

6. Karl Marx, quoted in Anthony Wilden, *System and Structure* (London: Tavistock Publications, 1972).

7. Herbert Marcuse, *Reason and Revolution* (New York: Oxford University Press, 1941). Marcuse is quoting Marx at the end of this passage.

8. Both the Renaissance painting and the mirror are two-dimensional rectilinear surfaces, conventionally hung to meet the standing spectator's eye-level view and flush with an interior wall, so that the wall functions both as an architectural (structural) support and as support for the painting or mirror. The mirror or painting's back surface and the area of the wall upon which it is hung are hidden from view; in their place is either the reflection of the opposite side of the space or a depiction of an illusionary "space." Both mirror and painting use the frame to orient the spectator's view, necessitating that he turns frontally and faces the picture or mirror surface, focusing his attention toward the center point (defined by the framed edges of the form).

A mirror literally inverts the Renaissance painting's perspective; it flattens the real, present world, reversing it 180 degrees to the spectator facing the mirror, so he can see himself physically in the picture (looking).

9. But an optical focus—which aspect of the world is perceived when one looks—is culturally determined.

10. The technological-utilitarian glass office structure derives from the Bauhaus's vision of an architecture built from elemental, ideal formal and social images. The total, utopian vision in theory could serve as an alternative to the dominant, conservative, bourgeois order, wedding science and aesthetics to a socially just and more rational notion of progress (scientific progress aiding social progress). The vision begins with, and is grafted onto, the mid-19th century notion of "art for art's sake," which proposed an art that would negate the existing world order through the creation of an interior order of art. In this vision, "Art"/"Architecture" attempts to create another (which is always "its" own) language—in order to transcend that of the existent, real world. The total new order could be seen as a negation of all existing values, the avant-gardist notion being one that radically denies the "old" in favor of the "new" (social-aesthetic principle); this is seen in itself as healthy. The structuralist version of "radical" art devaluation (e.g., Roland Barthes's *Writing Degree Zero*) is to purge the language of its (hidden) ideological contamination by reducing the text to purely elemental structure. The artist was seen as an "underground" but heroic figure, standing apart from the social order—the existence of his art as a radical negation, denial, of this order. It is a paradox, then, that the more willful and heroic the imposition of the art form on an environment perceived as sterile or antagonistically unaesthetic, the more transcendent and utopian the artist's or architect's initial vision (which the building/artwork symbolically expresses), the much more distanced (and arrogant) the message that the building/artwork conveys to the general social body and more impotent is its intended ideological corrective effect.

This text was written in 1979 and first published in Dan Graham: Video/Architecture/Television: Writings on Video and Video Works 1970–1978, *ed. Benjamin H. D. Buchloh (Halifax: The Press of the Nova Scotia College of Art and Design; New York: New York University Press, 1979), pp. 62–76.*

Dan Graham Interviewed by Ludger Gerdes

Ludger Gerdes

So Dan, what can you say about Conceptual art?

Dan Graham

The question was, also is, if Conceptual art was material, how can it have had any effect? One thing I think, the culture in the 60s was about immediacy and presentness. The present was detached from historical time. It was thought that one was to experiment in the here and now: thus life was a perceptual experience. These ideas came from both phenomenology and perhaps also drug culture. They also might have been, maybe, a way of adapting to this flow of new consumer goods that was flooding the market, maybe a positive way to respond, although on the other hand there was always an ambivalence—an awareness that consumer culture was a problem as well as positive, which was why both "hippies" and Conceptual art wanted to reject materiality. Conceptual art was context-dependent, it linked itself and drew its meaning from other things that were material, although a materiality that was often an "of the moment." Or it set up a process or connected itself to processes that would become material in a later point in time; from another point of view, it actually tried—this was the negating or deconstructing sense of Conceptual art—not to be material. It wanted to not have lasting material existence, but to exist only as a catalyst to change and help to deconstruct or to destroy existing material, established icons.

Gerdes

So one hand was doing what you call the deconstruction of the old order, and the other hand preparing kind of new models which the perceiver could use after having seen the artwork to make something different than what he knew from the other art.

Graham

Yes, with one exception, which is that these models weren't necessarily to be called "art"; they could function in culture generally. If Lawrence Weiner uses models inside language use—specifically he was relating his models to Chomsky's ideas of deep language—so Conceptual art often thought that it was both part of a vernacular common currency of culture *and also* making its own contribution to abstract scientific cultural investigations. It was populist in that is was using terms of the common language of information media. This was maybe a utopian conceit.

Gerdes

So in a way, concept art had similarities with Pop art in using populist motifs or contents or whatever, but on the other hand, it was not an art depending on icons or on objects. So what was the specificity of doing something which is conceptual?

Graham

Now I'm only speaking for myself. I didn't believe that there was such a thing as Conceptual art. Let's just say, it was the problematic relation between what was material and perceivable or what was structural and conceptual; say, the relation between the schema or the conceptual structure and what was there to be perceived at a present moment. It was combining the ideas of serial music *and* John Cage. On the one hand you had something extremely physical, and it was the quality of the actual perceptual process, of the spectator, receiving this material thing. On the other hand, the composition was generated from the most invisible, purely mathematical, structural kind of scheme. And the two didn't meet in any clear way, so there was this discrepancy between the two that was being investigated. If you want to put it another way, I was interested in the conceptual generating construct as against the material perceptual construct. And this issue was very focused on in all Conceptual art. The most simplistic way to see Conceptual art was that it could be just a concept "in the head," but I don't think that's exactly stating what the problem was. It was more a problem that was inherent in linguistics and structuralism to begin with, particularly when it met with phenomenology.

Gerdes

So could it be described as an investigation of finding basic structures of communication or of social groupings?

Graham

That's not a bad way to say it. That the paradoxes in this model, these models, became more evident. This wasn't just academic but—because these were problems that were inherent in, let's say, Modernist structures, in art, in music, from the beginning of the century—the issue was also whether you could communicate in terms of these structures, deep structures, and do away with representation.

Gerdes

Yes. But even for older Modern art, it had been an aim to find fundamental structures, whether these might be architectural or formal or sculptural or whatever.

Graham

These were more in the way of perceptual structures.

Gerdes

Right.

Graham

So I would locate them, people locate them, in different places. I would locate them in the relations of the spectator's sense perception. That's also why I would locate them in the area of information.

Gerdes

So it was a switch, not from the material entities but to the communicative procedures which are used to perceive these kinds of material.

Graham

I think that's very exact, what you just said; that would be a very good way to say it. That's close to what I would say.

Gerdes

Dan, you think Conceptual art was essentially influenced by political ideas? What is the political aim or content? Was the questioning of individuality to be believed?

Graham

Yes, one thing that was important was to destroy liberalism and humanism, I think that came from an attack on Abstract Expressionism where these things, the heroic and individual art gestures, were caricatured and made to seem absurd. In Pop art, Jasper Johns, in a very melancholy way, saw the death of the artist as, let's say, a seer or a prophet, a shaman, Faustian figure, in an extremely pessimistic way. This stance was ironically reversed in Pop art. As Andy Warhol said, well, maybe it's better if we all become like robots and machines. Conceptual art accepted the same thing, but saw it in terms of positive, affirmative, rather than negative possibilities, although it was always ambivalent about this. By affirmative possibilities, I mean those postulated by someone like Marcuse. It was also a time of phenomenology as a method, but unlike Sartre, who had a pessimistic view of existence, phenomenology was now turned around and made into a philosophy of simply experiencing perceptual immediacy for the sake of perceptual immediacy in itself, where life was an extended external present time. There was an enormous flood of new commodities which seemed to destroy any possibility of artists' own composition or creating new value, and seemed to devalue value. This devaluation was the result of an economy of less work and more time for consumption and leisure. But this devaluation could have possibilities. It was possibly meant that the receiver, the person who bought all of these things, might be made creative and liberated in his use of time. Life might become an aestheticized form of play. The art receiver could be a creative participant in art: art's task was to help make this aestheticized play available to everybody.

Gerdes

So then it was these old-fashioned Modern ideas that the artist would disappear?

Graham

In a certain way, the artist disappeared. He just set in motion different structures. The artist as a hero disappeared, that was part of the idea of composition disappearing at the time. A good example would be John Cage. In a way he was the most old-fashioned, because he was the most, sort of, transcendentally utopian postwar figure. But I think his work is a good model for the most optimistic aspects of Conceptual art. Information structure was a very important issue. In Baudrillard's recent writing it has returned in its most pessimistic form. Baudrillard's position was best stated in the 60s by a science fiction writer, Philip K. Dick: that art was a representation of a representation, that is, only a simulation of reality.

Gerdes

Dan, with concept art there was a certain emphasis on the use value that artworks could have, besides seeing an artwork just as an aesthetic entity. What was specific about this concept of use value?

Graham

I don't totally agree with that idea, or having art be reduced to simply use value. I don't think that was necessarily the correct reading of Conceptual art at the time. Later, some critics made those claims, but I don't think it's one hundred percent correct. It makes it seem that Conceptual art has no aesthetic value, which I don't agree with. I think my work has aesthetic value, I think if it doesn't, it's very bad, it doesn't work. My work, all work of that time, had a playfulness value. Marcuse said that he was in favor of aestheticized play, that this notion should take the place of art.

Gerdes

Aestheticized . . .

Graham

Aestheticized play would take the place of "formal" art. I think that goes too far also. But it seems to oppose itself to use value. In my case, maybe in other people's work, you have work that is a model for a kind of psychological/social/linguistic situation. It also has the form of a game. I can refer again to John Cage as a good example. It was the idea of game, rules of play, etc., which were important. And this playfulness, however ambiguous its relation to "art," liberated us from being essentially academic. The social-political models that were used, in my case, were popular cliches. I employed cliches in the same way that Pop art did. So if I took something that was a cliche, it wasn't necessarily serious, or kitsch, because it was critical of itself as a model and maybe critical of art as a model. It was both of those things at the same time. If it gave new perceptual information, that was a positive value as well. The main thing was that, like media cliches, the work wasn't designed to last forever. And its form—performance, video, language game—in one sense mirrored the way a video or theater actually was happening, outside of the area of art. But these works also related to history of art situations. For instance, Fluxus events or Happenings. Like Happenings, Conceptual art was about social or psychological language structures at that particular moment in time. Mine always involved the question of the audience, its perception of itself and of performance in the act of perceiving. Conceptual art, like performance events, was discardable. Because of the idea that society was a series of present moments, and as society changes the work was discardable, Conceptual work didn't have a historical dimension—other than de-emphasizing previous art ideologies. The only "art trace" left was remembrance of the piece by the performers and the audience, and its effects. This was the principle of my magazine pieces. So in that sense you could say it had an *immediate* use value, but it was discardable in the same way that a magazine article is discardable.

Was it aesthetic? Well, I would say it had to be aesthetic to work in design terms, but that's not as difficult a definition as for "art as art" terms. Is there an opposition between aesthetic and use value? I would say, no, there isn't. To see Conceptual art as absolute use value seems too puritanical, and most of the art of that time was anti-puritanical. But when you look back on it, it may look like it is puritanical. This is to confuse a concern with social idealism, a moralism coupled with "gallows" humor and a healthy nihilism, with today's "neo-Conceptualism" identified with either Baudrillard or Adorno. Critics discussing "Conceptual art" miss the contextual meaning and impose from their concerns today a very rigid viewpoint.

Gerdes

What about the use of reductionist structures?

Graham

Conceptual art, as well as Minimal art, was interested in what one calls reductiveness. One principle was that less is more. The idea was to reduce things—ideas, surface, content—to the point where they seemed to be blank or were tautologies, or had no obvious content in terms of representation or seemed not to be saying anything. They had no message. And yet behind the apparent black surface was often an incredible complexity. In literature, good examples are Michel Butor or Marguerite Duras or Robbe-Grillet, all of these French "nouveau roman" people, where it seemed everything was reduced to simple geometric ciphers.

Gerdes

The belief was in reducing them?

Graham

No, this was the way . . .

Gerdes

To find something universal?

Graham

The idea was that there wasn't anything universal. What was left was the phenomenological presence of the here and now of *reading* or seeing art in an architectural environment. I'm saying what it was getting rid of was subject matter. So it looks like a very simple blank structure, but behind it, in fact, are incredibly complex structures. But these structures which are exposed in a work were without traditional representational allusion—they had no overt meaning. They're ambiguous. A pretty good example is On Kawara, whose paintings' content may have appeared too simplistic, too literal, just the date; but in fact, he had this system dealing with political representation of time and the artist's place in this system behind it. What was being obviously gotten rid of was the idea that meaning was within the surface—representational meaning; and that the artist himself had any impact in the world. Conceptual structures were ones that were just to be found in the world without the artist's "discovery." It was analogous to the actual world, or the world discovered by modern physics. It was to be discovered in the spectator's perceptual take.

Gerdes

Also, humor was important for works like yours.

Graham

Well, I think the rationale for making work often *was* humor. But it was a humor where things seemed so simple that a child could have done them. Something approaching the idiotic. But to miss this humor is to miss the point of most of the work. It wasn't that it was about humor per se, but humor located where the real, let's say, philosophical or psychological edge was. I can think of very little Conceptual art that didn't sort of begin and end with Beckett-like humor. And I would say that half of my Conceptual pieces are certainly about this humor. Art is about transgression and also about camouflage. It also is a way to release some very strong feelings. Most of the strong feelings were actually expressed through humor—humor was the way into the work's ambiguities. I think you might grasp this from looking at Lichtenstein's dealing with women's emotions or war time. There certainly were elements of parody in the work.

Gerdes

Dan, also in your work and in works by colleagues like Michael Asher and Daniel Buren, there was an attempt at making an awareness of contexts where artworks usually are shown. Institutional contexts or formal, phenomenological contexts. In which way was this an important idea for works of yours?

Graham

My initial context was the gallery as presented in the magazine. I had a gallery in 1964 and I noticed that the gallery was dependent on magazine writing, advertising, photographs that were reproduced in the magazines to give initial value to the work the gallery was showing. In fact after we advertised a few times we got our first reviews, and our reviews had these photographs from the exhibition. My idea was that value came from a reproduction first, reproduction in magazines, before it came from people buying the artwork. The magazines are interesting to me because of their combination of photographs and words. I had been interested before my gallery experience in writing. After the gallery failed I started taking photographs of houses in suburbia. Being without money and having no formal art training, I turned to photography because it didn't cost any money or need any special skill. I wondered if you put photographs or art directly in the magazine with an article, whether the art/article bypassed the gallery. I figured if you had first shown it in a gallery it would have some value but if you didn't it wouldn't have any value.

My aim was to make an art which didn't have market value, but functioned in the same way as Flavin's fluorescents. I didn't want to show in a gallery setting. Flavin would take electric light fixtures—they were not "readymades"—and put them up as part of the lighting system of the gallery. This affected all the other work and made a reference to the gallery architecture itself. When the show was over the gallery removed them and they weren't really saleable because the context would be different in a home or museum setting. They were very context-dependent on the architecture of that show in that gallery. After the exhibition they went back to the hardware store. But in time some of Flavin's work was bought and sold out of context. This violation of the premise didn't make sense to me. I felt that works such as Flavin's made more sense like a magazine that was discarded after one month, thrown away. Like Flavin's lights, which modified the other work around it, my magazine placements were also dependent on context. In a magazine they took their meaning from what was around them in that issue, which modified their meanings, and they modified the other pages' meaning. That's how I came to the medium of information. Later, I got interested in the temporary pavilion for large exhibitions like "Documenta"; years later, I was invited to be in them.

The gallery is a very recent historical construct. The idea that it functions as emblematic of the Establishment or as a timeless, historically fixed form isn't correct. My article "Homes for America" was about the relation between the art and the urban or suburban environment. The gallery or museum must also be seen in terms of the relation of art to the urban and suburban surroundings. But in the 60s it was important to show how the Establishment, seen in Establishment terms of Establishment institutions, from the school to the museum, could be taken apart to expose its foundation in order to liberate it. This was the radical task of information: since it's revealed, it's liberating. It connected to the somewhat idealist, ironic and political gestures of that particular time. The deconstruction wasn't cynical. And it was more apocalyptic than pessimistic. Presently I'm not a believer in deconstruction. I don't think it's useful. But I think I share in the interest of that time, commonly shared by many Conceptual artists, of dismantling Establishment structures.

Gerdes

And the methods have been different in showing the structures of the gallery or the museum . . .

Graham

Hidden structures.

Gerdes

Hidden structures?

Graham

Yes.

Gerdes

And there was not so much of a look beyond the boundaries or the actual structures. But you in your writings have been one of the first not just to reflect on these structures, or the hidden structures, but to open up the mind for things outside the usual art world structures. Because you focused on architecture and on discussions which went on in architecture at that time, and tried to combine them with reflections in the art world.

Graham

I think maybe that was done through noticing that people such as Sol LeWitt, Flavin, were interested in films of Antonioni, Fellini, Godard, which themselves alluded to post–World War II architecture as kind of bureaucratic fascist architecture. I saw one content of Sol's work as an allusion to cliches of bureaucratic fascist vernacular architecture. I saw that Don Judd might be alluding to suburban architecture. But they didn't want to consciously represent that there was a subject matter or source for their abstract forms. Possibly by taking photographs of these phenomena it came to be more conscious to me. My references to suburban surroundings seemed to have appeared very early, in the first article, and in slide photographs I was taking.

Gerdes

So it seems that consciously—was it consciously or unconsciously?—colleagues of yours have been influenced or impressed by fascist gestures, fascist morphological gestures.

Graham

Well, I think it was a little more complicated. And it did involve some humor as well, ironic humor. America of that time, for that generation, was officially liberal, permissive. It congratulated itself on having stopped the fascist countries and in moving beyond that period. But consciously there was a troubling thought that these fascist structures had actually infiltrated mass psychological subliminal consciousness through advertising. I think Pop art was alluding to this—early Pop art, particularly Jasper Johns, early Warhol in the form of soup cans and beer cans and these mass advertising techniques, which of course were similar to the same mass psychological techniques that were used in Germany during the fascist period. Modernist architecture had entered into a phase—if you want, the Philip Johnson phase—where it was either cynical or very bureaucratic in its corporatization of modern devices, such as space grid arrangements, glass towers. You can see it in the work of people like

Artschwager, reflected in a humorous way. Sol LeWitt's first works reflected these architectural cliches.

And I think Minimal artists had a dilemma, because they, at the time, were very against official liberalism; this no doubt is reflected in a kind of mock fascism in their own work, which was somewhat contradictory and humorous. On one hand the work appeared to continue, but slightly revise, Constructivism. They were combining neo-Constructivist, Russian Constructivist forms with the forms of the period that came right afterward, late 30s fascist forms, and linking these two histories with the period of the present time, where you had a bureaucratic, late modernistic liberal style, if you want, "fascism," of housing estates. I think Gerhard Richter's early painting shows that, too. That's the contradictory imagery, it was "fascism" just under the surface. Next, LeWitt and these other people preferred to move toward abstraction. I couldn't do that if I was taking photographs, because you couldn't take abstract photographs of that phenomenon, and I was interested in magazine content, text and photos; what you would find in a magazine, where one finds representational photographs of phenomena, which could be grouped in a certain way with text, typographic design, and other overlaid, two-dimensional structures which were essentially informational structures. To work at making a translation, I couldn't make three-dimensional structures, for this required money. It was pretty important to do something that required no money and that wasn't collectible at that moment.

Gerdes

So in a way, concept art didn't survive in the way things changed in the 70s; and in the 80s there was a comeback of the object and of the artificial artwork. And you participated in that. What is the importance of this idea of the object, again, today?

Graham

Well, I think that Conceptual art only survived because the economy at that particular moment provided other sources of income. It seemed that there was enormous abundance for everybody, including artists, so there was no economic pressure.

Gerdes

The 60s?

Graham

Yes.

Gerdes

The idea of losing the object? The object as very important for artistic experience?

Graham

There were other movements. There were an enormous amount of objects. We "Conceptual artists" eventually had to realize that you had to be inside the Establishment, not marginalized, to affect the Establishment. The only way inside the Establishment was to make an object or a pseudo-object; either that or you became an academic, became only a teacher; we had to be more pragmatic about it. I think making an object didn't necessarily make you into a neo-Conceptual artist. A very good Conceptual artist is Bruce Nauman, and under normal conditions, his work never would have sold. He was making holograms, videotapes, photographs, all these unsaleable things. But because he had a very good gallery when he was quite young, because of the presence, even ironically, of the "artist's hand" and because he had a European base of museums that were buying his work, once that happened, the work always had the value, and always was treated as a collectible object, even if he didn't treat it that way. It was a valid strategy for Conceptual artists to make objects. The desire to communicate is the main desire of Conceptual art. It needed an audience, didn't want to be academicized, or marginalized. But the object produced was more of a "manifesto," an ironic, deceptive, pseudo-object designed in quasi bad faith toward an economy of consumers—and designed to infiltrate the system—or it was an information package. Conceptual art had begun to use "Pop" marketing strategies.

Gerdes

So the biggest issue was communication?

Graham

It might be. I think when you were speaking earlier about the idea of a model of some kind, making models, intellectual, communicational, whatever kind of models, I think that does require a particular kind of public context. And the public context definitely was itself shifting. In the 60s it was an extremely open, diverse one, which didn't have any fixed focus; it didn't need an object to focus on, didn't need a church, didn't need any architecture, didn't need a gallery, like an Arab bedouin nomad.

Gerdes

But at least for your purposes, elements of communication were very important, in terms of working out perceiving models, of perceiving somebody else and of perceiving yourself, or of interruption of perception of somebody else, or the ability of having an experience of yourself by the use of mirrors or glass or delayed videos. So in a way, again, it was not so much an autonomous, artificial object, which somebody could admire or experience in an autonomous realm of aesthetic experience. Your work was much more a tool for a social communicative process that you usually don't have either in art or in the everyday world.

Graham

I think if you don't have it in a gallery, then you can use the temporary museum exhibition that was thematized, which I would say were like world's fairs of art. Wolf Herzogenroth invited me in the video section of a large show, Projekt '74 "Kunst bleibt Kunst" in Cologne in 1974. I didn't have an existing object, but I thought up a work for that section, a didactic work for a large public. This is a specific kind of art, probably called *Demonstration Kunst,* or something. I like categories that are hybrid or have a double meaning. The art for magazines had meaning in terms of the magazine and of art. Or you can make art that has a private meaning, or conceptual meaning as a sort of scientific investigation—Nauman is a good example. On the other hand, you have something that's almost an art object, but it isn't exactly. I'm agreeing with what you're saying. You can't be too fixed about what an art object is. Because I think the art object often is what it is later in history, not at the moment that it was first conceived, and my first motive was not to make an art object per se.

Gerdes

And still, with your more recent works, you have this kind of double meaning, like the more contemporary pavilions: you can see them, on one hand, as objects coming out of highly Modernist or Minimalist morphology, and on the other hand you can experience them as a tool of, let's say, social interaction, between people hidden, people looking at other people, people being interrupted by boundaries, coming together across boundaries, and all these things.

Graham

I think they mimic these different conditions. They mimic these structures in the world, true, and they also maybe mimic the Minimal object taken outdoors or become almost functional as an architectural lobby or pavilion. The ultimate meaning, a lot of the meaning, comes from the particular use context. My present work isn't so different from its Conceptual art beginning point. I look for a context which is still of the moment but at least includes some of the future, some of the time that will pass between ten, twenty years from now and the future—what the work will become in a public context. But beyond that, I don't know. Basically, I'm not making a purely traditional art object.

Gerdes

Your new, different attitude toward time is also included in memory. Is this different from the Minimal objects which excluded memory or references to art or everything from the past?

Graham

Yes, except . . .

Gerdes

And the emphasis in your pavilions is more to make a connection between these forms which you use and the meaning they had in the past?

Graham

I think the Minimalist objects, although they were very aware of the past and took it into account and weren't as divorced from this as they pretended, had an ideology connected with the fact that it (the art) accepts that progress had come to an end and the only real value was the present. A Flavin had its ultimate value only from the particular present context that it was placed in—one which would never happen again. You had to experience it there and then. This was also a strategic way of being anti-museum, and anti-Establishment.

Gerdes

So the ideas which were important were the ideas of the here and now?

Graham

Well . . .

Gerdes

Actuality?

Graham

I think this led to a series of crises, because I think the idea of basing art on a strict phenomenology of the present and the work's visual presence assumed that every present would be equal to the present that just passed—that we'd have a series of presents, that they would be sufficient. My critique is that this devalues the former, just-past present. Walter Benjamin expresses this idea first. He notes that in consumer culture the importance of what has been recently passed and just discarded, like yesterday's papers, leads to an amnesia about that time period. I see a crisis in architecture where so-called post-Modern ideas replace so-called Modern ideas, only to have the post-Modernists' critique of Modernism (which was a critique that Modernism had no interest in the past, among other things) also tending to create a new denial of history—history of the just-past Modern movement. The Modernism it has discarded is immediately around it in today's real environment but not linked with or acknowledged.

I think that leaves my position as one that has ultimately to defend a kind of Modernism—one that critiques Modernism but isn't post-Modernist. Modernism has more value and power now that it's been discarded and is repressed—is part of the recent past. Its power is even stronger because it's been downgraded. In 1972 I did a piece called *Past Future/Split Attention,* a video. It's two people, one person is speaking about the other person's future, predicting his immediate future or far future, and the other person is speaking about the first person's just-past or remembered past. They speak at the same time and they are influencing each other. It all really takes place in the just-past. It's about the paradox of present time. Because neither stays in the present time as they speak or behave, it's impossible for there to be present time. The only thing resembling present time is a slight projection into the future, or into the just-past.

Gerdes

Do you make a difference between your work and the work of colleagues of the same generation? I would describe works like Daniel Buren's or Michael Asher's as being mainly interested in reflections of the known or unknown contexts of art in general. From my point of view, your work, since you started writing about architecture, has been more an attempt to look to situations beyond the normal boundaries of the existing so-called art world. So in the 60s and the 70s, unlike many colleagues, you opened up your opus to architecture and to discussions which took place in architecture of that time, and tried to look for a new area of artistic work. Is that any kind of correct description?

Graham

Yes.

Gerdes

You have been interested in post-Modern architecture, which, in contrast to Modern architecture, made an attempt to address public questions or questions of what is taking place in the arena of the city.

Graham

You remember that my first interests seemed to be the relation of the suburbs to the city, and this to the art world or the boundary between the two. I think I was drawn to Venturi's work by his similar interests. His second book used Ed Ruscha's parking lots and reread Pop art in terms of urban/suburban reality. I saw a reflection in architectural historical terms of things I was reflecting on from an art point of view. Reading from the way an architect sees art back and re-reflecting that view the other way. This is the type of boundary situation that I always got a lot out of. It was opposed to simply using architecture as emblematic of the gallery, and something which had to be deconstructed. I was also very influenced by two friends who were very interested in architecture, Michael Asher and John Knight. At that time I was tending to be somewhat critical of post-Conceptual Minimal purism. It was a time when I was switching from large video environments to museum situations. I was given a space in the Venice Biennale in 1976, a space which suggests an El Lissitzky demonstration room. I speculated as to what would happen if that enclosed space wasn't the pure white-wall gallery, whether it would be a problem if there was a window at the end instead of it being self-enclosed. Then it would be almost architecture. I thought of some situations where one could build a work which would have a similar situation to the Venice piece, but have a large window at one end and whose siting would be an actual suburban environment. Ideas that came from art and from analogous architectural practices at the same time could be similar to work done by architects. I also made, in model form, another group of things that were outdoor pavilions. These might be more readily doable in large exhibitions as "outdoor sculpture" pavilions. That would have an analogy to maybe Mies's Barcelona pavilion or to Rietveld's Sonsbeck pavilion. I became more involved in this context, which more specifically involved knowledge of architecture.

Gerdes

Nowadays we have a growing interest in making exhibitions that are not taking place inside the museum or the *Kunstverein* or the gallery but outside in cities. In which way do you share this interest?

Graham

I think these are conservative times, and I think the outdoor city exhibition is a way to solve a problem for museums. The city might spend a lot of money to build art museums for collections of a wealthy millionaire mogul type person, such as Saatchi or Ludwig or whatever, but there's a fear of buying something that's avant-garde. So you could take some of the same work which might not be purchased, put it outside, and call it sculpture for the public. It's not so avant-garde: it's a more traditional category called public sculpture, and no one has to keep the work around after the show, necessarily. Another thing that's happening in France, which is very similar, are the FRACs: the regional associations set up by the Socialist government to decentralize culture are buying a lot of work, but they often don't have the museums to exhibit it. One solution is to exhibit it in an existing garden on land which doesn't have much monetary value. So it's not expensive, you don't have to build a museum. You have created both a nature preserve and an art educational park. And you don't need so much work to fill it or to maintain it as a museum. These are pragmatic solutions, but I think there are deeper implications as to where this might be leading, which you'll have to ask me questions about.

Gerdes

I think, on one hand, we have to see that all Modern art was suffering from the reality that in modern times the artwork became something autonomous in itself. But since we have this kind of idea, and since the autonomous artwork was shown in specific situations which are prepared for these autonomous works, like museums, artists have had this feeling of coming back into contact with the real social world; so at least for the classic avant-garde of the 20th century it was a big attempt to come back into contact with social everyday life. And on the other hand I think what we see nowadays is that people from museums, curators or whatever, are using artworks to bring the museums outside in the context of the city. But there is no real situation of publicness because there is no real public need which is articulated and which is waiting for artworks, and there is no real communication between artists who are producing and certain parts of the public which need certain kinds of works for certain situations. So there is a kind of contradiction which you could polemically describe as an occupation or invasion going outside into the public realms of people. How do you see these two historical points?

Graham

Yes, I think that's a good analysis. But again, I'm going to relate to my own experiences working in a tradition that doesn't exist in America. Almost all of the work that I've been able to do that has had any effect in Europe has come out of the large temporary exhibition modeled on the world's fairs starting from the mid-19th century, the great expositions in Paris and London that then became trade fairs and then became "Documenta," "Projekt." These are art surveys for the general public, which usually involve temporary pavilions, pseudo-didactic categories of knowledge, themes. They are for a middle-class, educated public. The rationalization of art as knowledge and education is a little bit like buying an encyclopedia for your sons and daughters. The shows are justified by linking art to society. All of which I both do and don't take seriously, but which generates overall context.

Gerdes

I think that to compare our situation to situations of the past, where artworks have been used in public contexts outside of museums, you have to see a main difference, which is that till the beginning of the 20th century there have always been more or less general ideas of the shaping of the public—more or less a pictorial idea of shaping the world where the artwork had to fit in—and in cultural situations right now there's a lack, or there is not this kind of general idea where the artwork would fit in as part of a more or less general picture, like the traditional garden or landscape park was. So I think we have to be aware of this difference: if you take an artwork out of the museum and put it into the city, it's not comparable to the use of the artwork in other times in parks and gardens and cities. Even the classical Modernists, like Mies van der Rohe, had a more or less general idea of the shaping of the whole world, where the pavilion or the architecture or the work should fit in, and I think that at least since the Second World War this general idea of shaping the outside world has been lacking. So there is a difference if you go outside of the museum today.

Graham

I think you have two different things: I think the exhibitions are very programmatic in their themes, correct or incorrect; plus, one artist's work is aware of the other's work, so that there's a meaning by proximity to another work. In other words, context is a ruling factor in setting up a structure. There's also the context of the different areas of the city, historically and otherwise. In Venice, the Biennale pavilions are also in one location in the city. If you look in the catalogue for the Münster show, artworks are grouped, for good or bad, according to whether they're near the university area, the park area, the different areas, kind of a morphology of the city, a very vague kind of gestalt-like idea is supposed.

Gerdes

But the meanings . . .

Graham

No, there are a lot of meanings, but they're often extremely temporary and discardable meanings, because I think you're having a temporary exhibition, no better or no worse than the kind of really oddball temporary exhibitions they have inside museums for regular shows. You have a sculpture garden which supposedly gives work autonomy in relation to the neutral ground of the surroundings, a singular work in relation to the cosmos: the Münster show and "Chambres d'Amis" picked up existing urban historical relations of public and private spaces, and, in so doing, illustrated in terms of urban reality tendencies or meanings inside the art world for the public to read. This is precisely how a magazine functions—it represents a specialist area in terms of commonly approachable forms available to a general public; it uses temporary meanings and pseudo-categories of information and intellectual classification. When artwork remains after a show it could lose all its temporary, exhibition-related meaning. It's just a sculpture that's stuck there, but later it could come to memorialize a past event and time period. It's not the same as Mies van der Rohe, because the Barcelona pavilion was part of an exhibition and it was disassembled afterward, and not placed there permanently. This momentary cliche sense may not represent the real situation that's actually happening. Artists now are actually being asked to design more lasting aspects of urban design, to a certain extent. Conceptual artists such as Buren, Haacke, whatever, are being asked to actually design educational and art situations and are part of an urban design program with larger political goals in Paris. In a sense, the artist is placed in a middle-class, professional situation. This is something that is not new, but as the Socialist program does legitimize or reclaim some of the gains of 1968, it may be preferable to either the role of the outlaw or the role of the nihilist deconstructionist.

Gerdes

But I think the main problem is that by losing any kind of contact to a greater public, which was given to art in former times by the church, for example, the Modern artwork doesn't need any more to be part of any kind of city or whatever. And the situation now just reflects the situation that artists are more or less bored with showing their works in museums or in private collections and that they want to do something outside of these boundaries, which has been enforced also by the critical context works. But what this is leading to is just making jokes or fun or entertainment outside in the city. There is a problem of the real necessity of putting a work outside of the boundaries of the museum into something else. What is the something else, who defines it, and what could be done in the something else?

Graham

I'm not against the entertainment aspect of public art. Not in any absolute sense, because I think that historically that's always a given, art in an outdoor setting is partly designed to be entertaining, historically speaking—that the work has it as one of its attributes. I've never seen a work that was unentertaining.

Gerdes

There's a difference if a work is mainly entertaining or entertaining as a side effect.

Graham

It happens that at this moment the only work I seem to get funded is work whose place is usually in an exterior, public setting. Given my particular history and my position in the world or art market it seems the only work feasible now. So I have to reflect on that situation. I don't have the choice of doing other kinds of work for private collectors, although I'm not against this, because there is not the interest from a private collector; that comes out of a particular history of my work and my skills, etc. I can't easily change that fact. A public commission might be a way to do some things that I have wanted to do or it might not be. It's just the kind of work I get. But because I've worked in that area I have a somewhat different view of its possibilities. I think it's just as conservative as making art for private museums. But I don't think it's so simple. In America it usually involves a relation with corporations, as they are the sponsors of public art. In France it has to do with the regional art program, which is linked to recent social changes in culture and education. In Spain it has to do with the innovations in park design and the powerful, idealistic, popular role (as opposed to the Franco period) which art has in their culture as well as a Socialist urbanistic ideology. I can't give the idea of this choice that you are giving, because that doesn't apply to my present situation.

Gerdes

But if an artwork nowadays is presented in a context outside of the museum, what specifically can the artwork give in a public situation which couldn't be given by anything else except an artwork—that is, in your idea of giving a kind of education by the artwork?

Graham

The Enlightenment idea of art as part of education, I think, is built into Conceptual art. It seems that one place it's come up again is the integration of a museum as a humanistic, permanent educational fair that includes artworks as part of its program; in other words, a museum of science, technology and art in garden setting—like Parc La Villette.

Gerdes

What is the main thing that artworks should educate people about?

Graham

Well, that's too general a program.

Gerdes

What's the difference between artwork and scientific education, like school education or literal education or . . .

Graham

I think the middle class, which I guess I'm a part of, believes that art has educational value, and the mass taste believes it has entertainment value. I do believe that art addresses aesthetic values and isn't only or mainly educational or just entertainment. But some of its meaning does come from its addressing social and meaning assumptions of the audience and people who produce the art through funding it. These assumptions might be addressed and subverted by the work, but they can't be ignored. My own work is often quasi-philosophical—it might be a scientific, social or philosophical model which ultimately fails or doesn't work. It may touch assumptions about people in social groups, family structure, individual psychology or perception, so these assumptions of a quasi-social, education or scientific type which the audience brings to the work are useful in providing a setting for the work to function. This is like such assumptions in a play or a film—except that my work is still part of an abstract, formalist past tradition. My work in the early 1970s necessitated that the live audience bring an interest in "self-improvement" to it. This work involved the perceivers' perception of their own perceptual process. I'm aware of the rationale of those who produce work of mine for an exhibition. I know that many artists who sell a lot of their work do not want to be aware of the rationale of those who buy it. Their motives in producing work of mine may be very mixed, but they do not believe my work's meaning transcends their own cultural assumptions. They produce it because it fits into their general scheme for exhibitions, and this is usually somewhat didactic. Those who produce work of mine for its higher or spiritual value are people and situations I am usually suspicious about. My work can perform some didactic function in relation to other people's artwork and to an overall kind of scheme. Of course I would like to go beyond that beginning point and leave it open to other meanings.

Note

This interview was conducted in 1991. It is previously unpublished.

IV. Films

Film and Performance/Six Films, 1969–1974

A photographic image is a measure of itself as place. The recording camera's placement reflects its orientation in 360-degree space. Its orientation, shown as the recorded image, connects the rectangular front periphery of the camera to the mirror-reverse portion of the 360-degree environment the camera's frontal plane is aimed toward, reflecting the various closest light-reflective surfaces. (Reflected light defines, photographically, occupancy of space.) In a film, a series of images that have been sequentially recorded in the past are sequentially re-projected on, and as, a flat, rectangular surface a distance in front of the spectator's eyes; this is a plane parallel and mirror-reversed to the spectator's frontal body orientation and eye level.

A movie camera's viewfinder is placed on the performer's eye to identify the image seen on the screen by the spectator with the performer's perception of the world at the moment of performance. The viewer may also identify this image with his mind's eye. The lens and surface of the camera's body, its movement and orientation in space, constitute the media channel between the performer's presence and the spectator's perception.

A camera placed on another part of the performer's body or within his field of vision may be part of the performer's body feedback system. A camera's identity, in relation to the spectator's perception, may be part of the performer, one part of him but not another part of him, or not part of him (a separate mechanical object). Its image may be read as inside the performer or outside of him, or can be seen as both inside and outside of the performer, appearing as simultaneously subject and object.

Phenomenologically, the camera, its representations, and the spectator's view are the meeting point between, and can be seen to be any of, the elements of visual *consciousness*—if consciousness is partly *external* (situated in the object simulated in what is seen), partly internal (situated in the eye or camera), and partly cybernetic or *interpretive* (situated in the central nervous system or the process of attention which, with body's muscle/skeletal systems, achieves orientations in the world).

The visual field is topologically bounded by the retinal image of this body's nose, hands, feet and frontal shell of its cylindrical mass, which protrudes into the concave section of the larger 360-degree outside "space" which contains (within it) the body's cylindrical "hole."[1] A camera on the eye or on the body is the interface between the visual world ("outside") and the body's cylindrical perimeter bounding its own ("interior") 360-degree space.

Space cannot be apprehended except by movement of the viewer's eye's or body's place in time. The cameraman's visual field, when he moves his eyes or place in relation to the visual world (itself in the process of alteration, although usually at a slower rate), shifts in a topology of expansion, contraction or skew.

Visual perception is parallel to the perception of space in the process of orienting to a point of aim. In my films a performer's view is equivalent to what is seen by the optical surface of the front plane of the camera; thus the camera's frontal plane or orientation corresponds to the direction of the performer's attention in the time/space and films what it is orienting to. The process of physiological orientation—attention—of the performer(s) is correlated to the spectator's process of attention.

***Sunset to Sunrise,* 1969, 16mm, color**

The film is made by continuously moving a 16mm movie camera from a position oriented toward the sun on the horizon line at the moment of sunset, and proceeding in a slow spiral with gradual upward inclination toward the top of the sky. This spiral successively maps the complete topological surface area of the sky. The next morning at sunrise, from the same geographical site, beginning from the top, center of the sky, a reverse spiral downward in opposite right-to-left rotation is filmed, ending on the sun rising above the horizon.

The sun's light is simultaneously the point-source of illumination defining the surrounding 360-degree spatial "presence" *and* the source of illumination for the mechanical appearance of the film (document). The "spatial" presence illuminated is also the distance from the presence of the camera to the presence of the closest surface (placed in front of the camera's lens—reflecting its frontal orientation at each moment) reflecting light back to the film in the camera. As the camera is hand-held, it also reflects the filmmaker's body axis of 360-degree movement relative to the surrounding 360-degree space it documents (which the camera's image reflects).

For the spectator viewing the film, the continuous movement in time, read kinesthetically, is correlated to the identity of the filmmaker.

***Two Correlated Rotations,* 1969, two Super 8 films, black and white**

Two cameramen each hold cameras so that their viewfinders are extensions of their eyes and visual fields. They begin facing each other one foot away. They walk in counter spirals, the outside performer moving gradually outward while the inside performer walks inward approaching the center.

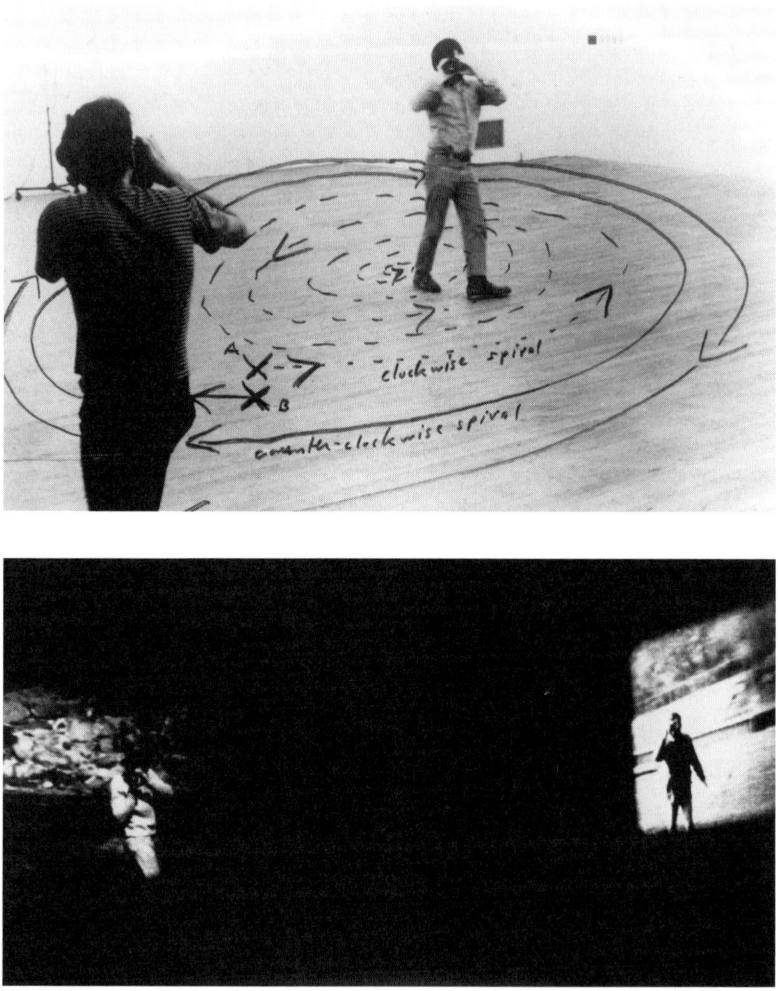

17
Dan Graham
Two Correlated Relations, 1969

Their aim, which is still in the state of a learning process, is to be as nearly as possible continuously centering their cameras' (and eyes') view on the frontal eye position of the other.

Geometrically the rotation of the performers' necks and of their paths keeps the camera/eye sight line of both cameras' images along the axis of the horizon line of the 360-degree surrounding space; the line of sight of both cameras' images when the cameras are facing each other passes through the center of the spirals and the interior of the 360-degree topological spatial enclosure.

Each performer's moves (and image of the other) reflects the other's in the reciprocal information feedback necessary to achieve continuous "aim," and the "aim" of the film, in the image read by the spectator's correlated rapid brain time apprehending the (feedback) relation of the reciprocal images. The two filmed images of the filmmakers, with cameras to their eyes (made by the opposite filmmaker), are simultaneously each other's subject (observer) and object. The spectator's attention is part of a three-way relation (circuit) between the attention of the two performers and the spectator's attention. In the spectator's view, it is impossible to separate the two cameras' mechanisms, the two minds and bodies from the feedback of reciprocal intelligence between them, read in the image by the viewer. The "self" is not an atomistic entity, but is imminent in the network of interrelationships or environmental structure.

In viewing the film on right-angle walls, both images are synchronous and simultaneously projected. Both filmmakers' and viewers' responses appear in the present time to them. The film-recorded time is "contained" in the mechanical operation of the cameras' and projectors' rotations. Due to mechanical irregularity, these may be slightly faster or slower in relation to each other in the screening, with subtle timing differences affecting the spectator's perceptual (brain's) reading of that time.

***Roll*, 1970, two Super 8 films (enlarged to 16mm), color**

The filming camera is an inert *object,* detached (although within the performer's visual field), while the other camera, attached to his eye, is both *subject and object.* The "objective" camera is placed with its base on the ground. After looking through its viewfinder to determine the left and right extremities which will frame its image, the performer positions his body and the second camera's front frame directly facing the inert camera's view and at the line of its left framing edge. With both cameras filming, the performer with camera to his eye rolls slowly toward the right framing edge of the other camera's

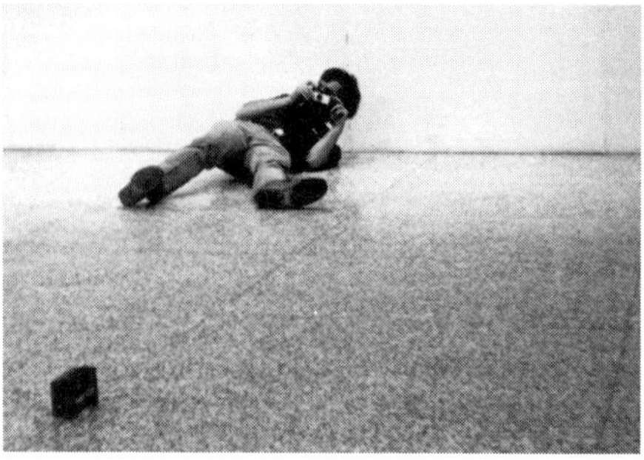

18
Dan Graham
Roll, 1970

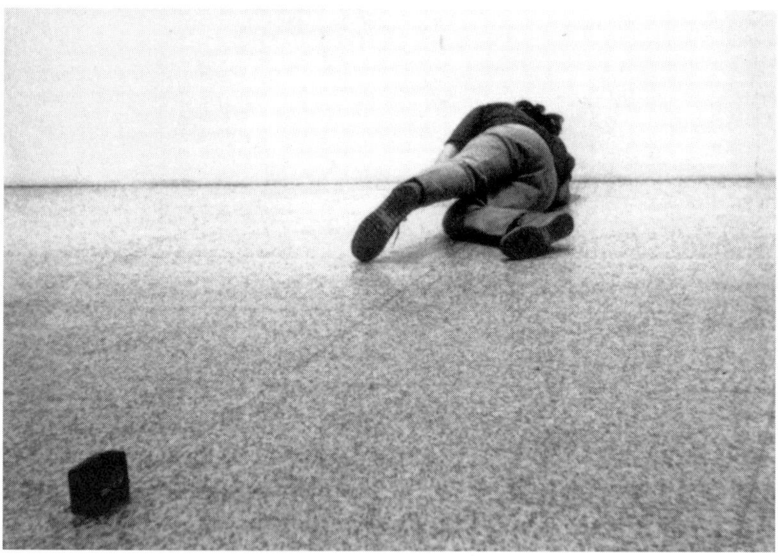

19
Dan Graham
Roll, 1970

view, with the aim of continuously orienting his eye/camera's view to center on the other camera's position (and image).

The performer's legs and frontal body trunk protrude at the bottom of the held camera/eye frame through which the performer must observe his shifting postural placement as feedback needed to achieve his orientation (and his image's). The spectator sees (from within) the body's kinesthetic sensations. From his eyeview inside the feedback loop he observes the body's shifts as it changes position in space in relation to the position of the aim (the fixed camera). The brain must correct the muscles to cause a skeletal alignment; this affects the camera's aim; it must be realigned by the neck's turning and the hands to keep open the visual feedback between the two cameras' images (upon which the perception of the piece depends).

The two films' images are projected for simultaneous viewing at eye level on distant opposite, parallel walls. Within the view from the body feedback loop, a continuously rotating image, the body appears unweighted. The view from the "objective" "black box" camera shows the body from outside as an object orienting with respect to universal gravity, opposing a stationary, parallel force and pressing the body's muscular/skeletal frame toward the horizontal.

***Body Press*, 1970–1972, two 16mm films, color**

Two filmmakers stand within a surrounding and completely mirrorized cylinder, body trunks stationary, hands holding and pressing a camera's back end flush with, while slowly rotating it about, the surface cylinder of their individual bodies. One rotation circumscribes the body's contour, spiraling slightly upward with the next turn. With successive rotations, the body surface areas are completely covered as a template by the back of the camera(s) until eye level (view through cameraman's eyes) is reached; then reverse mapping downward begins until the original starting point is reached. The rotations are at correlated speed; when each camera is rotated to each body's rear it is then facing and filming the other, where they are exchanged so that the camera's "identity" "changes hands," each performer handling a new camera. The cameras are of different size and mass. In the process, the performers are to concentrate on the coexistent, simultaneous identity of the camera describing them and their body.[2]

Optically the two cameras film the image reflected on the mirror, which is the same surface as the box (and lens) of the camera's five visible sides, the body of the performer, and (possibly) the eyes on the mirror.[3] The camera's angle of orientation or view of the area of the mirror's reflective image is determined by the placement of the camera on the body contour at a given mo-

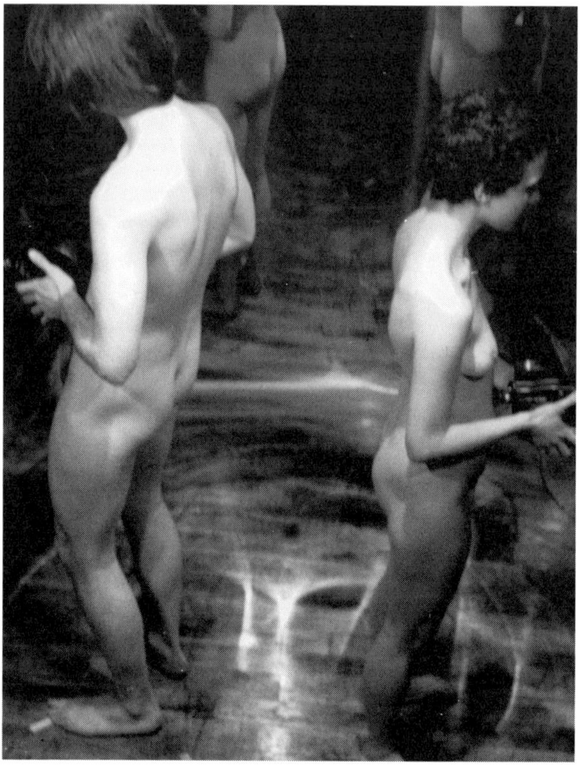

20
Dan Graham
Body Press, 1970-1972

ment. (The camera might be pressed against the chest but such an upward angle shows head and eyes.) To the spectator the camera's optical vantage is the skin. (An exception is when the performer's eyes are also seen reflected or when the cameras are seen filming the other.) The performer's musculature is also "seen" pressing into the surface of the body (pulling inside out). At the same time, kinesthetically, the handling of the camera can be "felt" by the spectator as surface tension—as the hidden side of the camera presses and slides against the skin it covers at a particular moment.

The films are projected at the same time on two loop projectors, shown very large on two opposite but very close walls. A member of the audience (man or woman) might identify with one image or the other from the same camera, or might identify with one body of the other, shifting his or her view each time to face the other screen when cameras are exchanged.

***Binocular Zoom*, 1969, Super 8 film on a split screen, color**

Two Super 8 movie cameras with identical zoom lenses are placed with the viewfinder flush to each of my eyes. Each of the cameras' images is focused on the sun somewhat obscured by a cloudy sky. The image of each camera corresponds to the double retinal images of the right and left eyes. Filming begins with both cameras simultaneously. Initially, the images synchronously are extreme close-up views, maximum disparity between the right and the left images being caused as they "halve" the sun. The two zoom lenses open their respective fields of view at the same rate until reaching their fullest extent. Both images diminish in size to a "distance."

For viewing, the films made by the two cameras are simultaneously projected as a "split-screen" image.

21
Dan Graham
Binocular Zoom, 1969

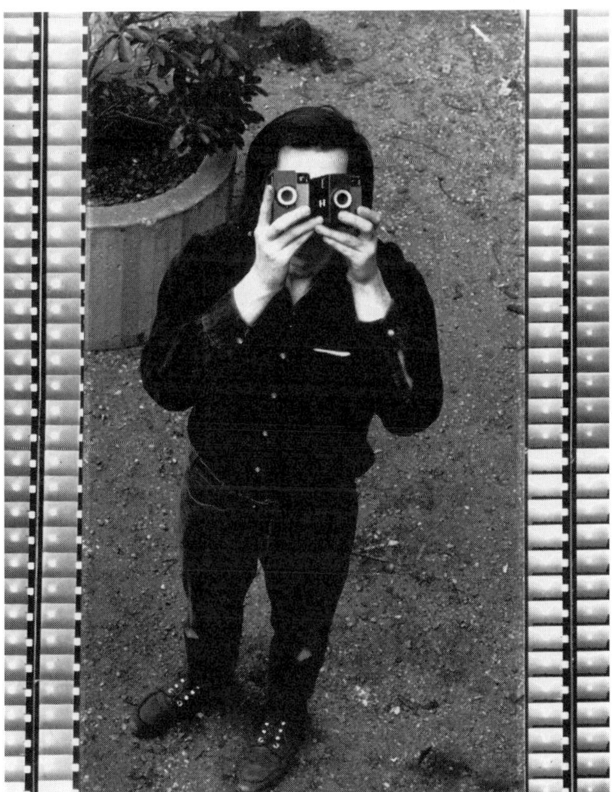

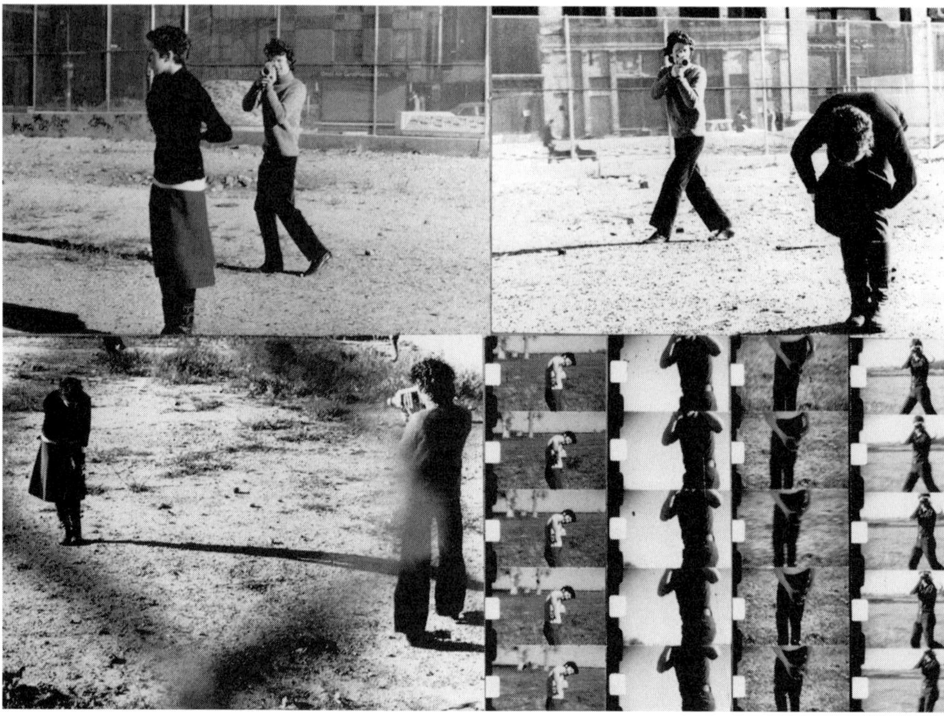

22
Dan Graham
Helix/Spiral, 1973

Helix/Spiral, 1973, two Super 8 films (enlarged to 16mm), color

A stationary inner cameraman slides the back end of his camera while pressing it flat against his body. It moves in a gradually descending helix from eyes to feet so the entire surface area of his body is topologically covered. As the camera rotates, circumscribing the body, it films the outside 360 degrees of the surrounding space. At each moment and point on the body the specific angle of the body's contour determines the camera's plane or angle of orientation. Each second it is filming the light reflected from the particular environmental plane facing parallel to the camera's front plane, while the other, obverse, side of the filmed exterior is the negative, cylindrical "hole" in the larger 360-degree topological whole occupied by that person's body.

At a distance on the horizon of the inner filmmaker's view, a second filmmaker with the camera's viewfinder to his eye walks inward in a gradual spiral whose center is the position of the first filmmaker. In walking he maps in his spiraling the complete topographic surface area in 360 degrees between the inner performer and his initial distance. He reaches the point of the inner filmmaker when this performer has taken his camera to feet or ground level. The outside man's aim is to continuously center his camera on the inside camera while continuously having himself centered in the view of that camera. To achieve this as he spirals, he adjusts his forward movement relative to the rate with which the inside cameraman manipulates the camera around his body.

The filmed images reflect all outer "edges" that meet at a given moment on the two films' surfaces. Kinetic reverberations of the images are caused by the camera's movement against the inner cameraman's changing contour, and the instability in the outside cameraman's image is caused by his feet moving across the irregular topography of the land. Both cameras' lenses film the visual surfaces of the outside environment, film the other camera's front plane and lens, film both performers' "subjective" "mind's eye" views, and film both performer's observed exteriors. At each moment in their camera's continuous rotation, each projected film's view is the opposite 180 degrees of the surrounding 360-degree space.

The two films are projected for simultaneous viewing on opposite walls.

Notes

1. Consider that the performer/filmmaker's body is a 360-degree cylindrical surface occupying a part (from its point of view, the center part) of the 360-degree larger, circumambient, semispherical space within which the smaller cylinder of the body is contained.

2. The camera may or may not be read as an extension of the body's identity.

3. In projection, what is seen by the spectator.

This text was written in 1976 and first published in Films *(Geneva: Éditions Centre d'Art Contemporain/Écart Publications, 1977).*

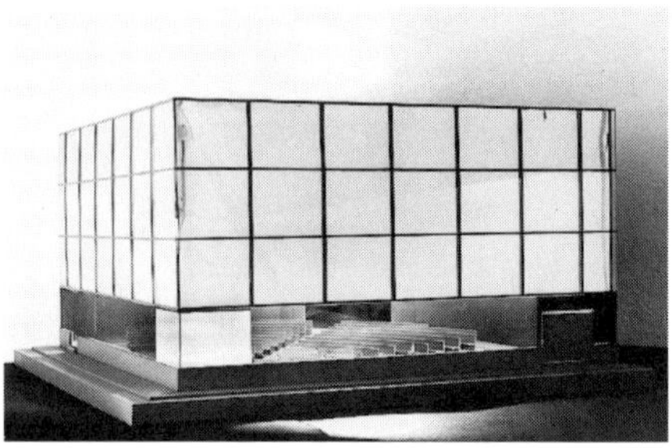

23
Dan Graham
Cinema, 1981

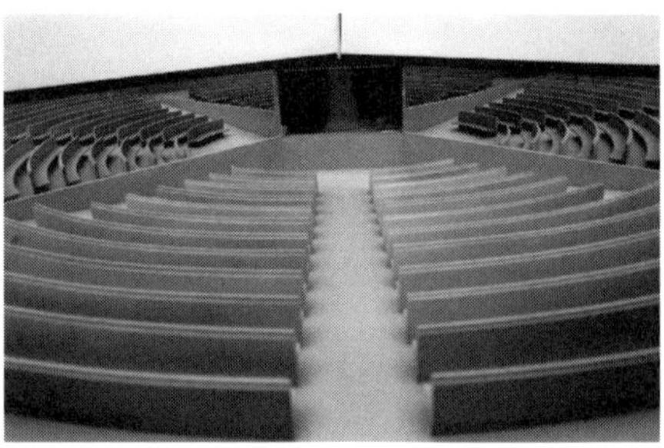

24
Dan Graham
Cinema, 1981

Cinema

A cinema, the ground level of a Modern office building, is sited on a busy corner. Its facade consists of two-way mirrored glass, which allows viewers on whichever side is darker at any particular moment to see through and observe the other side (without being seen by the people on that side). From the other side, the window appears as a mirror. When the light illuminates the surface of both sides more or less equally, the glass facade is both semi-reflective and partially transparent. Spectators on both sides observe both the opposing space *and* a reflection of their own look within their own space.

STAGE I: *The Film Is Projected; the Interior Is Dark*

A two-way mirror screen is substituted for the conventional screen. Located at the front of the building, it forms the longer side of an equilateral triangle whose apex is the front corner of the building. Because of the properties of the two-way mirror, when a film is projected, the mirror functions as a normal screen for the interior film-goer and also projects the film image so that it can be seen, in reverse, from the street through the building's facade. Although it is placed seven feet above the heads of the front row interior audience, the screen image appears at a street viewer's eye level. Further, when viewed from the street, the screen's image can be looked through to see the frontal gaze of the audience watching the screen. This is because the light of the projector falls on the interior of the screen, making the reverse side of this two-way mirror darker relative to its front and therefore slightly transparent.

STAGE II: ***The Film Is Not Projected; House Lights Are Up***

The house lights in the cinema are turned on after (or before) a film is projected. Interior spectators see the screen, as well as the side windows, as reflective mirrors—reminiscent of mirrored cinema lobbies. Where the Renaissance framing of the screen has, a few seconds ago, been a "mirror" for the spectator's subjective projection of his body, which, disembodied and invisible, has been "lost" to his immediate environment in its identification with the film, the screen itself and the sides of the theater now become literal mirrors (as opposed to the illusionary "mirror" of the film), reflecting the real space and bodies and looks of the spectators. The spectator sees his real position represented on the mirror, relative to the presence of the rest of the audience, whereas in the fictional world of the film he was the phenomenological center of an illusionary world. He sees himself looking in relation to the looks of the others in the audience. Outside, the psychological position of the spectator also reverses for he is now able to look through the window, himself unseen. Awareness of *his* body and *his* environment is lost. His position as voyeur becomes akin to that of the movie audience the previous moment.

In my cinema project it is the screen, instead of the machine, and the system of voyeuristic identifications, which are exposed. It is assumed that the cinema is prototypical of all other perspective systems which work to produce a social subject through manipulating the subject's imaginary identifications. In the cinema all looks are intersubjective: it is difficult to separate the optics of the materials of the architecture from the psychological identifications constructed by the film images. The psychological circuit of intersubjective looks and identifications is echoed in and is a product of the material properties of the architectural materials, whose optical functioning derives from the properties of the two-way mirror glass. In this "CINEMA," unlike the cinema which must conceal from the spectators their own looks and projections, the architecture allows inside and outside spectators to perceive their positions, projections, bodies and identifications. Topologically, an optical "skin," both reflective and transparent inside and outside, functions simultaneously as a screen for the film's projection. Dialectically, it is seen in the outside environment as well as in the normal cinema context as a point of transfer for the gazes of the inner and outer spectators, in relation to each other and the film image.

Note

This text, written in 1981, has been published several times. The original version appeared in Anne Rorimer, Dan Graham: Buildings and Signs, *exh. cat. (Chicago: Renaissance Society of the University of Chicago, 1981), pp. 47–50.*

Dan Graham Interviewed by Eric de Bruyn

Eric de Bruyn

The first work that is listed in the filmography of your *Films* catalogue is in fact a "proto-cinematic" piece called *Project for Slide Projector* of 1966.[1] Did you develop other slide projections at the time?

Dan Graham

The photographs of *Homes for America* were shown as a slide projection during the *Projected Art* exhibition at Finch College in 1966.[2] In *Project for Slide Projector* I was interested in the interface between speeded-up slide projection and film. It was like the photos for *Homes for America*, I wanted to do the same things that I saw in Minimal and Pop art in a flat, photographic situation. I wanted to re-do the modules of Larry Bell or Donald Judd as a slide projection.[3]

de Bruyn

You did not further pursue this line of work?

Graham

No, it was too technically complex and expensive. In fact, *Project for Slide Projector* was one of the student projects that I suggested to the Nova Scotia College of Art. As they had the equipment, I could do film and video. In Halifax I could do the things that I had in my head, like the slide project, by calling them student projects. At the time I was living in a tiny apartment without a studio and without any money.

de Bruyn

Who invited you to the Nova Scotia College of Art?

Graham

David Askevold contacted several Conceptual artists for a course called "Projects," which consisted of instructional projects for students to do. Lawrence Weiner recommended me to Jerry Ferguson who was teaching in Halifax with David. David and I had an incredibly sympathetic conversation, an immediate rapport, and I realized that Halifax had a lot of video and film equipment, particularly video equipment, since I wanted to move into video. I basically invited myself up there for three weeks.[4]

de Bruyn

Who was working with video in Halifax?

Graham

Nobody.

de Bruyn

Sunset to Sunrise was shot in Nova Scotia.[5] Was it your first film?

Graham

Actually I attempted to shoot the film before on Super 8 film. The Nova Scotia version was on 16mm.

de Bruyn

Sunset to Sunrise was shot in two takes?

Graham

Yes. I thought Nova Scotia had the most beautiful scenery with its rocky coast and the clear uninterrupted sky. I was going for the cliche. And maybe ideas I got from Bob Mangold's paintings: the rounded paintings that have a modulated sunset or sunrise, like the one I own. I guess Roy Lichtenstein was working with the same concept, too. *Sunset to Sunrise* also relates to the video pieces where I was putting the camera to the eye and making a feedback loop between my body and the TV monitor, that is, the TV camera wall situation. In *Sunset to Sunrise* you have the body and the eye of the camera person, the camera being moved by an actual person, so in a way you're inside the person's visual field, but you also have the surrounding 360-degree sky, which is the outdoors. In a way, the exterior space relates to the eye; in other words, it's another hemispheric situation. So, from the eye to the next outdoor area that is furthest removed from the eye, which is the sky. And as you rotate around, the body is rotating, so it's actually the 360-degree space of the body.

de Bruyn

Sunset to Sunrise, then, is similar to *March 31, 1966,* in which you tabulate the distance between the retinal wall of the eye to the "edge of the known universe" in successive steps.[6]

Graham

Yes. It also relates to the still photographs of Richard Long, where he is making "landscape" through his walking. *Sunset to Sunrise* is a landscape piece. It is also about life which is film, which is what film is about.

de Bruyn

Could you further specify the interest that Richard Long's work held for you at that moment?

Graham

I thought Richard Long was the big innovator, and also Bruce Nauman, who went a step beyond Minimalism. Richard Long represents a somewhat ironic return to the landscape, and with Nauman you have the body of the artist, the artist as performer. Richard Long, and also Gilbert & George, were using ideas of the Romantic poet, of the Victorian dandy, as an ironic comment directed against avant-gardism. In a sense they were doing performances.

de Bruyn

But how does Richard Long's reference to the tradition of landscape painting relate to your own film work?

Graham

It is rare that I do landscape pieces, but my interest in landscape was through Long: the notion of the artist being inside the landscape. But in the case of *Sunset to Sunrise* there is also the influence of Michael Snow.

de Bruyn

You are referring to his film *Back and Forth?*

Graham

Exactly.

de Bruyn

By that time Michael Snow had shot both *Wavelength* (1966–1967) and *Back and Forth* (1968–1969). Did you attend screenings of these films in New York?

Graham

Yes.

de Bruyn

And did you see other examples of the so-called Structural film like Paul Sharits and Hollis Frampton?

Graham

No, I saw no other films. I knew Michael Snow through Steve Reich to whose music I was drawn.

de Bruyn

You did not perceive a link between the "avant-garde" film scene in New York and the contemporary art world?

Graham

No, there were only Andy Warhol and Jack Smith, which was probably not avant-garde filmmaking. It is the same situation as with Bruce Nauman. He was a member of Anne Halprin's dance group and he took a lot of things from Simone Forti. When I met Richard Serra in 1968 he talked about Simone Forti and Nauman as his biggest influences, so I immediately found out everything I could about Simone Forti, but I didn't know anything about dance. I was tracing things backward through word of mouth. When Steve Reich mentioned Michael Snow I wanted to see everything he did.

de Bruyn

Let's talk about your interest in Bruce Nauman.

Graham

The main show at the time was *Anti-Illusion: Procedures/Materials* at the Whitney. It was the first time I saw a Nauman performance.[7] Nauman was important for everybody except the Minimalist artists. Serra and Dennis Oppenheim both knew Bruce Nauman from San Francisco.

de Bruyn

After *Sunset to Sunrise* you made *Two Correlated Positions* and *Roll*.[8] Each film consists of two reels which were shot simultaneously with two different cameras. How would you describe the structural difference between the two films?

Graham

In *Roll* the camera is passive, it is totally objective, not objective and subjective. In other words, in *Roll* the camera is not attached to the eye of another performer. The philosophical base for the films with the camera attached to the eye, such as *Two Correlated Positions,* is that the camera was objective, a mechanical box attached to the subjectivity of the gaze of the performer, which is also the gaze of the spectator. The spectator identifies with the performer, identifies with what the performer is looking at, which is another performer. The camera is objective, but the gaze can be both objective and subjective. In *Roll* the camera was placed passively on the ground. It was therefore absolutely objective.

de Bruyn

In *Roll* you were rolling across the floor while aiming your camera at the other camera. How was *Two Correlated Rotations* set up?

Graham

There are two performers rotating around each other in a kind of a helix situation.

de Bruyn

How does the structure of *Two Correlated Positions* differ from your film *Helix/Spiral* of 1973?[9]

Graham

In that film one of the cameras was sliding against the body of the performer. The performer is stationary, but the camera is making a map of his body as in *Body Press.* And the second performer is spiraling out, away from the first performer.

de Bruyn

In *Helix/Spiral,* then, one of the two cameras is not held in front of the performer's eye but pressed against his body, in contrast to *Two Correlated Positions,* where the camera is always on the eye.

Graham

The camera is always on the eye and both performers are in motion. The film is mapping out the ground space between the two people, as well as mapping along the horizon line the same distance you have in *Sunset to Sunrise*—the most distant surface, the sky—and it is also mapping out the 360-degree surface of the body. The film was shot near the Loeb Student Center in New York on my return from Halifax. It is now in the collection of the Tate Gallery.

de Bruyn

Binocular Zoom was shot during the same period?[10]

Graham

Yes.

de Bruyn

What kind of recording and projection equipment did you use?

Graham

The films were shot on Super 8 and shown on technicolor loop projectors.

de Bruyn

How did you install the films in the gallery?

Graham

The films were projected in different manners. *Sunset to Sunrise* was shown on a single screen, *Binocular Zoom* on a split screen, *Two Correlated Positions* was projected at right angles in the corner of two walls.

de Bruyn

Why did you chose this specific set-up for *Two Correlated Positions?*

Graham

I wanted the spectator to experience something of the panorama that exists in the actual filming. As the performers are rotating around each other, you see part of a circle, part of the horizon line, and I wanted the spectator to be able to see both parts at the same time, unlike *Roll* where you had to turn to look at one screen or the other. *Roll* and *Helix/Spiral* were projected on two opposite walls, like *Body Press.* In other words, I used all possible permutations.

de Bruyn

Why is *Body Press* dated 1970–1972?[11]

Graham

It took a long time to realize.

de Bruyn

Didn't you make two versions?

Graham

Yes, an original version in Super-8 and a 16mm version in 1972.

de Bruyn

In other words, the idea of *Body Press* dates from 1970. Did the technical realization of the film prove difficult?

Graham

Yes, the building of the mirrorized cylinder. The problem was that the back surface of the Super-8 camera wasn't flat, so you couldn't flatten it against the body. And also the reloading of the cameras was very complicated. I wanted something that you could reload immediately. Of course, the earlier films were done with the Super-8 instamatic camera, the Super 8 simple rectangle, which contained film cassettes of 3.5 minutes.

de Bruyn

And would you loop them together.

Graham

No, the film were very short.

de Bruyn

And *Sunset to Sunrise?*

Graham

Sunset to Sunrise was not shot on 16mm.

de Bruyn

The films *Binocular Zoom* or *Two Correlated Positions* were therefore all Super-8 loops of 3.5 minutes in length.

Graham

Yes.

de Bruyn

I presume that you preferred to work with the 16mm camera in *Body Press* because of its weight.

Graham

Yes, the weight and the quality. In other words, I wanted to make a very good skin flick.

de Bruyn

The films shot before *Body Press* are concerned with the relation of the spectator to the body and to the object, that is, the camera that the spectator appears to be looking through. In *Body Press,* because of your use of the mirror, there exists an intermediary moment when the camera is being crossed over between the two performers. At this point the perceptual character of the camera's view is radically altered. Perception becomes, as it were, detached from its roots in the body. The formerly distinct image of the performer's body is totally distorted in the anamorphic reflection of the mirrorized cylinder. It is this aspect of *Body Press* which distinguishes it from the other films, or video pieces.

Graham

And there is a moment of acclimatizing the camera to the body when the performers take on the other camera. The camera represents not only something objective but something that comes from the other body.

de Bruyn

You have the two identification possibilities, male and female. But there is also this in-between moment when there is a distortion of the image, the two bodies optically merging together, and the body parts appear hanging in front of the camera . . .

Graham

Right.

de Bruyn

The spectator sees the other camera, the two cameras are, as it were, looking at each other, but there is a sense of the camera floating through space which the spectator can't immediately connect to any body.

Graham

Well, it also has the notion of exchange.

de Bruyn

How did you conceptualize the piece?

Graham

I think it is a matter of identification with the camera and the person at the same time. Do you identify with the camera or the person, and then how do people identify with the camera that is being used to map their body? The camera is at first a foreign item coming from somebody else; then eventually it is merged with themselves when they put it around their body.

de Bruyn

The only film you made after *Body Press* was *Helix/Spiral* in 1973?

Graham

Yes.

de Bruyn

What were your reasons to stop making films?

Graham

Body Press was very expensive. There was the difficulty of presenting the films. The fact that I exhausted the possibilities of camera to eye to body. It was like a permutational set of possibilities. The fact that I preferred to do live performance with video. And I guess that I was fascinated by the possibility of cable and other uses of video. What I tended to do was take a particular area and exhaust it.

de Bruyn

You were using video at the same time that you were working with film. Film, however, occupied a minor part of your time. Once you attempted all the different permutations with a specific set, you lost interest in the medium of film?

Graham

I was attracted to film for the same reason I was attracted to the photos of Conceptual art. It was because you could use a fixed-focus instamatic camera and you had these very inexpensive technicolor loop projectors. So the presentation was simple, basic, elementary, cheap and it fit into what some other artists were doing using the loop projectors. I wanted to put more into the films in terms of their philosophical model or one-of-a-kind uniqueness. Within their own point of view they were structuralist. And I think they come from the live video piece *TV Camera/Monitor* of 1970, which was a problem because it had to be set up as a performance. First of all it damaged the camera; secondly it was very artificial. It was not transportable, unlike the films. The great thing about the films was that I could do them outside the studio.[12] They became landscape pieces. It's an advantage that you couldn't get with video at the time.

de Bruyn

Then you could have conceived of doing the same works with video?

Graham

Only later.

de Bruyn

Was there something specific about the medium, besides the particular equipment you used, something about the materiality of the medium that interested you?

Graham

I think cinema is more hallucinatory. Certainly with *Body Press* you get yourself into a hallucinatory, meditative situation. It's also more voyeuristic than video.

de Bruyn

Because of the way it is being presented on the screens.

Graham

. . . the way it's presented on the screens. I'm thinking of spectator perception. It's like what Marshall McLuhan said about video: it's participatory, it's tactile, it's not distanced, it's not voyeuristic. It presupposes a kind of real time, participatory, not another time.

de Bruyn

In *Body Press* you use mirrors for the first time.

Graham

There was also the slide piece. The panes of glass as they accumulate become very mirror-like. You can see the camera and the photographer.

de Bruyn

That piece doesn't exist anymore?

Graham

It was done temporarily. I have the slides.

de Bruyn

You have pointed out a connection between *Body Press* and the *Rooftop Urban Park Project: Two Way Mirror Cylinder Inside Cube* (1981–1991) at the Dia Center for the Arts.

Graham

The Dia piece has all the things that the films have: there is the relation to the body of the spectator, the spectator's relation between a rectilinear form and a curved form. The film's rectilinear form was the box of the camera. There is the relation to the surrounding horizon line . . .

de Bruyn

The rectilinear form being, of course, also the projection situation . . .

Graham

. . . the projection situation, the walls of the interior.

de Bruyn

Was the relation to *Body Press* on your mind when you conceived the Dia piece or did the relationship become clear retroactively? In other words, did *Body Press* present a kind of cumulative moment in your earlier work to which you wanted to return?

Graham

Before the Dia piece there was a model for something very similar. But there I was using the cube and the sphere. In *Body Press,* although the camera wasn't a cube, in the first version, the Super 8 version, the camera was a cube—cube inside a cylinder. It is also about the flatness of one surface against the curvature of the body.

de Bruyn

Is the Dia pavilion the only piece that has one form completely enclosing the other form?

Graham

There are models for other ones, but it is the only one that was any good. Actually, they were too expensive to be built.

de Bruyn

At this point, I would like to turn to your *Cinema* project of 1981, which bears an obvious relation to your pavilion structures.[13]

Graham

The idea was based on the Modern office building sheathed in glass that was transferred from the Bauhaus into corporate architecture. It was a Productivist idea, where one could see into the building. After a certain time period, with the introduction of two-way mirror office glass, the surfaces of the city became like cinema surfaces.

de Bruyn

Is "cinematic" a term you would also use to describe the ever-changing appearance of your pavilions due to their reflective surfaces?

Graham

I use it to describe the surface of the city. In other words, when you see glass or two-way mirror glass it's cinematic. The mirror is also hidden. When you're looking in the window of a shopping arcade there is a mirror image of yourself that you scarcely see projected on the goods, which is similar to the idea of Christian Metz—that you are projecting yourself onto the characters and then you become a bigger person, a better person, or a whole person by accepting the goods.

de Bruyn

How did you conceive of the *Cinema* project?

Graham

It was because I became interested in two-way mirror glass and two-way mylar, the stretched plastic that could be a cinema screen, and the fact that I was interested in the two-way mirror office building. So I wondered what could fit into the two-way mirror office building: the Modern cinema. I had not yet seen Duiker's *Handelsblad Cineac* in Amsterdam. But obviously there is a relation to Duiker after the fact.

de Bruyn

When you designed the *Cinema* you did not know about the Duiker building?

Graham

No.

de Bruyn

You have referred to the historical model of Productivist architecture. Duiker's *Cineac,* which exposes the projection apparatus to our view from the street, is obviously related to this model. Were you also interested in Constructivist film?

Graham

I never saw it.

de Bruyn

You weren't interested?

Graham

No, I just didn't see it. I was interested in the gaze and the gaze relative to people on screen, and what you could do with the two-way mirror, what I was later doing in my other buildings. You could see the gaze of the person inside superimposed on the gaze of the person outside, and that they are in complete flux as the sun is changing; with the *Cinema* there is also a complete flux and the part of the film that is projected, that is very light, is going to be reflective on the inside and transparent on the outside, with people looking through. When it's a very light image people outside can look through and see people on the inside gazing at the screen.

de Bruyn

But not the machinery behind it all that is creating the illusion.

Graham

No, I'm saying what is more interesting than the machinery is the gaze and the surface of the buildings in the city . . . the screen, the skin, as opposed to the actual machinery.

de Bruyn

That which you hollow out in the building—the screen, not the projection booth.

Graham

Exactly.

de Bruyn

You have on occasion stressed the importance of the "sociological" film method of Jean-Luc Godard. Were you referring to your *Homes for America?*

Graham

That was before I saw Godard. The only Godard that fits is when he was doing sociological things like *Two or Three Things I Know about Her* and maybe *The Married Woman.* Those are like my magazine pieces.

de Bruyn

The relation is to the magazine pieces and not to your film work.

Graham

Well, it was also everything in *Contempt.* From the architecture with the steps of Sartoris. The steps were very important. And the Brechtian showing of the apparatus of the film within a film. The Godard was a film about film. They are shooting a film in *Contempt.*

de Bruyn

You're referring to *Body Press.*

Graham

Yes, but the biggest influence of Godard was on the Dean Martin article. I remember that nobody in the world missed a Godard film.[14]

de Bruyn

Where did you first show the films?

Graham

John Gibson organized an evening of screenings at the Loeb Student Center in 1970 and I came out with a publication called *Performance 1.* My films were shown and I performed *TV Camera/Monitor.*[15] The films were shown in group shows. *Two Correlated Positions* was also shown in 1972 during my first one-man show at Lisson Gallery, at Galleria Toselli in Milan, and at the Protech-Rivkin Gallery in Washington, D.C. Galerie MTL in Brussels also showed my films in 1973. *Roll* was sold to the collector Andre Goemine.

de Bruyn

How did John Gibson become involved with film?

Graham

John Gibson showed films by Gordon Matta-Clark. But his main advisor was Dennis Oppenheim. John Gibson, however, was more interested in flat photo documentation which would be saleable.

de Bruyn

Are you implying that his support for film was short-lived?

Graham

Well, it was one of the forms in which we represented Nauman-like performances. I think that everybody wanted to make films. It was the time when Castelli and Sonnabend had their film and video distribution, which was what the artists wanted. Lawrence Weiner was also making films. Artists basically wanted to do films and videos.

de Bruyn

Can 1970, in retrospect, be considered as something of a breaking point for the artist film?

Graham

Yes.

de Bruyn

Of course, several artists were working in film before 1970.

Graham

Yes, but I think that the idea of using film and video came from Nauman.

de Bruyn

Was it not more over-determined? What about the other filmmakers in New York during the sixties?

Graham

But I think that Michael Snow was part of the art world.

de Bruyn

More so than Hollis Frampton or Paul Shartis, I gather from your remarks.

Graham

Absolutely.

de Bruyn

Artist films are usually omitted in the history of the so-called avant-garde or structural film in New York.

Graham

Except for Andy Warhol.

de Bruyn

Indeed. The history of experimental film is generally written in terms of a formal evolution. Within this perspective, artist films are often judged to be merely derivative, if not "amateurish." However, the artist film does not stand within the same tradition. It partakes of a different artistic genealogy and operates within a separate institutional context.

Graham

Well, what is lost in these histories is that both filmmakers and artists were often doing it for fun. For instance, I would say that Michael Snow's *Back and Forth* is basically a pun on sexuality. Ed Ruscha's film *Crackers* is obviously humorous.

de Bruyn

Ruscha's *Crackers* is a narrative film. It is completely different from what you were doing.

Graham

True.

de Bruyn

. . . or Nauman.

Graham

Well, Nauman's video tapes are based on philosophical and literary humor such as *His Black Balls.* The punning, literary aspect of the work comes from William T. Wiley.[16] We saw films as a popular medium. In other words, film and video were something everybody could do, or it was a kind of artist's "home video." The medium was accessible and artists even had fantasies of mass distribution.

de Bruyn

During the sixties there was a certain euphoria surrounding the emergence of the "new media" of communication. I'm thinking, for instance, of the writings of Marshall McLuhan. Did you perceive your work as opposed to his ideas?

Graham

No, I was very influenced by McLuhan.

de Bruyn

Did you adhere to his utopian view of the new media?

Graham

In a video, like *Production/Reception (Piece for Two Cable TV Channels)* of 1976, you have two cable stations and a normal station; you're watching a local news program, and then one cable station shows how it is being produced, live, and the other one shows how it is being received in a typical household. There are many projects like that, which are, in a way, both structuralist and utopian.

de Bruyn

What is utopian? The structure of the work appears more indicative of the spectator's alienation by the media.

Graham

It also shows that cable allows anything. It allows an anthropology.

de Bruyn

Ideally, yes, it would allow that to take place. But, of course, it didn't happen.

Graham

But that was later. We believed that you would have all these local art stations.

de Bruyn

All the same, were you not attempting to subvert the dominant structure of the mass media system?

Graham

In *Two Consciousness Projections* of 1972 there is a live TV set-up. The woman (or sometimes a man) watches the image of herself on a monitor, and a man, or woman, is looking through a camera from the other side of the monitor. They are both describing their consciousness, which is the view of the woman as she views herself and the way the man views the woman. The audience hears the consciousness, or Freudian projections, of both performers and they can see the actual situation. Again, it is both subjective and objective. The woman is subjective, but the man makes her objectified. At first the audience is identifying with the man, but later, when it becomes obvious that he is projecting, and not dealing with the actual situation, they start identifying with the woman, and he becomes very shaky.

de Bruyn

Yet, how does this exchange of identity, the mirroring of the other, these kind of psycho-sexual games, relate to McLuhan?

Graham

In other words, the mysticism, the Catholic mysticism supplanted from what he thought was James Joyce onto TV as a medium and onto corporate culture as the avatar of this new mysticism.

de Bruyn

There is McLuhan, but also somebody like Gene Youngblood and his book *Expanded Cinema* in 1970, who made futuristic prognoses about the beneficial impact of new media such as computers, video, and TV on contemporary culture.

Graham

My position is always in-between. It's structuralist anthropology and McLuhan at the same time, reading back McLuhan to what his real source was, namely Walter Benjamin. I did not know Benjamin then, but obviously there was a remnant of the latter in McLuhan. Or, my interest in the genre of science fiction, which is both utopian and dystopian at the same time, or in popular cliches that are both things. In other words, I'm agreeing with popular psychology as a kind of Pop media thing. I agree with it, but on the other hand it is temporary and you can throw it away, just like Pop art. You can use the media to show these theories. In my approach to these ideas I was following the magazine *Radical Software.*

de Bruyn

Radical Software?

Graham

It was a utopian video magazine. It was into television, communalism, topology, topological furniture. Their editor was Paul Ryan. He wrote about cybernetics and the sacred. He was one of the great video philosophers and pioneers. His work was about topology and creating sacred situations, meditative objects through video.

de Bruyn

What was *Radical Software* propounding?

Graham

McLuhan was just the tip of the iceberg. Video art came out of this magazine. It was communal, sociologist, geology was important, drug culture.

de Bruyn

What is topological furniture?

Graham

In other words, furniture that made topology move your own body together with somebody else's body. The metaphor of topology was very important. The topology metaphor and R. D. Laing were how I structured the video piece *Past Future/Split Attention.*[17]

de Bruyn

You are referring to the book *Knots* by Laing?[18]

Graham

Yes.

de Bruyn

Where did the notion of topology originate?

Graham

Topology is a very nineteen-sixties idea that the inside and the outside were the same surface and that you could make a loop, like a Möbius strip, identifying inside and outside.

de Bruyn

You're saying that the idea was out there at the time and that there was no specific source.

Graham

Well, again, I got a lot of it from *Radical Software.* I guess it was the dominant mathematical metaphor.

de Bruyn

The cover illustration of the *Films* catalogue is a drawing by Ernst Mach of his visual field, in which we appear to be peering out into the world from within his skull. The image is partially framed by the arch of his eyebrow and his nose, while his reclining lower body is seen below, extending into space, but seemingly detached from his visual consciousness.

Graham

That was related to my discovery of James Gibson.[19]

de Bruyn

Whom you refer to in *Subject Matter.*

Graham

Yes. He was a psychologist who was interested in the fact that we discover things visually by moving our body in a particular location. The visual experience is something that happens in a real extended time period as we move around in space. There is a feedback between the part of the body that we see, which is the part of the body below the eye, not just the eye, and the actual environment that we are in. And that we apprehend things in series.

de Bruyn

In series?

Graham

In other words, in overlapping moments. It is not a Renaissance perspectival idea of visuality. It's something we experience as part of an ongoing physical, perceptual process.

de Bruyn

An embodied viewer.

Graham

An embodied viewer which I combine with an interest in feedback and feedback loops.

de Bruyn

Does the idea of short-term memory that plays such an important role in the video installations come from Gibson as well?

Graham

No, I got that from the feedback loop in real time, when we see ourselves. Actually, the first time I experienced this was with Steve Reich, who actually got it from Terry Riley, the idea of a loop which repeats what you heard five seconds ago. So it was inside your short-term memory, giving you a kind of extended present time.

de Bruyn

So you can contract the two moments together?

Graham

It's a kind of drug time, where you have an extended present time. It is also what happens when you see your own feedback. You do something, you see the feedback, which influences what you're doing, which, again, is re-influencing what you're doing, so that you're looped within your own body perception. . . . In short, we have two different things. Gibson is writing about the kinesthetic feeling of your body being a part of the perception process, which is of course against Renaissance perspective. And the idea of an extended present time, which is very much 1960s, early 70s, coming from drug time. It is what you get when you see yourself on a feedback loop in video. In other words, when you return to an image of yourself or to the image that you're seeing. You return to your own perceptual process within a very short period of time. It comes from Terry Riley by way of the structuralist Steve Reich.

de Bruyn

The use of shifting phase movements?

Graham

It was before the phase. It was the *Come Out* piece of 1966—the piece Reich did with the black boy speaking the words "come out," about squeezing open a bruise so that the bruise blood could come out. Reich made loops on a tape recorder, five- to six-second time delay loops. Nauman and I did the same thing with video perception. Nauman made a five- to six-second time delay in all his early works. Everybody was doing it. It originally comes from Terry Riley and Steve Reich.

de Bruyn

In the Nauman films there is also the accidental occurrence of a dissynchrony between sound and image.

Graham

More simply, Nauman discovered the use of super slow motion in film. Because then you have an opening up of an extended present time.

de Bruyn

In contrast to the notion of the present as being discontinuous.

Graham

Which, again, was a Renaissance notion.

Notes

1. Dan Graham, *Films,* exh. cat. (Geneva: Éditions Centre d'Art Contemporain/Écart Publications, 1977). The catalogue contains descriptions by Dan Graham of all his films. *Project for Slide Projector* consists of a carousel slide projector which continuously projects a series of eighty slides. The slides were made by rotating a camera around the panes of a glass box. The depth of focus changes with each shot according to a fixed schema. On completion of a full rotation new glass panes are added onto the box structure. The resulting twenty slides are shown in their original order and in reverse. The procedure is duplicated for the remaining forty slides. Dan Graham explains:

> The effect of light changes: initially it is light through the transparent space, the "illusionistic" effect of complex exterior and interior mirroring develops as successive boxes within boxes are added and filmed; finally the surface becomes more or less a mirror and the light opaque. . . . What is seen must be read in terms of the conventions of still photography: two-dimensional objects which appear at once solid and also as transparent (pp. 3–5).

2. Graham refers to his projection piece at Finch College in his essay "Photographs of Motion": "The use of the inherent 'flat,' serialized space was why I turned to the 35mm slide (color transparency) as art structure in itself in a series shot in 1965 and 1966 of architectural alignments and another series of transparent-mirror 'spaces'." See Dan Graham, "Photographs of Motion," in *End Moments* (New York: Dan Graham, 1969), p. 34.

The photo-essay *Homes for America* was first published, in truncated form, in *Arts Magazine* 41, no. 3 (December–January 1966–1967).

3. In "Photographs of Motion" Graham situates his *Project for Slide Projector* in relation to both an "archaeology" of cinema and the practice of Minimal art:

> Ironically it wasn't the new medium of cinema which devolved from Edison's invention, but the steps along its path—the analysis of motion—which first "moved" artists. Marey's work is recalled by the Futurists and most notably, by Marcel Duchamp's paintings. . . . Léger, Moholy-Nagy and others did utilize the motion picture (also Duchamp at a later date), but only as an available tool and not in terms of its structural underpinnings. It wasn't until recently, with the "Minimalist" reduction of the medium to its structural support in itself considered as an "object" that photography could find its own subject matter.
>
> See Graham, *End Moments,* p. 34.

4. Dan Graham visited the Nova Scotia School of Art during the early Spring of 1969.

5. *Sunset to Sunrise* (1969, 16mm, color). "The film is made by continuously moving a 16mm movie camera from a position oriented toward the sun on the horizon line at the moment of sunset, and proceeding in a slow spiral with gradual upward inclination toward the top of the sky. . . . The next morning at sunrise . . . a reverse spiral downward in opposite right-to-left rotation is filmed, ending on the sun rising above the horizon." (Dan Graham, *Films,* p. 11).

6. *March 31, 1966* appears in *For Publication* (Los Angeles: Otis Art Institute, 1975), and was first exhibited at *Art in Series,* Finch College Museum of Art, New York, Winter, 1966–1967.

7. Graham is referring to the performance *Bouncing in a Corner* by Bruce Nauman, which he performed with Meredith Monk during the exhibition *Anti-Illusion: Procedures/Materials* at the Whitney Museum of American Art in 1969. Graham writes in "Subject Matter" about the seminal importance of this event to the development of his own critical position vis-à-vis Minimalism. ("Subject Matter" was first published in *End Moments.*)

8. *Two Correlated Positions* (two Super 8 films, color, 1969) and *Roll* (two Super 8 films, color, 1970).

9. *Helix/Spiral* (two Super 8 films, color, 1973).

10. *Binocular Zoom* (1969–1970) was shot by Dan Graham with two Super 8 cameras held before both eyes. Both lenses gradually zoom out from a close-up of the sun.

11. *Body Press* (1970–1972, two 16mm films, color). Graham describes the filming procedure of *Body Press* as follows:

> Two filmmakers stand within a surrounding and completely mirrorized cylinder, body trunk stationary, hands holding and pressing a camera's back-end flush to, while slowly rotating it about, the surface cylinder of their individual bodies. One rotation circumscribes the body's contour, spiraling slightly upward with the next turn. With successive rotations, the body surface areas are completely covered as a template by the back of the camera(s) until eye-level (view through cameraman's eyes) is reached; then reverse mapping downward begins . . . when each camera is rotated to each body's rear it is then facing and filming the other where they are exchanged so the camera's "identity" "changes hands" and each performer is handling a new camera.
>
> See Graham, *Films,* p. 21.

12. *Body Press* is an exception, since it was shot in a studio.

13. *Cinema* (1981) exists as an architectural model for a cinema to be sited on the ground level of a modern office building. An extensive description of the project can be found in *Rock My Religion: Writings and Art Projects 1965–1990/Dan Graham,* ed. Brian Wallis (Cambridge: MIT Press, 1993), pp. 168–69.

14. See Dan Graham, "Dean Martin/Entertainment as Theater" (1967), in *Rock My Religion,* pp. 56–65.

15. *Performance 1* (New York: John Gibson Gallery, 1970) lists the following films: *Two Correlated Rotations, Roll, Sunset to Sunrise, Binocular Zoom of Highlight.* The catalogue also contains descriptions of *(Like),* a tape loop piece, and the performances *Lax/Relax* and *TV Camera/Monitor.*

16. The California artist William T. Wiley was a teacher of Bruce Nauman's at the University of California, Davis.

17. *Past Future/Split Attention* (videotape, b/w, 1972). The following citation comes from Graham's own description of the video performance:

> Two people who know each other are in the same space. While one person predicts continuously the other person's future behavior, the other person recounts (by memory) the other's past behavior. . . . For the performance to proceed, a simultaneous, but doubled, attention of the first performer's "self" in relation to the other's impressions must be maintained. This effects cause-and-effect directionality. The activity of the two is joined by numerous loops of feedback and feed-ahead words and behavior.

See Dan Graham: "Past Future/Split Attention" (1972), *Rock My Religion,* p. 66. Also see below in this volume.

18. R. D. Laing, *Knots* (New York: Pantheon Books, 1971).

19. James Gibson, *The Perception of the Visual World* (New York: Allen & Unwin, 1950).

This interview was held in New York in March 1996, and was initially published in Gloria Moure, Dan Graham, *exh. cat. (Santiago de Compostela: Centro Galego de Arte Contemporanea, 1997), pp. 195–205.*

V. Performance

Lax/Relax

A girl is instructed to say the word . . . "lax" . . . to herself and then to breath in and out, then to repeat this word . . . and to continue this pattern for thirty minutes. This is tape-recorded. The girl may be hypnotizing herself.

In front of a live audience, I say the word . . . "relax" . . . to myself, breath in and out, then repeat this pattern for the length of time of the recorded girl's voice tape. I speak into a microphone connected for amplification to a tape recorder whose self-contained speakers are playing (on one side) the girl's pre-recorded voice and (on the other side) my voice. Through absorption, the girl's recorded voice and my voice are tending in vocal intonation and in my body's posture to "identify" with our particular phrase.

In the initial stages of performance my awareness is focused upon: myself (self-relation), the voice of (and my relation to) the girl, and the audience's responses. My initial outward responses, my timing and phrasing, reflect my consciousness of all three inputs. But as I concentrate, gradually my awareness shifts to only myself and relating to the girl's voice; then finally I am centered in only self-absorption.

The performance begins with both words spoken in phase: the breathing reflects my (and the girl's) "distance" as the words move in and out of phase with irregular breathing modules; as the piece continues and the breathing regularizes in phase.

The audience may become involved in its own breathing responses and thus locate the surface of its involvement; its attention is somewhere between "inside" my breathing and its relation to the girl's or its own breathing. It may become hypnotically affected.

Note

This text was written at the time of the work's first performance, which took place at the New York University Loeb Student Center, May 1969. It is reprinted here from Dan Graham, Performance *(New York: John Gibson Gallery, 1970), p. 4.*

Dan Graham

Past Future/Split Attention

Two people who know each other are in the same space. While one person predicts continuously the other person's future behavior, the other person recounts (by memory) the other's past behavior.

Both performers are in the present, so knowledge of the past is needed to continuously deduce future behavior (in terms of causal relation). For one to see the other in the present (attention) there is a mirror reflection or closed figure-eight feedback/feed-ahead loop of past/future. One person's behavior reciprocally reflects/depends upon the other's, so that each one's information of his moves is seen, in part, as a reflection of the effect that his own just-past behavior has had in reversed tense, as perceived from the other's view of himself. For instance, the expectation of the person predicting the other one's behavior may be thwarted if the other person deliberately alters the course of his future behavior and establishes an alternate or negative series of actions. However, unconsciously (conscious to an outside observer in a longer span of time) he may perform as predicted, but in a displaced or altered sequence of responses which reflect his reaction to the reaction of the other, to his projecting a "past" identity upon them. Or he may be projecting the behavior that the other person is anticipating from him onto the other person's past, trying to affect that person's future predictions, and so on. (As part of the thinking process in terms of time continuum of cause and effect, the observer, in dealing with what he sees, extrapolates from the observed's past behavior projected in a line to the future.) For the performance to proceed, a simultaneous, but doubled, attention of the first performer's "self" in relation to the other (object)—the other's impressions—must be maintained by each performer. This affects cause and effect directionality, as does the discrepancy in time between words as linear projections and the very different (but also linear) sequential direction of behavior. As videotape is a continuum (unlike film, which is discontinuous, an analytic re-construction) with separate sound (verbal) and visual tracks, it is an ideal medium for presenting this sequence.

Note

This text was written in 1972 and first published in Anton Herbert, ed., Dan Graham: Théâtre *(Ghent: de appel, 1982), n. p.*

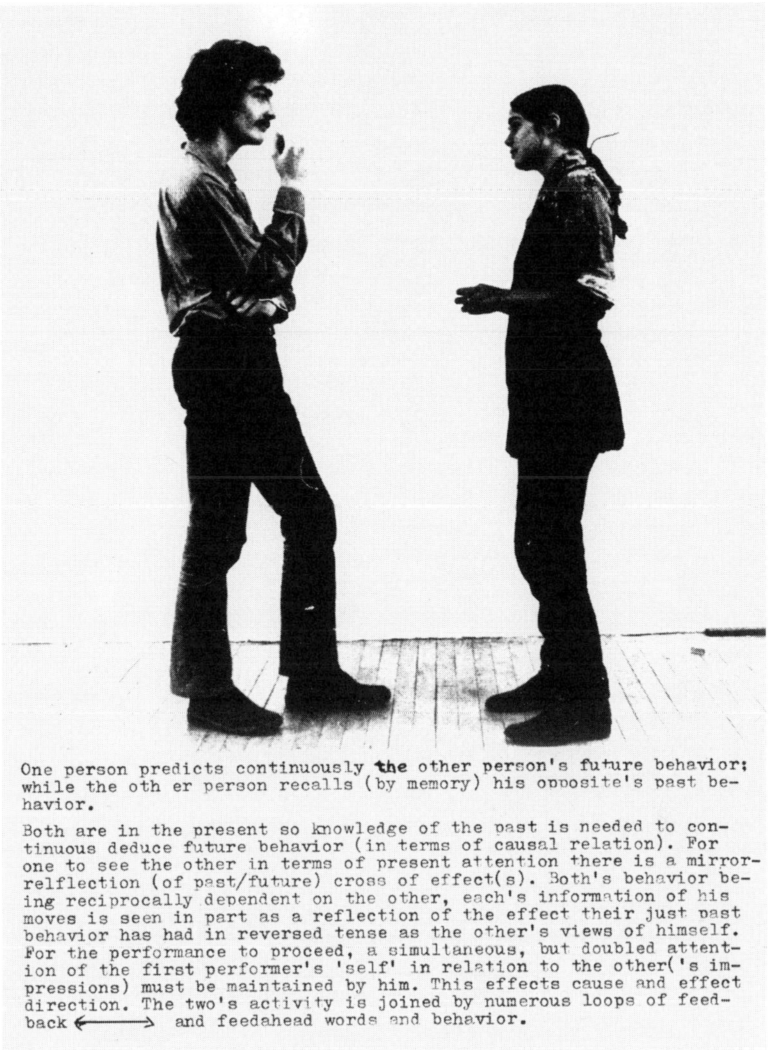

25
Dan Graham
Past Future/Split Attention, 1972

Dan Graham

Performer/Audience/Mirror

A performer faces a seated audience. Behind the performer, covering the back wall (parallel to the frontal view of the seated audience), is a mirror reflecting the audience.

Stage 1

The performer looks in the general direction of the audience. He begins a continuous description of his external movements and the attitudes he believes are signified by this behavior for about five minutes. The audience hears the performer and sees his body.

Stage 2

The performer continues facing the audience. Looking directly at them, he continuously describes their external behavior for about five minutes. (See Observation 2.)

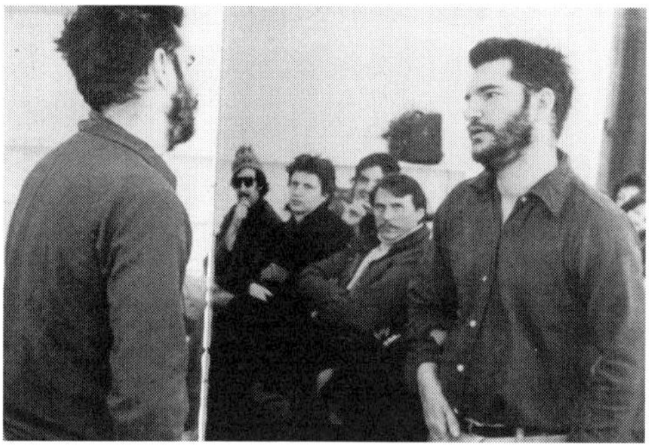

26
Dan Graham
Performer/Audience/Mirror, 1977

Stage 3

The performer faces the mirror (his back turned to the audience). For about five minutes he continuously describes his front body's gestures and the attitudes it may signify. He is free to move about, in order to better see aspects of his body's movements. When he sees and describes his body from the front, the audience, inversely, sees his back (and their front). The performer is facing the same direction as the audience, seeing the same mirror-view. The audience cannot see (the position of) the performer's eyes.

Stage 4

The performer remains turned, facing the mirror. For about five minutes he observes and continuously describes the audience who he can see mirror-reversed from Stage 2 (their right and left now being the same as his). He freely moves about relative to the mirror in order to view different aspects of the audience's behavior. His change of position produces a changing visual perspective which is correspondingly reflected in the description. The audience's view remains fixed; they are not (conventionally) free to move from their seats in relation to the mirror covering the front staging area.

Observations:

1. Through the use of a mirror the audience is able to instantaneously perceive itself as a public body (as a unity), offsetting its definition by the performer. This gives it a power within the performance equivalent to that of the performer.

2. In Stage 2, the audience sees itself reflected by the mirror instantaneously, while the performer's comments are slightly delayed and follow, as they are verbal discourse, a continuous temporal forward flow. This effects cause and effect interpretation for the audience. First, a person in the audience sees himself "objectively" ("subjectively") perceived by himself; next, he hears himself described "objectively" ("subjectively") in terms of the performer's perception. The slightly delayed verbal description by the performer overlaps/undercuts the present (fully present) mirror-view an audience member has of himself and of the collective audience; it may influence his further interpretation of what he sees. Cause and effect relations are further complicated when members of the audience (because they can see and be seen on the mirror by other members of the audience) attempt to influence (through eye contact, gestures, etc.) the behavior of other audience members, which thereby influences the performer's description (of the audience's behavior).

Transcript of the second performance of *Performer, Audience, Mirror,* at P.S. 1 (December 1977):

Stage 1

> I'm sort of sliding around in place . . . umm . . . wearing a very bright carmine red shirt with one hand completely in the pocket finger, thumb stuck out, the other thumb in the pocket, hand stuck out, knuckles kind of touching the edge of my pocket as I turn rotating on my right leg . . . uh, more so than the left arm; now it goes back . . . both, uhh . . . actually the, the right arm is just slightly akimbo, pressed back against the body as I rock back pivoting now and actually balancing on my . . . left . . . leg . . . my left foot, which is on the audience's right side. Hands haven't changed,

very subtly the foot is changing, the heel kind of peeps up . . . creeping up . . . creeping down as if peeping . . . peeping, at the audience . . . but it's not moving very much. . . . The mouth speaks and now the head is rotated slightly toward the audience on the right side; it continues to rotate. The whole torso—actually it's not the head, it's the torso . . . but the feet are stationary, they haven't moved an inch. Now the head goes up looking at the corner up near the lights toward the window at the back and going a little bit higher, uhh . . . the shoulders haven't moved an inch. Now the head goes up looking a little bit . . . uh, there's a little bit of movement now as the knees become a tiny bit looser and the body now rocks back and forth in a stable position . . . feet slightly spread . . . uh . . . a good center of balance . . . and perhaps slightly more relaxed. The head, which was looking straight up, now looks down . . . uhh . . . at a spot on the floor, perhaps, or at the first chair and as this happens the knees now, now the whole bottom part of the body is bending towards the audience's left and almost losing its balance for a second . . . there was a stutter in the speech as the balance was almost lost, almost regained, but now moving again in that direction almost compulsively . . . repeating the same pattern as before. The hands haven't changed much, uh . . . except the knuckles aren't touching. Umm . . . maybe it's, uh, it's not a fist as much as it was before on the right side and, as this happens, as if to accent that, uh, there's a pivot on the right, uh, the right leg, the leg on the audience's left side, on the heel so it's now at right angles to the other foot, only now the head looks down looking at that formation . . . and there's a movement, uh, in that direction as if walking in that direction to the side of the room, which has commenced . . . and I'm walking . . . walking in that direction . . . to the side of the room offstage; it stops at the word "stage," hesitates on the toe of the left foot, which is unbalancing the body as I can't stand properly, and now starting to walk backwards . . . with a kind of trembling, a kind of lack of balance and an attitude of, uh, hesitation . . . and there is a rocking on the knee, the knee on the side closest to the audience . . . rocking up and down and kind of puffing . . . maybe an impatience and a slight anger . . . it might stop but it hasn't stopped and now the body rotates, uh, very slowly, deliberately looks at the audience; it's slightly moving now toward the room, though, as if pivoting again on the top of the torso. The feet staying stationary so there's a bisection between those two parts of the body, torso and the top; the head looks up again, staring above the audience . . . at, uh, a very bright, uh . . . lighted wall, uh, above, looking, uh, continuing, it's as if once movement begins it's, it's like a tripod, it keeps just going higher and higher, pivoting, panning back, looks down, slight eye contact with the audience for a second, and now the body pivots in the other direction . . . on the audience's right . . . the foot on the, uh . . . inside. Now the foot on the on the audience's right side now is at right angles and the head is looking at the foot but there's no movement this time . . . a kind of rocking back and forth . . . uh, the hands haven't moved at all . . . and, umm . . . now looking directly at the audience . . .

Stage 2

The audience is looking down, particularly the audience in the front row looking down toward my feet . . . no . . . not much eye contact . . . uh, the eye contact, uh, is now more established in the middle than in the front rows and in the back rows the audience is less distracted than it was, umm . . . a few seconds ago. Umm . . . there is a kind of eye blink, umm . . . by a number of people, uh . . . the eyes make contact, blink, go down, umm . . . the people seem a little bit, uhh . . . uh, they're a little bit startled, umm . . . umm . . . the expression is now that some people are frowning as if disagreeing with that, puckering at the edges, uh, the very edges of, of, the, uh, of the lips. Umm . . . now . . . a couple of people move their head or shake their head, uhh . . . which is a head movement instead of an eye movement . . . and there's a little bit of lip movement. There's been no sound . . . there's only a tiny snicker in the front row, but no one else; now everyone is snickering, but not the same way; it's kind of an acknowledgment snicker, um . . . saying you agree with, uh . . . um . . . now there's much more blinking and much more coquettish kind of attitude in the blink rather than just a kind of distancing—not trying to look. And people smile a little bit, slightly smirking, slightly smiling, somewhere between the two of these; these, uh, tend to be people in the center, uh, which is where I'm looking . . . um, uh, not people, not people in the front. Umm . . . everyone . . . uh, other people now touching their bodies scratching themselves or moving a little bit in position (I say everybody, I don't mean that, I mean about half of the people in one . . . tends to be people that I'm looking at that, uh, move this way, other people I'm looking at I catch aren't) . . . someone's parting their hair; someone looks back . . . um . . . now the difference between the people in the back is, is they seem much more stone-faced about the whole thing . . . they're hiding, they're hiding in the back . . . they're either very serious or they don't want to be seen. Umm . . . people in front, um, seem to be staring slightly down not looking up, uh, well, uh, they're, uh, now they're looking up . . . I guess it's rather hard for them to see me on an eye contact basis. It's the people in the center that, uh, are the focus of my attention. And now it's funny, all the people seem very disparate with what they're doing, not that they're moving much but they're taking separate poses, kind of defining their individual selves as statues posing, uh . . . now everybody smiles at that; uh, the smiles are not . . . of a uniform type . . . uh, people now are not . . . no, they're—some people are making eye contact; a lot of people shifted . . . and there's a kind of laughter . . . uh, a laughing and looking away, uh . . . uh . . . a number of people. . . .

Stage 3

I'm looking at myself and my face looks almost as red as the shirt I'm wearing. As I look back and I'm scratching at the acned face—as I look at that, the eyes are red too, the rims of the eyes, uhh, the face is rather round, umm, the shirt is open in a kind of triangle and my hands are in my pockets, one thumb in the pocket . . . uh . . . on one side and the hands in the pocket with the thumb sticking out on the other side. The feet are kind of, one foot is forward in a very angular way from the other, umm . . . a very dynamic pose although there's no motion . . . um . . . involved in it . . . and now a kind of violent shrug of the shoulder, uh . . . rather aggressive, and a rocking so that the one hand is akimbo; it goes back and forth; the other hand doesn't move, umm . . . and then the feet kind of kick each other, kick around the place . . . a kind of hop, skip, and jump: a semi-dance . . . it's hard to know what that signifies; it's much more aggressive as I move onto that foot . . . it is a kind of dance pattern trying to communicate something, and then a shuffle . . . and. . . . I'm looking down again and, uh, from the side, uh, not much more information uh, about the . . . except the shoulders seem even more, um, hunched, uh; but as I do that I shake my, umm, arms, somewhat loosening them up, and now they're out of the pocket and I'm making a fist and the fist goes up in a pugilistic, uh, boxing sense and I hit the mirror for a second, look down, look up, uh, the eyes, uh, they look a little bit deadpan, umm, the lip, the lower lip is a little bit loose, it could be a half pout . . . uh . . . um . . . it's tired; it looks tired, somewhat tired . . . the eyes look somewhat tired, um . . . I also see wrinkles around the edges, the edges, the corners of the eyes, as I look. But the face is very dead, very deadpan, very straightforward, very unexpressive, except perhaps for the lips as I talk . . . um . . . it seems like the upper lip is more aggressive, umm . . . umm . . . goes up . . . and now I'm moving the arms akimbo as if I might communicate something, perhaps contradicting that last message; again, hard to know what that means precisely, uh . . . I'll try to guess . . . umm . . . perhaps it is some kind of disagreement; and now I just spread my legs totally, so that cuts off movement, uh . . . as the legs are very far apart; it creates a center of balance; the head is down; I'm not even looking at myself; it goes up as I do, I detect a smile or a semi-smile, just the beginning of one, and, uh . . . the expression, it's a little more light-hearted, and now [much laughter in the background] . . . and now you can see my teeth . . . [more laughter] and also the smile . . . and that [more laughter] takes away from the redness and, uh, it's a kind of humorous, humorous gesture . . .

Stage 4

As I'm looking at the audience back here the audience seems, uh . . . mildly amused . . . uh, all the audience . . . uh . . . and there they got their heads, uh . . . hanging, ostensibly just to look at my eyes, which is very hard for them to see—they're actually just seeing my back. . . . Uh, but they're craning themselves in order to do that so they look a little bit more angular. Umm . . . it's like, reversed . . . collectively, they seem much more similar . . . rather than individual, and they all seem content, umm . . . they seem fairly, umm . . . content . . . and they laugh with a sound for the first time . . . licking the tops of their lips some of them, well, uh . . . different people have different ways of expressing, of expressing this, but the faces are not as symmetrical; it's not a kind of, "I'm O.K." smile, more, uh, relaxed, um, than previously; I also see, um, the eyes are much more alive than they were previously and there's less of them blinking, umm, perhaps because I'm not looking directly at them. Let's move around here . . . um . . . now this side of the audience . . . which is, um, now on my left side, which is the audience's left side, umm . . . well, a moment ago they were smiling, now they're very serious. Umm . . . and now there's a half smile that comes up to a full smile in the case of a couple of people . . . umm . . . and now I see two people in the third row and then a woman who wouldn't smile if nobody else did—that's where my eyes were directed at the time—which was strange . . . and everyone else was not . . . um, people in the back, in the back row, are dead [much laughter]; either their head and faces, uh, have, uh, have a beard which hides them or glasses or a kind of professional look, uh; the same could be said of the people standing in that position—of course, when I said that, that was not true, but they all, uh—well, the person with a beard has a camera and is taking pictures; they're all trying to disguise their expression in various ways . . . it's very different from the people in the middle who—where I look—who seem much more natural in a funny way. The people in front are just looking up because they're very low, um, like kind of footlights. I'm looking at the other side now; I see peoples' heads quite askew um, in different ways; I think they're trying to catch my eyes, umm . . . from here it looks like they probably do from where, from where they are and their heads kind of move but they're not looking at me as they move their head. Umm, people are . . . people . . . um, on that side they're um, um . . . How can I do that? . . . I have to define them as being different from the people on the other side, I guess; I guess I can't, uh, really, at this point, except that they seem to be, uh, able to look at, at my eyes so that they're looking at me from a much more angular view and, um, testing that, uh, situation. Further back, um . . . . [laughter] everybody laughs . . . umm . . . and as they laugh . . . um, they move their heads and it's a much more animated laugh than before. . . . It's funny, people, a few people have touched their body with their, uh, um, hands, but most people haven't . . . there's very little body movement; a, uh, a lot of head movement . . . eye movement but very little body movement. Uh, a few people are clutching their hands together. In fact, everybody in the first row seems to have that posture. Now the people in the second row, um, seem to be holding, um, their body together; rather than clutching their hands they're clutching their body, uh; a lot of people in the second row are doing that. In the third row, well, it's impossible to see, but I think that it also seems to be true; it seems to be rather uniform, that situation in the piece. Umm . . . some people in the back row are moving, sort of, sort of shaking their heads, but maybe because I'm not concentrating on them they feel they can do that. Uh . . . many yawns, uh, about half the yawns in the front row, uh, people in the second row are very amused as as a whole group [laughter], uh . . . on the left side quite amused [some laughter].

Stage 5, Stage 1 repeated

Now as I pick up the stride, and deliberately scuff the floor as I move from one side to the other, my hands are very loose at my sides. . . . I'm twiddling my fingers somewhat, a little bit like a kind of monkey, uh, pose as I walk back, certainly much more relaxed than before as I scratch my head, walking to the side, not even looking at the audience, just making a corridor, uh, walking back across from one side to the other, um . . . somewhat, uh, very . . . loose, somewhat, and, uh, somewhat slower than I normally walk and when I do that I kind of twist on my hips, uh . . . as if I'm, uh, at a party and I want to dance, um, but I can't really do it [laughter], and, uh, now I put my hands out in front and they're almost prayer-like . . . I guess that's what that represents, umm . . . gesture bringing the hands up and down, up and down, I'm looking at my hands as I do it and now the hands go down to the side; they're very loose, almost too loose . . . uh . . . almost artificial; when they do I kick with my right foot on the audience's left, and now I bring my knee up so I'm balancing on the other foot, which creates a kind of playful, um, pose, perhaps I could fall. . . . Um . . . and I look up . . . I look up for a second for a confirmation from the audience, um, now the foot goes down . . . um, but it's still a little— . . . here seems to be a little unsteadiness, um, involved. And now suddenly there's a decisive gesture . . . the feet are splitting apart and, um, a kind of clutching one ear, the ear on the audience's, uh, right side . . . umm . . . and scratching it, taking the wax out of it, looking at my finger [some laughter], uh, looking—now I'm looking up at the audience—the audience, um, has made some reaction, uh, I look over the audience, now I look down at my body; it's as if I'm checking out parts of my body, semi-aware of the audience and semi-not aware of the audience. At one point I, um, well, this actually continues because I'm looking at a fingernail on my, uh, left hand—audience's right side—um, seeing that they're dirty, um, quite, dirty, um, and while I've done that the finger, the thumb has gone back inside the pocket on the right on my side. Hands now, instead of clutching against the corduroy pants, are actually, the fingers are actually outward as if they were about to take off, and I take it out of the pocket and look at it for a second . . . now a very decisive move to the side. . . . For the first time that I turn around and make a fist, scratch the ear again and, um, look at the audience, and I look at the audience.

Stage 6, repeating Stage 2

As the audience, uh, has just completed, uh, very individual gestures, uh, coughing, uh, things that have nothing to do with reflecting what I'm doing, umm . . . and now they're, umm . . . um . . . gradually coming around to look at me. It's funny . . . now some are very serious . . . a little sad . . . and some are very happy . . . umm, I guess that's the way people are: they're either one way or the other . . . um . . . so maybe they're acting more natural and this amuses some people and it doesn't amuse other people. Umm . . . I'm looking for, um, the hand, things that I noticed before. . . . I'd say that the people in the front row haven't changed at all; they're generally clutching, uh, their hands together, uh, but not their body, and some people in the second row have loosened up their hands and they're not clutching their body; other people are, uh, that's true of the people in the third row, uh, and, uh, and I can see it's probably less true of the people in the fourth row who are more natural with their hands, and now they have a semi-yawn and, umm . . . um . . . a loose smile at that; it's a time for some people to yawn and loosen up their heads a little bit at this moment, and look away for the first time; I'm losing some people's attention, umm . . . which has a little bit to do with physical tiredness; now some people are actually communicating rather than responding, that is, they're moving their face or their lips, uh, as if they're actually looking at me directly to say something individually; um, people are much more individual and it's become a little closer to a dialogue, um, I see more yawns; it's as if it's given people permission to express that, um . . . um, that feeling that some people must have . . . um . . . the people who are standing in the back and probably not seeing the mirror seem, uh, really to be quite serious . . . um, extremely serious . . . . Uh, um, the people in front are not looking at me, they're looking at the mirror and probably at themselves or the other bodies [inaudible] . . . uh . . . more people yawn . . . someone's parting his hair; other people look away . . . people express something with an aside . . . an asymmetrical gesture with the sides of their mouths, which, uh, I take to be, uh, uh . . . through its lack of symmetry a kind of, um, loss of interest. Now everyone . . . people are leaving and other people shuffling, uh, shuffling into position . . . um. . . .

Stage 7, repeating Stage 3

I looked very strange for a second, lips are together, um, looking down . . . hands in the pocket . . . pockets, a kind of exaggeration, seriousness, bewildered humor at the same time . . . uh . . . again the stance is half aggressive . . . with the feet bending, bending with front torso forward in the way the feet are splayed in that kind of asymmetrical fashion as if about to move, when the arms are akimbo but because the head is down, um, and the shoulders somewhat up and I just moved them up again to emphasize that, uh . . . there's a kind of timidity or fear, and now they go back and relax and the opposite happens, um, there is a kind of confidence . . . and, um, semi-grin is more of a [inaudible] and also a little bit of frustration and a little bit of relaxation and now a little bit more serious expression emerges. It's very hard, uh, the changes in expression are so rapid it's hard to even see them, and as I do this I'm again moving—straddling to the side slightly, um, balancing on one foot and raising the other foot up, up to the toe and then rotating. A very stiff, strange kind of gesture, uh . . . um . . . sort of more a dance gesture. The hands are different from the last time in that the, um, two hands, both fingers are in the pockets; the two thumbs are out, uh. . . . My body is basically symmetrical, which it hasn't been in a long time. Just as I do that, uh . . . I kind of make a gesture with one shoulder to make it asymmetrical a little bit . . . but because the arms are a little akimbo (the entire body spreads out a bit). What this means probably is that, um, uh, the performance has settled into a kind of balance . . . um . . . situation. Um . . . maybe I have a more balanced view of myself. Uh . . . maybe I don't because I just kicked the cinder block which indicates a very great level, uh . . . is that humorous or what? [laughter—especially loud from one woman].

Stage 8, repeating Stage 4

Now the audience is . . . is, uh, is actually laughing, uh, pretty loudly . . . uh, horsey laughs, and, as I say that, everyone kind of lets their laughs and their heads go . . . [inaudible] impersonating their looks as if to de-emphasize the fact that they even did that. Um, of course, some laugh and some don't . . . they're very aware of me. Their mouths are open; people's mouths are a little bit more open and talking, uh . . . that means they're probably more, um, relaxed again, uh . . . it's funny, now people are amused but in a different way, some look at me and some look the other way . . . that is, they're listening. Uh . . . as I said that everyone's eye goes back to look at me sometimes very sneakily, which is odd because their bodies are asymmetrical; they may be looking one direction, uh, pointing the body in one direction and looking in the other direction. Um . . . it's very hard to get people in the very back, uh . . . they seem to be more attentive than before, um . . . well . . . they're more relaxed; they're less serious, but they're also very uninvolved, um . . . in different ways, either, um, chewing or looking to the side . . . um. . . . Again, it's quite hard for me to see this, um . . . it's more of a guess than anything. Also, the people in the direct middle, um, it's difficult, um . . . to see it, but as a group they're quite serious at the moment now; of course, everyone seems a little serious . . . it's as if I'm about to make a philosophical point, which I'm not . . . um . . . they're expecting that and, as I say that, everyone laughs again a very relaxed laugh, um . . . and, um . . . people are nervously moving their hands a tiny bit, um . . . but it's as if there's a kind of semi-communication, where they're smoking, they're, they loosen up their hands a little more than before, and, as I say that, one of the persons in the front row moves his hands together, clutches them, had his hands, uh . . . normally clutched, unclutched, and then he clutches them again, um . . . um, more people scratching just as I say that, scratching their face . . . some people looking away, uh . . . um . . . also tension . . . some blinking . . . umm . . . someone deliberately trying to get my attention um . . . in a theatrical way, uh . . . uh . . . that's like, well . . . people broadly smiling in the area that they normally have been, which is like the third row . . . second, third row are the most active ones, um [laughter], and they now look at each other nodding as if they're collectively [laughter] aware of this fact, um [much laughter], as a group [laughter]. Umm . . . this, by the way, is on the left side . . . my left side . . . their left side . . . our left side . . . um . . . now we got some action in the fourth row, too [loud laughter], as well as the third row, for the first time. . .um. . .I must say that it's the left side that's the, um, people who seem to like it better . . . appreciate me more . . . though I don't see any humor in this piece, um . . . uh. . . . These remarks affect more one than the other side . . . 'cause I'm looking in that direction . . . that may be a constant tendency . . . uh, seeing what happens on the other side . . . now the more serious people, uh, it's hard to make judgments but, uh, some of them are the ones that are not—are—they're not really laughing; the others haven't really changed . . . ummm . . . too much.

Stage 9, repeating Stage 1

Well . . . I'm looking down after looking up for a second and I just moved forward with one foot. . . . As if scratching in place . . . uh . . . the body is kind of rigid, the arms are akimbo as they have been all along, as I move directly in on the audience, um; I'm stopping in front of the audience, and, um, kneeling on a chair for a second, shaking a little bit, going back, um; I'm making a semi-fist; there seems to be a kind of semi-aggressive attitude but I don't know whether it's more toward myself or toward the audience—it's always aborted. Um . . . there's, um, a tiny bit of kicking and, um, a sort of semi-kick. . . . It's funny how the feet are now splayed apart. They're always asymmetrical, as if the audience, as if I deliberately want to unbalance myself; but I don't move; I'm stationary; I don't move in one direction or the other. I'm in the center, uh . . . this is where I tend to station myself during the performance. . . . Now I'm turning, um, and actually kind of looking at the direction of the audience on, on the audience's left side, and, as I do this . . . do that, I do something I did last time but different, raising my hands, they're together, they're at right angles to my body and, uh, now the fingers are pointed directly at the audience and, uh, it's as if it's a calisthenic gesture; now I bring the arms apart and down again, uh, and then relax them. What this signifies, um, I don't know. Maybe because it's I'm in school, P.S. 1, that's uh, that's why this is happening. . . . It's a little bit like, uh . . . gym class or something . . . although all these things are aborted and now there's a kind of rocking, uh, on the hip, back and forth in place. The feet again are, uh, akimbo, I guess that's the rather . . . it's about . . . it's as if I'm about to move very suddenly but I don't do it. Um . . . and then they freeze . . . and there's some bending of the knees, which causes both balance and lack of balance, and now I try to correct the balance . . .

and just, [sound] just snapped my two fingers together [again, the sound of fingers snapping], did that again . . . rocking back and forth; it's that kind of semi-parting, um, gesture but, um, it doesn't really mean that much. Now I go back a little bit again . . . backing up a kind of hop, semi-trot . . . O.K . . . thanks [applause] . . . [applause continues loudly].

Notes

This text was written at the time of the work's first performance, which took place at de appel, Amsterdam, Holland, June 1977. It was followed by a second performance at P.S. 1, New York, December 1977, and a third at Riverside Studios, London, England, March 1979. The text was first published in Anton Herbert, ed., Dan Graham: Théâtre *(Ghent: de appel, 1982), n. p.*

Musical Performance and Stage-Set Utilizing Two-Way Mirror and Time-Delay

An earlier performance set design involving video and a two-way mirror screen, done in collaboration with the composer, Glenn Branca, involves both the performers' *and* the audience members' self-awareness of their perception process: *Musical Performance and Stage-Set Utilizing Two-Way Mirror and Time-Delay* was shown in 1983 at the Bern Kunsthalle as part of a Dan Graham exhibition.

The audience is seated on the right; the three musicians are on the left and arranged in a triangle, with Branca at the front or apex. Audience and performers face a wall-sized two-way mirror. Behind this two-way mirror is a video monitor, whose image is luminescent enough to be seen through the mirror. The monitor image displays a view of the entire space. Its image comes from a camera mounted behind the two-way mirror, next to the monitor. A tape delay system causes the image to be delayed six seconds in the past.

The musicians must look toward the two-way mirror for cues from each other. They also may look to the six-second delayed image as a compositional metronome.

The audience's best view of the musicians comes from looking at the mirror and the monitor projecting behind it. They see other members of the audience gazing, as well as their own looks. When the musicians look toward the mirror image to see other musicians playing or to see the six-second-delay video, the audience members' views are placed between the intersubjective gazes on the three musicians.

Note

This essay was written in 1983. It was originally published in Dan Graham, Dan Graham-Pavilions, *exh. cat. (Munich: Kunstverein, 1988), p. 48.*

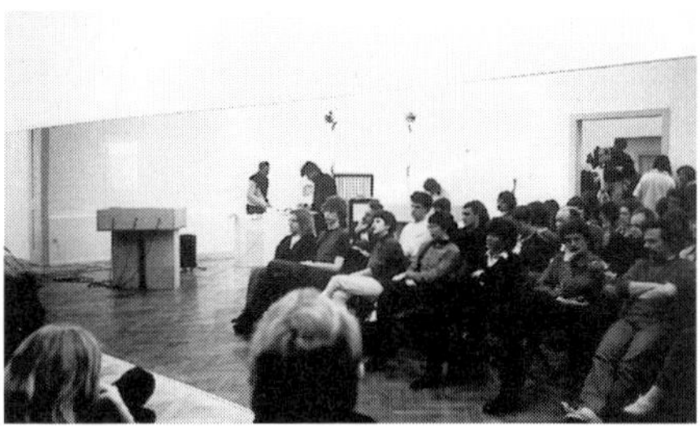

27
Glenn Branca and Dan Graham,
Musical Performance and Stage-Set, 1985

Stage-Set for *Guaire*

I designed a stage-set using a video time-delay and a curved, two-way mirror showing the audience an anamorphic image of itself, for a play by the artist James Coleman. It was performed at Dun Guaire Castle in Kinrara, Ireland, and set in the 16th century. The audience was seated in a "period room," the restored "throne room" whose mock "medieval banquets" were now normally held for tourists at this castle. Seated at a long narrow table, to see the play performed by a single actress on a tiny stage where the king had once sat, the audience's position was identical to that of the traveling poets or bards. They sat in on banquets in various Irish courts and provided information and commentary to the ruler.

Behind the "king" was a curved, two-way mirror, which, when the lights were on, showed the audience an anamorphically distorted image of themselves. For most of the performance a recorded video was projected onto the back of the two-way mirror. Its image was of the throne room from the king's point of view. In the play's development the king's commanding view is gradually lost as he takes the position of his ruled subjects. The video-recorded image was a plastic death mask of the king—a skull-like form. Projected into the two-way curved mirror, it was seen distended anamorphically. The performer turned to face the video image through the mirror. Suddenly, the lights were turned on, and the audience saw an image of its own gaze superimposed on the combined images of the performer and the video-recorded image of the death mask of the performer. After the lights were again dimmed, the video was switched to a live image, photographed by a camera to the side of the stage on an eight-second delay. Next, the performer lifted her mask. Turning back to the video image in the mirror she saw a masked image of herself, and made a gesture as if she could not bear to look at herself. Then, as she looked back at the mirror, the image appeared to catch up in time and become simply a reflection.

Note

This essay was written in 1985. It was initially published in Dan Graham, Dan Graham-Pavilions, *exh. cat. (Munich: Kunstverein, 1988), p. 48.*

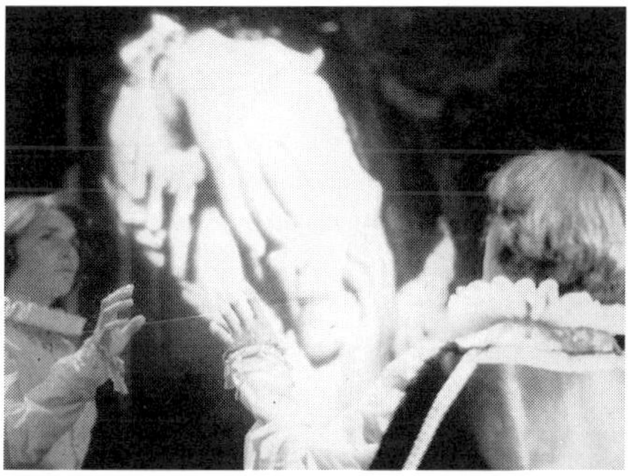

28
James Coleman and Dan Graham
Guaire, 1986

Theater-Cinema

Italian gardens of the Renaissance and Baroque periods were both *al fresco* museums and theaters in which the spectator doubled as performer. These gardens took their design from rediscovered Roman texts describing Roman country villas and gardens, augmented by archaeological discoveries, often on the precise site of the particular Roman garden. These excavated ruins, along with remnants of Roman statuary, were linked with newly built grottoes, fountains, waterworks, and perspectivally organized allées and green theaters. The logic connecting "rooms" and "streets" often was based on a Roman literary text; Ovid's *Metamorphoses,* in which the natural is transformed into the unnatural, was one primary source. The Italian garden might display, as well, scientific curiosities, botanical species, and various artifacts from everywhere in the world. Italian gardens, as museums and as metaphoric and actual theaters, came to represent the world as microcosm and as macrocosm.

The first gardens were built on a hill, their vistas stretching below the owner's villa. They were entered through an apse-like addition to the ground level of the villa, which gave an ideal view of the garden below. Once in the garden the spectator was like an actor wandering through scenes in a play. Theater set design and garden design influenced each other. The garden, treated metaphorically as a vast, outdoor theater, itself usually contained one or more theater whose architectural boundaries were constructed from box hedges, grass, stones, statuary, and fountains, all of which formed part of the stage-set and the seating area. Similarly, the axial perspective of Italian gardens was ideal for translation into sets of a perspectivally based stagecraft. The set designer Torelli produced stage-sets of gardens which recreated what audiences would see in neighboring villa gardens. Inigo Jones, in his masques presented in royal gardens, involved the audience's experience of moving through a garden to confront narratively the mythological programs. The garden as a theater and the garden theater within the garden gave a sense of a representation within a representation. To add to this effect, many of the plays performed within the garden's "green theaters" had garden scenes.

Often the "real" garden (where the play was being performed) would become part of the stage design. An opera performed inside the Barberini Palace garden in 1656 had a painted set of a garden, while across the proscenium arch ran a row of fountains from which actual water was piped. A theater in a Madrid garden in the early 17th century had a rear wall which opened to show beyond the illusionist garden scenery of the stage.

My *Theater-Cinema* (1966–1986) is a model that functions as part of a museological exhibition using various modern artists' models, and slide projections. The concept and schematic layout were designed by Rüdiger Schöttle. The models and the slides are to be projected into a large landscape model of a complete Baroque garden. This exhibition, titled "Bestiarium," is based on the idea of the theater-garden.

As Schöttle had previously used a model of *Cinema* (1981) in his "Louis XIV tänzt" exposition, I decided to reuse both *Cinema* and the relation to Versailles in my contribution to the new project. The cinema would be attached to a "green theater" located in a garden like Versailles. As in some of Torelli's and Inigo Jones's set designs for plays performed in outdoor theaters in gardens, the set would be a scene depicting an adjacent area of the same garden. The set's perspective would be nearly identical to the perspective that the spectator would have from the area in which he was positioned. The actors on stage would wear costumes which were nearly identical to the nobility who observed the play.

The rear of the stage set is designed as a two-way mirror which reflects the gazes of the nobility viewing the play and the garden's hedge-lined allées, in diminishing perspective. This rear stage–set as two-way mirror also functions as a rear-screen projection screen, superimposing images of the film being shown in the cinema, Rossellini's *The Rise to Power of Louis XIV* (1964).

Two-way mirror mylar provides a normal (not transparent) screen for viewers located in the movie house. Because of its properties of being more transparent on the side which receives less light, at moments of greater image brightness in the film, spectators in the theater also see the faces of the viewing cinema audience through the image of the film. At this point the mirrored backdrop is giving superimposed images of the image of the theater audience; images of the "real" garden allées, looking in the reverse direction of the stage; images from the film; and the image of the movie audience (confronting the image of the theater audience gazing at themselves and the theater actors).

Rossellini's *The Rise to Power of Louis XIV* was made for French television and later released for the cinema audience. The scene used in this project shows the young king and his entourage of court aristocrats walking in the garden of Versailles. This film focuses on Louis XIV's consolidation of his power through his reduction of the nobility to manipulated actors in a continuously staged spectacle. The king has become author and director as well as prime actor in a continuous theatrical fiction which is staged to reinforce an elaborate bureaucratic hierarchy, based on codes of court etiquette. He defines each courtier, all of whom are forced to live at court to preserve their roles, in terms of the limits of their function and position at court, through dress and dining codes and minute codes of court manners and ritual. The king as director has created a vast mise-en-scène, indistinguishable from "real" life. Rossellini shows the king creating an ideology of the unity of French nationhood which depends upon recognition of Louis XIV as Sun God and absolute monarch of all of France. Rossellini's film films Louis XIV's performance or creation of his self-representation; it attempts to "show the actor showing himself" and thereby show the actual historical creation, through Louis XIV's premeditated scenario that produced his (and France's) fiction of power. Rossellini's film is also a film about the film director's—Rossellini's—position as someone manipulating actors to create a fictional spectacle which purports to be historical reality.

The difference between Louis XIV's era and the present era is that royal stagecraft in the 17th century was linked to theatrical representation. Today political power and historical "reality" derive from the subliminal effects of film and television, which substitute media representations for historical memory. In the age of Louis XIV, the monarch's power was represented through his positioning within theater architecture at the central point at which all perspectival lines culminated. His perspective was the ideal one; he was the viewpoint to which all the actions on stage were addressed; he was the central actor in a court drama which he staged and in which all the others functioned as foils.

Today's ruler's image is produced and manipulated in the same way that the film or television actor is made into a "star." Rossellini, in this educational film, tried to overcome the tyranny of this "star" system and also the tyranny of his own hegemony as director, by giving all the roles, including that of Louis XIV to unknown, French peasant non-actors from the Versailles region. Politically, Rossellini attempts to reawaken popular memory, the peasant class's potentially subversive historical view of the nobility, as against the media stereotype, controlled in the interest of those in power today, of Louis XIV's role in history. Rossellini wishes to show how non-foreordained Louis XIV's power and creation of a national myth of French nationhood were.

Theater-Cinema takes the premise of Schöttle's exhibition, a return to archetypal German (and European) architectural, garden theatrical and urban typologies and proposes that in the present time the garden as theater and as museum still does have enormous importance—but as an "educational" "amusement park" influenced by cinema. The theater-cinema garden is based on the scenography derived from film's fantasy images and Hollywood set design. Disneyland and Parc de La Villette depend on the replacement of theater as generator of education and political mythology by post-filmic representation.

Note

This text was written in 1986. It was originally published in Dan Graham, Dan Graham-Pavilions, *exh. cat. (Munich: Kunstverein, 1988), pp. 54–55.*

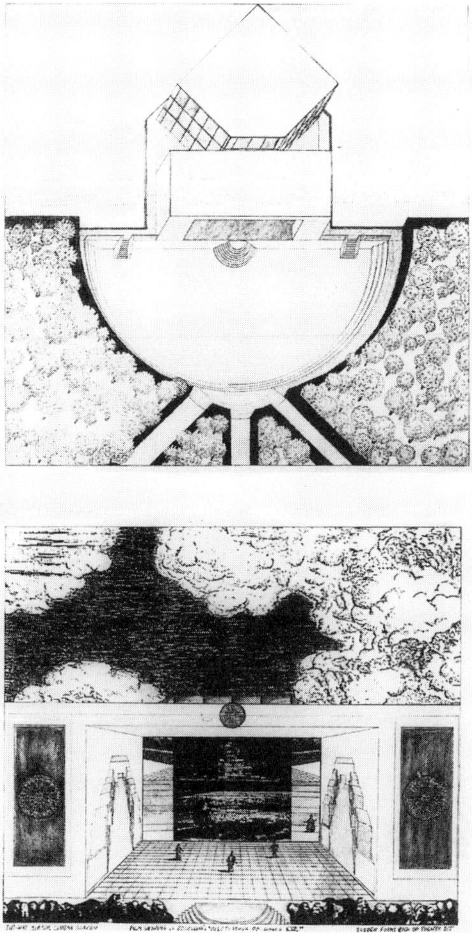

29
Dan Graham
Design for *Theater-Cinema,* 1986

30
Dan Graham
Theater-Cinema, 1986

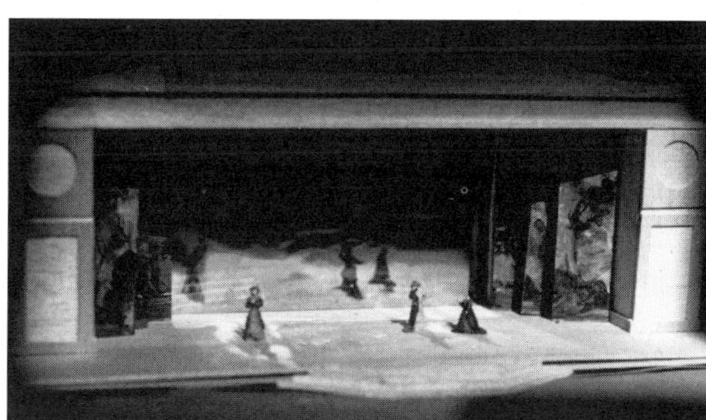

Dan Graham

Performance: End of the '60s

I have a dilemma discussing 60s or 70s works of mine at this end of the 1980s moment, where they may appear as "utopian" alternatives to the present situation. These performances used as background assumptions some of the psychological and sociological instant-utopian ideas which seemed to be alternatives to the Establishment or academic beliefs of the moment. The hope was that the (inter) personal could re-politicize the body politic. Radical psychology, ethnology, consciousness-altering states induced by meditation techniques, and feminism generated new models of personal and group behavior and possibilities, which were shared simultaneously by artists and the so-called "counterculture." These models provided assumptions which I knew the audience shared with me and which the art world also shared. My performances utilized these models of behavior as a structure, while testing the "utopian" premises in the actual performance situations. They both "worked" (created a certain effect in performance) or didn't "work" as viable philosophical premises. The structures of these works were hybrids, with a combination of various methodological assumptions underlying current art practice. The performances were predicated on sets of assumptions from art practice and philosophical postulates then in intellectual vogue. For example, new psychological theories of consciousness, derived from meta-psychology, and drug and meditation experiences were combined or contrasted in a performance structure which might adopt a literalized, philosophical-phenomenological description. My performance works existed, like my earlier "Conceptual art" involving the use of magazine pages, on a boundary between formal, self-enclosed art and popular cultural assumptions and the temporary, perhaps disposable, readings of that moment.

I did performances because many other artists then also did performances. I was not interested in being a "performance" artist, I was more interested in the position of the art-guru (enhanced by media reproduction and occupied by artists such as Joseph Beuys, politicians such as the Kennedys, rock figures such as the Beatles), or in illustrating the ideas of psychologists such as R. D. Laing and Gregory Bateson.

Formally, in art terms, my performances were a way out of my earlier Minimalist and structuralist assumptions based on a phenomenology of presence. The performances were based on the present-time consciousness of the artist (who in the performance was temporarily replacing the art object) and the spectator's present-time perceptions. The performances also subjected this new present-time presence of the artist, in relation to the perceiving audience, to a critique. In introducing my own subjectivity, as well as giving primacy to the spectator's perception process, the work constituted an abandonment of the hermetic, anonymous information quality of earlier "Conceptual" work.

The aim of the performance was a therapeutic belief that the "personal was political." "Consciousness raising" in women's groups and what I learned of psychological "encounter groups" from media sources were combined in these performances with a belief in face-to-face community "consciousness raising" in the New York art world to solve economic and political problems. This new art world belief in the decentralized small community group was being tried out in local democracy experiments, from Santa Monica to smaller, rural settlements connected to the "back to the earth" or ecology movement: perhaps through performance discussion, social groups could effect social change through personal change. Artwork might be based on working with the body politic in terms of the direct honest baring of feelings. The art world as a personal community could be emblematic of society in general and both community discussion and performances might effect a change in the structure of the art world. The "alternative spaces" which had been created by artists as alternatives to the Establishment gallery and museum system were the most characteristic venues for the performance form.

I first tried performance as a visiting artist in an art school in Canada. The "performances" were projects for students or models of art-making which the students and I could perform informally as "learning exercises." They were not performed, at first, with the aim of media documentation and never as saleable art for gallery exhibition. For me and for the students participating in the performances, they were merely try-outs, ways of testing situations or means of expression uninhibited by the need to make perfect, finished artworks.

I did performances in the art world because artists I admired or knew personally also did performances. It was a democratic mode, where young artists who did not have access to art galleries or enough money to produce studio art for exhibition could show their work quickly to other artists in the community. It was assumed that the more experimental works would be seen in the forms of performance, artist's film and video in alternative spaces by the community before being displayed in galleries and disseminated through the media. They were also "fun"—done in situations not unlike informal rock concerts.

A premise of 1960s "Modernist" art was to present the present as immediacy—as pure phenomenological consciousness without the contamination of historical or other *a priori* meaning. The world could be experienced as pure presence, self-sufficient and without memory. Each privileged present-time situation was to be totally unique or new. My video time-delay installations and performance designs use this "Modernist" notion of phenomenological immediacy, foregrounding an awareness of the presence of the viewer's own perceptual process, while at the same moment they critique it by showing the impossibility of locating a pure present tense.

Note

This text was written in 1989. It is previously unpublished.

Dan Graham in Conversation with Brian Hatton

Brian Hatton

One piece which is often referred to as a starting point in your work, although it is by no means the first thing you did, is a magazine piece called *Homes for America,* a series of photographs of houses in the suburbs of New York, which appeared to replicate the formats and configurations of Minimal sculpture of the time, and which you described in a rather deadpan journalistic way. What emerges through the course of that reading is that the piece operates on several levels: on some levels it was a documentary article about architecture, on another level it was a reflection on Conceptual art, and on another level the magazine article itself was a piece of art. Reading it, one became conscious of the mediation involved in introducing art into the systems of public consumption. This may seem quite a long way now from your current piece at the Serpentine Gallery, which continues your investigation of the genre of the pavilion.[1]

Dan Graham

I've also been interested in the garden, in the history of the park: it involves hedges in relation to one-way glass. The magazine pieces were hybrids between things you could see in the art gallery as art, and normal magazine pages. I had envisaged all these articles at the time with photographs of suburban houses as a sociological, semi-political comment about the suburbs. There was also the perception that Minimal art was using the materials of the suburbs, and relating, in a certain way, the urban situation in which the art was placed in the gallery to suburban architecture. I related this to the magazine genre, and I think what I am doing now relates historically to the picturesque labyrinths of the Baroque period, using hedges which are reflected and re-reflected; using one-way mirrors, which are emblematic of the Modern office building in the city.

Hatton

When you visit the piece, you also see yourself reflected, sometimes alongside the reflection of others, and it seems to me there's a double articulation: on the one hand, it's dealing with the relationship between nature and the city, and also between the work of art and the public realm, and on the other hand, it explores the relationship between a private experience and a socialized experience of encountering yourself amongst others.

Graham

You become conscious of the fact that the materials of modern life, showcase windows and one-way mirror office building windows, in many ways involve psychological projection.

For example, when you see things in showcase windows, you are projecting an image of yourself or of your body onto the commodity, which makes you conscious of losing an ego which you would find again in buying the commodity. In the earliest pieces involving mirrors and glass, I set up a situation where public space would function like a showcase window, except that the spectators would see themselves in place of the commodity, gazing at themselves, or other audiences gazing at them as a second audience on the other side. The pieces are always involved with the psychological aspect of your seeing your own gaze and other people gazing at you. In another sense, they are philosophical models of consciousness.

Hatton

I find it interesting in these works that you've taken devices such as one-way mirrors and, before that, video, which were originally developed in systems of surveillance and control in alienating circumstances. One-way mirrors, for instance, were used in psychological laboratories, video has been used for security purposes. But you are actually unravelling them, in extremely alienating circumstances. Is it the case that we are surveying ourselves?

Graham

The one-way mirror was used in psychology laboratories so that the patients who were being examined by doctors in training would only see a mirror image of themselves, and would not be aware that they were actually being surveyed by students on the other side. It's the same situation with the one-way mirror office building. There was the Bauhaus idea of simple clear glass which would show people on the outside exactly how productive the corporation was on the inside. Although spectators would only see accountants and clerks and bank tellers, they wouldn't really see or hear what was happening inside, and they wouldn't see the people who were heading the corporations, who would actually be at the top looking down. That became a very empty metaphor, and the new metaphor the corporation took up was the metaphor of ecology. The one-way mirror office building showed you a view of nature on the outside, except in a city like Toronto where there are so many one-way mirrored office buildings that they're just images of other one-way mirrored office buildings replicated indefinitely. Also, it was very helpful in terms of insulation: it cut down energy and heat consumption inside, because it reflected the light back on the outside and it gave the people inside a privileged, transparent view looking outside, but not being seen by the people outside. So what I've done is to place the one-way mirror in an open situation where it's both transparent and reflective at the same time, which in a way contradicts how it's normally used. Also, it's creating a self-consciousness of people in a public space, in a public situation, something like the Brechtian idea that the audience should be made self-conscious of itself, the way performers should call attention to themselves and their performance by making themselves and their gestures self-conscious.

Hatton

In your piece at the Serpentine, the inside/outside duality, which is disrupting if not deconstructing, seems to be linked with a recollection of a certain type of interior, the so-called open plan, with space-dividers. The Mies van der Rohe Barcelona Pavilion comes to mind, except that there's something strange, because this isn't an interior, it's an exterior. I recall that in an interview with Daniel Savioni you refer to a piece you made, *Alterations of a Suburban House,* in which you could see into the interior of a suburban house from the street. You described it as a violation of public space, even more than it was of interior space.

Graham

This particular project dates from 1978, when I showed projects which would alter vernacular suburban architecture, reflecting both on high architecture by Mies van der Rohe, Robert Venturi and others, and on the convention of the picture window and the same kind of suburban houses as those I photographed in the *Homes for America* article you mentioned.

I showed these impossible kinds of projects: another project was for a cinema in a one-way mirror building. The screen was also a one-way mirror, so that on the outside you could look through the screen and see the film which was showing inside, in reverse. At certain points you could see the gaze of the people inside looking at the cinema. People inside the cinema could look outside and see the lights of the city. When the lights were turned on and the cinema was over, they would have a view of themselves as an audience, seeing themselves in the mirror, realizing that in fact cinema involved this narcissistic spectator-identification with people in the film. In this space they would be made self-conscious of this situation.

In this series there were also works which were sculpture pavilions. They were half like pavilions, such as Mies van der Rohe's Barcelona Pavilion, but they could be seen as conventional sculpture in a sculpture park or the grounds of a museum. These were the first works actually to be constructed.

Alteration of a Suburban House is the best example of an unrealized suburban house project. It involved making the picture window one transparent plane in front and then bisecting the center of the building, which was a kind of ranch-style horizontal American house. Half-way back there was a mirror plane, so that people on the outside could look and see the front spaces, which were the living room and dining room. The mirror actually had doors that would lead to the private space in the back, being typically the more hidden area of the house: bedrooms, study, bathrooms.

In one sense, it was a little like the Mies van der Rohe Farnsworth house or the Philip Johnson glass house. In another sense the mirror reflected back the buildings from across the street, filling them in as a facade, and made the entire building, if you saw it from a car, a kind of billboard display for a typical suburban house situation: new housing projects that you might want to buy, except you were actually seeing the reality you were in. What it in fact violated was the kind of space that people, walking by or in their cars, were in, which is the sort of space which exists outside the private house. I think it was much more transgressive of this public space in relationship to their normal voyeuristic view through the picture window of a private house. So it's a relation between the conventions of private space and public space that interests me.

Hatton

You made a video called *Rock My Religion,* which was an attempt to map onto certain aspects of rock music the same aspects found in the ecstatic tradition of Protestant sects. There seems to be a communal, utopian dimension to the public implications of this work. (Perhaps the audience is familiar through illustrations of Dan's work with rather cool-seeming prisms of glass and mirror in sharp geometrical configurations which wouldn't immediately connote an ecstatic experience. It took me some time to bring these things together.)

Graham

I think most of the spaces are meditative spaces. You are not alone with yourself, you are aware of your relationship to other spectators and other people in a group situation. So they involve the communal aspect of public space, and the spectatorship isn't necessarily that cool: it's referenced to earlier ideas or sensations which you can experience in the buildings of Mies van der Rohe (his projects for early glass skyscrapers have an almost mystical, transcendental idea of nature) and the psychological relationship in a piece called *Two Adjacent Pavilions,* which are both one-way mirror glass and contain space for five or six people standing up in each pavilion and maybe two or three people lying down. The top of one of the pavilions is transparent so light will flood into it, and it becomes equally reflective and transparent at the same time, but that's very much determined by the sunlight; so they're referenced very much to the sun and the moon, like Chinese garden pavilions. The other pavilion is opaque in terms of its roof, so it's dark, and on the inside you're much more transparent: people on the outside see you in a reflective way. But these relations are always in flux and always relative to nature, so in fact they're evocative of some of the transcendental sensations which one gets both in the Chinese and the English garden.

Hatton

I think you were referring to pavilions when you said, "I always use a mirror with something else," so there is interpenetration. It seems to me that part of your work is directly phenomenological: it seems to address directly one's experience of being there, seeing through things, seeing your reflection, encountering others, being aware of the light and the present moment, as opposed to the moment a few moments ago, or the anticipation of a few moments from now as you move around. These things have a long history in your work, and your video *Delay Rooms,* in the seventies, explored them intensively.

However, there's another—we might way allusive—level to your work, which depends on cultural readings. You see the glass as a suburban picture window or as a stage, and you refer modern modes of vision such as video to earlier modes, and make a conscious transferral of things such as perspective to contemporary modes of vision. In some cases these allusions become specifically defined: for instance, in the pavilion you made in Austria, which has an iconographical allusion in its configuration.

Graham

The Schloss Buchburg pavilion in Austria is in the form of a Jewish Star of David. It superimposes two triangles. One triangle is a water basin, and the other triangle, which would make up the Jewish star, has one-way mirror on all sides and the top is transparent. I had qualms about showing in Austria, as a Jewish person, and also it was the time when there was a great controversy about how they suppressed their anti-Semitic period. At the same time I wanted to make something that was a pleasure pavilion for the local inhabitants, that related to the water-works, an ecological dam nearby. It's in the moat area of the castle, and what you have are three triangular basins which make a good picnic area, and then you can go inside the glass pavilion: first over stone, then you go to the center, which is a continuation of the water triangle, and you're walking on a grid over the water, seeing the reflection of the water which is re-reflected in the crystalline sides of the one-way mirror. Probably people are not aware that it's the Star of David. You become aware of it when you walk over the drawbridge going to the castle and look down.

I've also made a pavilion which is a kind of lobby or meeting place, in the Carnegie Museum in Pittsburgh, in the shape of an open heart. I realized that this very empty place in the lobby was for meeting people, and I was quite interested in anamorphic curved glass, so that on the inside you are actually seeing a double anamorphic image of yourself and other people, anamorphically enlarged when you're inside the pavilion. On the outside of the pavilion you have a convex reduction of the image. It alludes to the sentimental romantic cliche, very much the sensibility of Pittsburgh:

on the one hand, the very tough city which produced *Night of the Living Dead,* on the other hand very much involved in Hallmark cards and sentimental romantic cliches. Just behind the pavilion were ten Andy Warhol silver paintings of Elvis.

Hatton

What your work often does is to bring these allusions to the phenomenological present and disrupt them in a certain way, through the channel of the phenomenological disruptions you're working with. For instance, the question of inside/outside is enlarged and amplified by a mapping, a reference or an allusion to the question of the status of the work, as to whether it's in the gallery or out of the gallery, or whether it's in nature or in the city.

Graham

Or whether it's in your body or in the architecture.

Hatton

I think it's not accidental that you particularly focused on indeterminate places: waiting rooms, lobbies. Arcadian limbos or even railway station atria, those kinds of places which are on a cusp, which have not really been adequately defined.

Graham

Also, since I realized that the works go into a park city I think they allude to conventions, historical and present, of park architecture. So I have a pavilion for skateboarders, realizing that in normal park architecture we have things for children—playgrounds—we have things for older people, adults, adults with children, but not teenagers. So in a way it's very much like a music gazebo, it produces a very kaleidoscopic experience because it uses one-way mirrors, a canopy in the form of a four-sided pyramid with the top cut off, a kind of new Ledoux or Boule, the kind of neoclassical architecture you find in Canary Wharf and also in Battery Park City today. However, it's tied into a saucer-shaped bowl where the skateboarders perform, as they go up at the edge and experience themselves free of centrifugal force, almost floating. They can see a kaleidoscopic view of themselves in relation to nature, in relation to the sky, and a diamond image which comes out of the hole I've left in the top. They fit themselves into the park as a mediation between the city experience and the private pleasure one gets in films or amusement parks and suburban backyards with swimming pools. In using hedges as boundaries, or taking motifs from nineteenth-century parks and placing them in a kind of family backyard garden situation, a social Arcadian space, the work tries to coalesce public and private.

Hatton

The skateboard is famous for having colonized indeterminate spaces: for example, the undercrofts of brutalist complexes like the Hayward Gallery in London.

Graham

That's exactly where I had the idea, seeing skateboarders under the Hayward Gallery.

Hatton

This leads to a question about the utopian aspiration in your work: to situate itself in some place which could never be institutionalized. The eighteenth-century pavilion in a landscaped park owned by an aristocrat was a place defined as outside the rules of the main country house, but nevertheless it fell within the landscape park, which was under the monopoly ownership of the aristocracy. So it was a strictly contained version of Arcadia. Now you're working with a putative democracy, not an aristocracy, and also with the city as a system of public and private estates and planning authorities. You are also working with the institution of art, which requires a certain ontology of practice, so it's as though you want to locate, but you don't want to be located.

Graham

I think the tradition the work can be related to stems from Abbé Laugier's "primitive hut," which was a very simple emblematic representation in trees and branches, but using allusions to Greek architecture of a very elemental kind that could be in the park and be critical, in an Arcadian way, of the modern city. The idea was adopted by modern architects to make each architectural masterpiece into a kind of blueprint for a utopia. In fact, we deconstructed that idea: architects half believe in it and half don't believe in it, and I think maybe the same is true of art—the idea of art as a kind of utopian critique of existing society is both believed in and not believed in. I think my work is in that ambiguity, between being utopian and being anti-utopian. Sometimes it comes from humor and satire, and also it's a matter of presentation. The skateboard pavilion and the one-way mirror hedge at the Serpentine were actually proposed for International Garden Year in Stuttgart, which was a redesign of the center of the city into a new urban plan and a park plan. Both were rejected, and what they accepted was something called *The Gate of Hope,* a triumphal central arch. In fact, the skateboard pavilion will probably be constructed in Holland, because it fits the Dutch democratic tolerance of everything from teenagers to drug culture by tolerating it inside the culture so as to contain it; and the one-way mirror hedge labyrinth may be the central motif for a park, constructed over a parking garage, which I'm working on in association with a young architect in Nantes. So both of these will be going to socialist situations in places other than where they originated, and probably the origination of the pieces was somewhat transgressive. I didn't think they would be accepted. Maybe they are accepted now, but in another cultural situation.

Hatton

There's an element of populism in your work which accepts certain developments in the city of consumerism, such as the suburb and the corporate atrium. You see urban and suburban as interchangeable, but at the same time in your works those meanings change as they are used by many people. As I become one person among many others experiencing, using the environments created in your works, they take on a number of meanings which I didn't know were there.

Graham

Of course, that generates other works, and some of the works actually come out of specific programs or even compromises or changes that I have to make mid-route. There was a children's pavilion built for the *Chambre d'Amis* project in Ghent, in which artists were commissioned to work in private spaces, the homes, backyards, and gardens of people who lived in the city. I was building what I thought would be a winter garden for an architect, who was moving from his house at the end of a backyard into a new house he had designed facing the street. He wanted the old house to become his office, so he could lead people through his garage, along a boardwalk, and through this pavilion in the center of the garden to his old home/new architect's office. The problem was, first, that his children, who played in the old backyard—which was now a garden—were excluded from it; second, the plot was very narrow, and if I made a pavilion this long it would have dwarfed his own work. His purpose really was for people to experience his own work as an advertisement for what he might be doing. My solution was to make a children's pavilion. I made it on a playground scale. It was after seeing this work on video that Jeff Wall had the idea of making Cibachrome photographs of children, and for me to design a children's pavilion on a very large scale to house these photographs. This underground pavilion is an enlarged earth mound/children's magic mountain with a concave/convex one-way mirror occulus opening at its top.

Because of the way I used the sun and moon in some of the pavilions, and also the overlay of nature and reflections of nature, sometimes mystical quasi-religious ideas come back, as if they had been denied in early modernism. There was an early project for a large video projector outside a modern suburban house, which would be projecting outside whatever TV program people were watching inside. I saw it as being located in a city like Los Angeles or Houston, a completely suburban city, and at night it would reference itself to illuminated billboards and neon signs, but at the same time it would also refer to the moon, the stars and the sunset.

Hatton

Would you say that this mystical moment is situated in a dialectical way in your work? Robert Smithson laid claim to a dialectical approach to landscape, wanting to place the sublime in the context of the banal.

Graham

I think there is a close parallel—in the idea of the banality of normal suburban existence, which you see in that period in the mid-sixties when it was referenced in films by Jean-Luc Godard, in songs by the Beatles or the Kinks. One would find it in hybrid locations, such as the suburbs, highway culture, theme parks, which are now becoming educational theme parks and which are, in fact, the new outdoor museum. I think Smithson's outdoor works related to this context.

I have been asked recently if I would make work using virtual reality technology. I think that my work has been situated in that area of the cinematic, hallucinatory, kaleidoscopic, which virtual reality will now fill—a cinema/amusement park sensibility—so maybe virtual reality will lead itself to the next development in my work.

Notes

1. Hatton is referring to *Two-Way Mirror and Hedge Labyrinth* (1989–1991), described by Graham in part VI of this volume.

This conversation took place before a live audience at the Institute of Contemporary Arts, London, in March 1992. It was initially published in Talking Art (London: ICA, 1994), pp. 53–65.

VI. Pavilion Sculptures

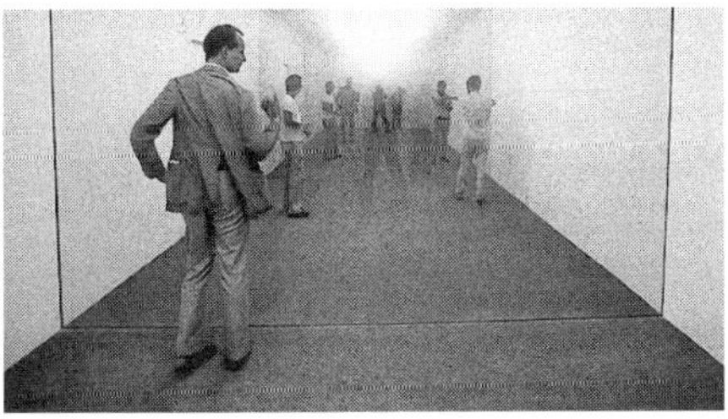

31
Dan Graham
Public Space/Two Audiences, 1976

Notes on *Public Space/Two Audiences*

Public Space/Two Audiences was one of a number of individual room-environments enclosed within a large building housing "Ambiente," a thematic exhibition presented by the Italian government as part of the 1976 Venice Biennale. The Biennale functions as a showcase for recent developments in art. It is organized as a series of separate exhibits housed in separate buildings by each of the participating countries, plus a number of thematic exhibitions, such as "Ambiente," organized by the Biennale itself. Each national display is a "showcase" for the culture of that country; likewise, individual artists are often shown in room subdivisions of the national pavilion's space—this space then becomes a showcase for characteristic examples of that artist's work. Collectively, the ensemble of "spaces" is to represent a socially relevant, topical, and unifying viewpoint or framework on the theme of that particular Biennale. The theme of the 1976 Biennale was the environment, with reference to architecture.

Public Space/Two Audiences was constructed to work in a specific container of "Ambiente." I wanted it to function doubly as art and as simply an exhibition pavilion (for itself), following the examples of Mies van der Rohe's Barcelona Pavilion or Lissitzky's two exhibition rooms. The artwork "placed on display by my environment" was the architectural container, as its own material structure; at the same time it was designed to be a display container for the viewers inside (observing themselves), the container's structure, and what effects the specific materials employed in its construction had on their perceptions. A first effect for the spectators might be to see the structure and materials in purely aesthetic terms; after a time in the space, and only if other people were present in the space as well, the psychological and social aspects of the materials and structure would become evident. Within the art context it is often only the aesthetic effects of glass and mirror which are noticed; whereas, outside the exhibition frame, these same materials are employed to control a person or a group's social reality. Glass partitions in the customs area

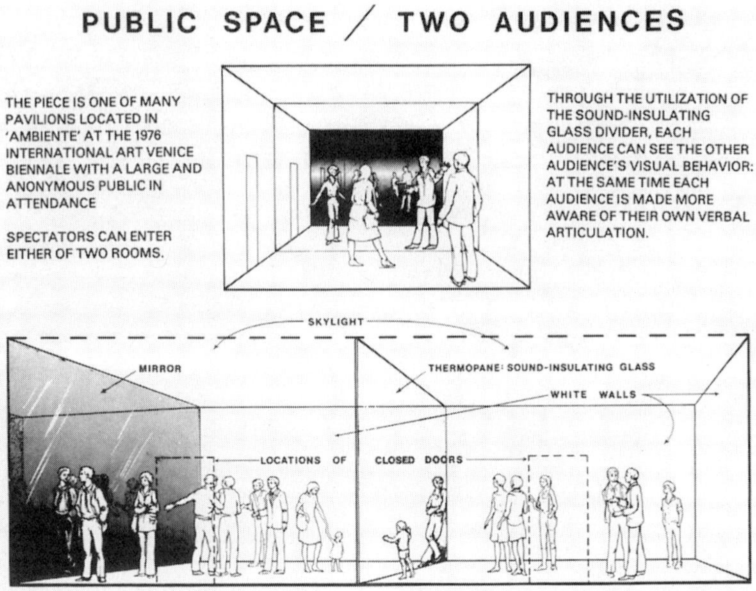

32
Dan Graham
Public Space/Two Audiences, 1976

of many international airports are accoustically sealed, insulating legal residents of the country from those passengers arrived but not "cleared." Another example is the use of hermetically sealed glass in the maternity ward of some hospitals, designed to separate the observing father from his newlyborn child. In this instance, the institution, having separated the child from the mother, medically, in the interests of public health, claims rights to its body from the "natural" father. Both the public institution and the father are given a visual perspective; the child is conditioned to allow the institution and his parents the permissible rights to total visual, clinical observation.

Unlike examples of "Minimal" art environments, "West-Coast, USA" perceptual environments using physiological effects of natural light, or post-Bauhaus architectural use of pure materials or the material elements of its construction, *Public Space/Two Audiences* is not entirely abstract or materialistic. "Minimal" art as well as environmental/perceptual art (of the kind built by such artists as Robert Irwin or Maria Nordman) would reduce the individual spectator's perception of the materials, structure or sense-data to a purely phenomenological presence. Ultimately, this work depends upon the construction of a privileged position for the single viewer's perception. The difference between the two forms is that in "Minimal" art the art object is objectified and factually material, while environmental art constructs the spectator as transcendentally subjective. Both forms depend upon perceptual immediacy: a phenomenological consciousness which connects the perceiving subject to what is perceived. "Perception has no time-span," says Robert Irwin. Both "Minimal" art and environmental art deny connotative, social meanings; the art experience is pure; there is no acknowledgement of social or historical mediation or temporality (especially in the case of environmental art). This is a restatement of Kantian idealism, which separates the experience of the purely aesthetic from the socially utilitarian. In this new form of Kantian idealism the isolated spectator's "subjective" consciousness-in-itself replaces the art object to be perceived-for-itself; his/her perception is the product of the art. Thus, instead of eliminating the physically present art object, environmental art's meditative approach creates a secondary, veiled object: the viewer's consciousness as a subject. All this is aligned to the psychological cult of the self-realization of the individual.

Psychologically, in *Public Space/Two Audiences,* for one audience, the glass divider is a window showing, objectifying the other audience's behavior (the observed, second audience, becomes, by analogy, a "mirror" of the outward behavior of the audience observing); simultaneously, the mirror at the end of one space allows the observing audience to view themselves as a unified body (engaged in looking at the other audience or at themselves looking at the other audience). A parallel, but reverse, situation exists for that second audience. In looking at the other audience, both audiences seek objective confirmation of their respective subjectively experienced social situations. (The spectators of one audience tend to see the other objectively, while their own subjectivity seems insulated from the subjective experience of the opposite audience. Normally, neither observed nor observer on opposite sides of glass can be part of the other group's intersubjective framework.) This effects a double reversal, for while the glass partition places a distance between opposing spectators and individuals in both audiences, the co-presence in the mirror of themselves looking and the others looking makes for a visual, intersubjective "closeness."

The complexity of this relation of the spectators to their image, and to the image of the other, reciprocal spectators, is echoed in a second reflection (in addition to that of the mirror). Because glass is itself partially reflective, observers in the room distant from the mirror, looking in the direction of the mirror through the glass divider, see a double reflection of their image, first in the glass and then, smaller in size but better delineated, in the mirror. This is similar to the effect of a showcase display window, upon which is often projected the "ghost" image of the spectator gazing at the products inside. Because of the particular lighting of the glass to enhance reflections, and because of the white wall as neutral background, an observer within the room with the mirror, looking in the other direction directly at the opposite audience, will see partially reflected on the glass's surface a specular image of the space of both rooms—this image being reflected from the opposite mirror's surface to fill in the blank surface behind the glass.

Because of the asymmetrical use of a mirror at one end of the blank wall at the other end, the two audience's perceptual situations differ. A spectator in the room with the mirror can choose several alternative ways of looking: he may look only at his own image in the mirror; he may observe himself in the mirror, but also observe his relation to his group; he may, as an individual, observe in the mirror the other audience (seeing himself in relation to the other audience and perhaps the audience observing him at the same time as he observes them); feeling himself a collective part of the audience, he may observe both audiences observing each other. If the spectator changes his position and looks away from the mirror, he may observe his own audience face to face (as in normal life). Finally, if he faces the glass divider, he may observe members of the other audience but not see an image of himself looking (because the far wall of the other space is blank).

In contrast, members of the other audience tend to look collectively in only one direction, as both the image of the other audience and the image of themselves are to be found by looking toward the distant mirror. When members of this audience look there, they will always see their own image (an image of themselves looking) reflected in the mirror and the glass.

The observer is made to become psychologically self-conscious, conscious of himself as a body which is a perceiving subject; just as, socially, he is made to become aware of himself in relation to his group. This is the reversal of the usual loss of "self" when a spectator looks at the conventional artwork. There, the "self" is mentally projected into (and identified with) the subject of the artwork. In this traditional, contemplative mode the observing subject not only loses awareness of his "self," but also consciousness of being part of a present, palpable, and specific social group, located in a specific time and social reality and occurring only within the architectural frame where the work is presented. In *Public Space/Two Audiences* the work looks back; the spectators, inversely, see their projection of "self" (conventionally missing) returned specularly by the material (by means of the structural) aspects of the work.

Note
This text, which supplements Graham's Public Space/Two Audiences *(1976), was written in 1978 and originally published in* Aspects, *no. 5 (Winter 1978).*

Alteration to a Suburban House

The complete front facade of a conventional, suburban "ranch-style" house has been removed; it is replaced by a sheet of transparent glass. Inside the house, a sheer sheet of mirror hides the private bedrooms and bathrooms in the back from the visible kitchen, hall, pantry, and livingroom in the front. There are doors which lead through the mirrored pane to the back rooms. The mirror, as it faces the glass facade and the street, reflects not only the house's interior, but the street and the environment outside the house. The reflected images of the facades of the two houses across the street appear, surrounded by the outside suburban lawn and street environment behind the glass in the mirror. In a sense, seen particularly from a moving car on the street, the view through the window is a metaphoric billboard, but one depicting a non-

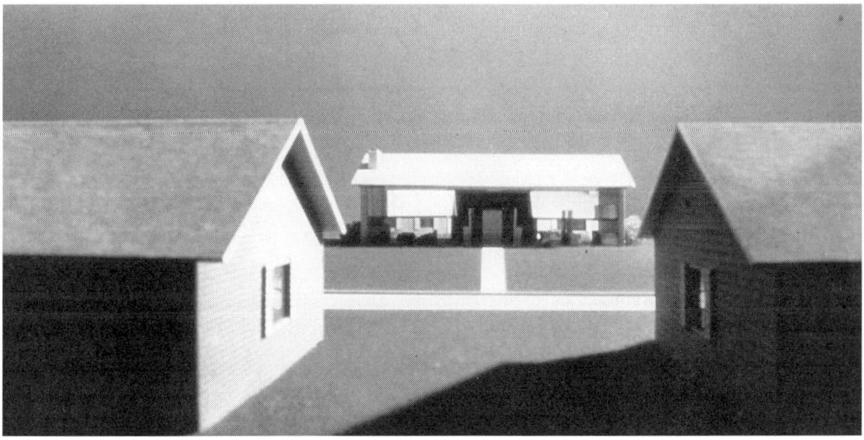

33
Dan Graham
Alteration to a Suburban House, 1978

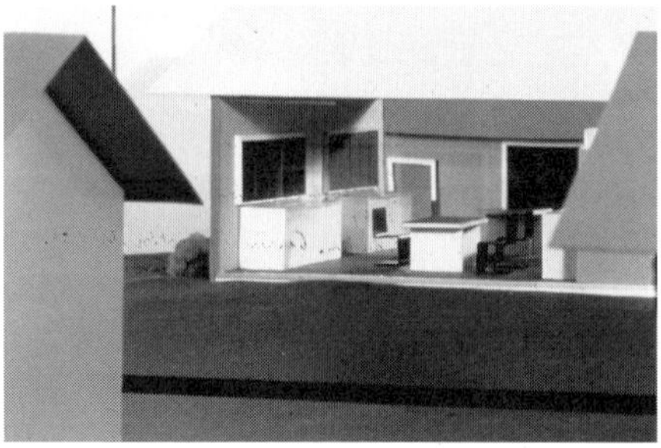

34
Dan Graham
Alteration to a Suburban House, 1978

illusionistic view. The view is of a typically desirable, conventional house surrounded by greenery. To a pedestrian the glass facade reveals the interior living quarters and displays them like a shop window. But the mirror, situated behind the glass pane, reveals this external observer within his conventionalized suburban environment—an image perhaps more powerful than the visibility of half of the private interior because it invades the public space in front of the property lines.

In many houses, the limited view of the interior provided by the "picture window" simply gives outsiders a picture of accepted conventional normalcy. Other conventional ornaments placed in front of the house also express the homeowner's individual identity.

Alteration to a Suburban House, by substituting the actual place of the conventional sign, strips the house of its community-defined "personal" identity. The project might be read as architecture, by architects as well as by the general public. It might also be read as the owner's "do-it-yourself" home modification. It is different in one aspect from its architectural references (Robert Venturi, early houses of Michael Graves or Frank Gehry) in that my house modification radically disturbs, through its visible intrusions into private space and from private space into the street, codes and property lines that socially containerize private from public space. While some radical architects deconstruct an extant, vernacular house, the cuts, while providing unconventional views of the outside environment, never allow those outside a similar view of the inside. The glass houses of Mies van der Rohe and Philip Johnson, which are transparent on all four sides, are set in isolated, aristocratic nature preserves, and are therefore never visible to the exterior public (except via photographs).

Alteration projects back to the artificial suburban Main Street environment its own meaning. Writing about Mies' 1930s houses, Tafuri and Dal Co note:

> Nature was made part of the furnishing, a spectacle to be enjoyed only on condition that it be kept impalpably remote. . . .Nature could be replaced by a photomontage. . . .The glass walls of Mies become the glass over the picture.[1]

In Mies' 1940s Farnsworth house, the vertical glass curtain wall skyscraper pioneered by Mies in urban Chicago becomes a horizontal glass belvedere, a patrician's retreat. The glass walls relate to daylight and nighttime differently, as Jeff Wall observes:

> These huge window-walls create a play of reflection and transmission of light according to the daylight's character. Shifts in its direction, quality and intensity create moments when the gaze's play with itself becomes apparent. . . .From the outside, the tremendous reflectivity of the glass wall can screen the interior from view behind a mirror image of the surrounding landscape. . . .[This] gives the interior a stage-set character. From within, in daytime, the landscape is intensely introjected while remaining immured behind glass, which may reflect the occupant somewhat. . . .
>
> Theoretically, invisibility is. . .the primary condition produced by the symbolism of the glass wall. In the glass house, this condition is superimposed upon a controlled image of nature. . . .Within the house, the occupant engages in a complex game with nature and with day itself. . . .The house, then, effects control of nature and the natural flow of time and light. As long as the house's control remains uninterrupted, euphoric absorption can occur, and the anxiety inherent in theoretical invisibility can remain suppressed.
>
> At night. . .the landscape disappears in blackness. . . .The interior artificial lighting necessary at night transforms the interior surface of the glass walls into gigantic mirrors. . . .In its nocturnal play with the nothingness of nature's withdrawal. . .the house invokes a state of terror. . . .In the hours of darkness. . .the Romantic. . .fantasy. . .of vampirism must constitute the regulation of the house's game with itself. . . .In the night. . .the power of absorptive gazing, of inspection, is transferred to the invisible eye of nature. Nature abruptly takes on vampiric powers. . . .Nature, which is at night actually invisible, is. . .endowed with an inverted vampiric intelligence. . . .The glass house is a crypt.[2]

Wall believes that my *Alteration to a Suburban House* is "centered in the exposure and enlargement of the veiled vampiric discourse which suffuses. . .the glass houses. . .[and] the glass tower." He notes that one variant of the vampire myth is an account of an assault on the castle-crypt by the terrified peasants. In this they embody "inspired revolutionary daring" as well as a "frenzied, compulsive violence" in which the villagers become like vampires as they fight them. Wall notes that my *Alteration*

> makes an ordinary tract house function as a partial glass house. . .to impose the vampiric discourse of exhibitionism and alienation upon the site which has been constructed as an illusory haven from vampirism.[3]

Unlike Mies of Johnson's house, which keeps the outside at bay through a play of compositional wit,

> In. . ."Alteration" the regime of wit is interrupted. . .by the overbearing presence of a mute and relentless reflective mechanism. . . .The perspective established by the mirror, in overriding the reflectivity of the glass, indicates that the occupant is now on an equal footing with the passersby, who. . .have become more important. The villagers of the vampiric symbology approach the mirrored crypt. . . .They mirror, the new facade of a new interior, clasps within its optics occupant and passerby, and explicitly identifies them with each other, just as it identifies itself with the other houses which it also reflects.[4]

Notes

1. Manfredo Tafuri and Francesco Dal Co, *Modern Architecture* (New York: Harry N. Abrams, 1979), p. 157.

2. Jeff Wall, "Dan Graham's Kammerspiel" (1982), in Gary Dufour, *Dan Graham,* exh. cat. (Perth: Art Gallery of Western Australia, 1985); subsequently published in *Dan Graham's Kammerspiel* (Toronto: Art Metropole, 1991). Graham is citing here from an earlier (unpublished) draft of Wall's essay.

3. Ibid.

4. Ibid.

This text, written in 1978, first appeared in Anne Rorimer, Dan Graham, Buildings and Signs, *exh. cat. (Chicago: Renaissance Society of the University of Chicago, 1981), p. 35, from which this version is drawn. An extract was included in* Rock My Religion: Writings and Art Projects 1965–1990/Dan Graham, *ed. Brian Wallis (Cambridge: MIT Press, 1993), pp. 206–207.*

35
Dan Graham
Pavilion/Sculpture for Argonne, 1978–1981

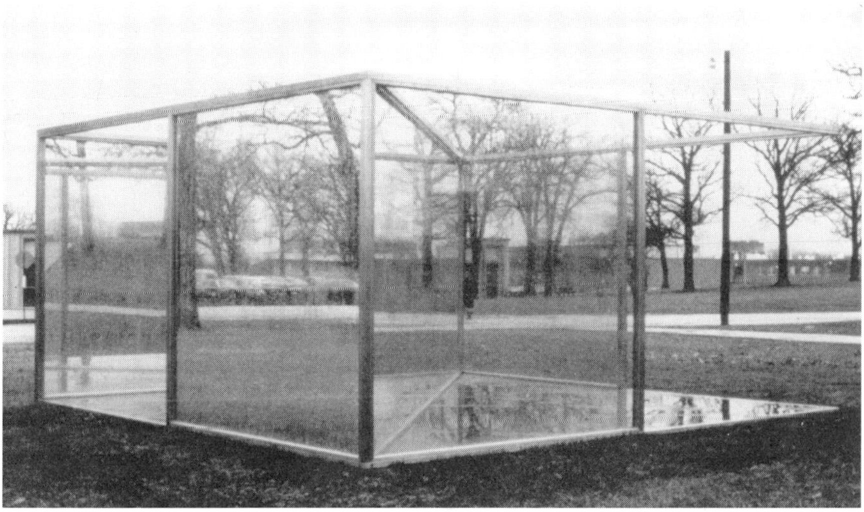

Pavilion/Sculpture for Argonne

Argonne National Laboratory, an emergency research facility twenty-eight miles southwest of Chicago and jointly directed by the University of Chicago and the U.S. government, commissioned this work, a structure measuring 7½ feet high × 15 feet wide × 15 feet deep. Each 15 foot side is subdivided into 7½ foot square frames. These frames have either mirrors on both sides, or transparent glass, or remain open. A sheet of transparent glass diagonally divides the form into two equal triangular units. A spectator is able to enter through one of the open frames, finding himself, because of the diagonal divider, in either one audience area or the other.

Pavilion/Sculpture for Argonne is literally reflective of its environment. Reflections on its mirror and glass and the shadows from the framework are subject to continual variation from overhead sun and passing clouds. At the same time, the form is also architectonic, with inside and outside space, and open to use.

Because of its double function as architectural pavilion and as sculptural form, a comparison could be made to Rietveld's sculpture pavilion in the sculpture park of the Kröller-Müller Museum, which is both a sculptural and a utilitarian form. Pierced cinderblocks, a high interior window and one completely open side admit air and light and provide unobstructed views of the outdoor works in the surrounding park. There is an ambiguity as to whether the art it displays is in an exhibition space or is outside and still part of "Nature." A shelter for both the sculpture it displays and for people observing the sculpture, it makes spectators looking at the art within its space into a cohesive group and, at the same time, it imposes an order on the works it groups for display. *Pavilion/Sculpture for Argonne* creates its own social order, one which is based on two sets of social divisions. The first is between two audiences within the pavilion on opposite sides of the diagonal division. The second is between those inside the work and those outside.

The pavilion/sculpture will be situated in a wooded area at the front and to one side of a new administration building designed by Helmut Jahn. This building makes use of a solar energy-efficient design which also symbolizes the sun as energy source. It is a semi-circular, glass-sheathed form, flat in the front, with the rest of the implied circle completed by a reflecting pond. Angled frames on the front facade are designed to accommodate solar collectors, should this become economically feasible; they would also prismatically reflect the sun. In this setting *Pavilion/Sculpture for Argonne* is analogous to a small, rustic or rococo pavilion in relation to the larger building's (technological) Versailles symbolism. The sculpture/pavilion is aligned with the point where the building's front facade ends and its left side begins to curve. It is also aligned with the curve of the access road on its other side. It can either be seen from a car (where it is larger in scale than the administration building behind it) or approached on foot. Its orientation is such that the two interior mirrors catch the sun's reflection during the morning, creating prismatic reflection in relation to the angled, sun-reflecting elements of the building. The diagonal element of *Pavilion/Sculpture for Argonne,* if extended toward the building, would perpendicularly bisect the floor of the building.

Note

This text dates from 1978–1981 and first appeared in Anne Rorimer, Dan Graham, Buildings and Signs, *exh. cat. (Chicago: Renaissance Society of the University of Chicago, 1981), pp. 27–33.*

Two-Way Mirror Cylinder Inside Cube and Video Salon: Rooftop Park for Dia Center for the Arts

This project took as its program the reconfiguration of the function of the museum space of the Dia Center for the Arts in New York City as a social and artistic showing space, while at the same time it functioned as an autonomous artwork within the existing Dia program of elite artists realizing perfect works under ideal conditions.

This piece is both an optical device and an architectural modification of a previously unused rooftop, giving the Dia exhibition complex a variety of new functions. The interior spaces of the Dia building had previously been used as meditative and "ideal" exhibition spaces for "great" artworks or installations. The art was meant to be viewed by individual spectators, under prime showing conditions. My work necessitates a large public audience aware of each other's, as well as their own, gazes at the artworks under continually altering outdoor solar and sky conditions.

The total work is an open-air, rooftop performance space, observatory/camera obscura/optical device/video and coffee bar/lounge, with other multi-use possibilities.

36
Dan Graham
Two-Way Mirror Cylinder Inside Cube, 1989

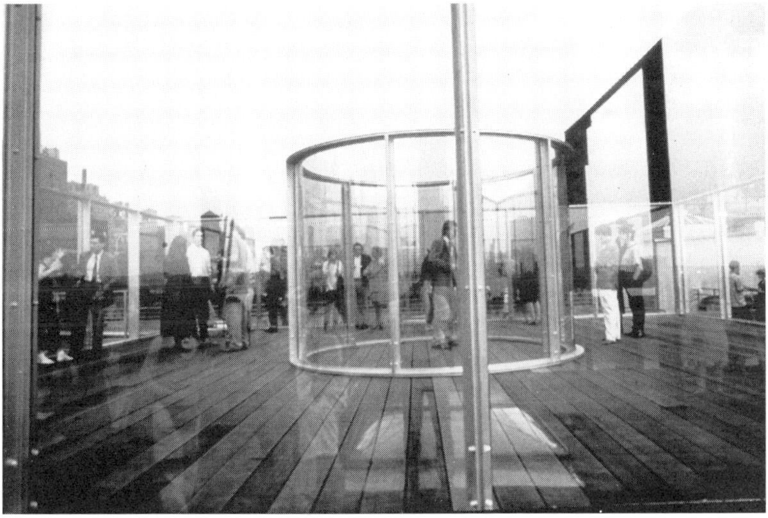

In the center of the roof is a raised boardwalk-like wooden platform containing a two-way mirrorized cylinder with a door, allowing spectators to enter its interior. The interior view shows spectators a concave, enlarged anamorphic view of themselves against the sky and urban landscape. The exterior view shows spectators a convex anamorphic view of themselves.

At the margin of the raised platform is a two-way mirror cube. The cube represents the urban grid of New York's midtown street plan. The cylinder directly relates to the overhead water tower and has the same circumference. It reflects the 360-degree horizon line.

There is a dialectic between the perception of oneself and other bodies perceiving themselves, making the spectator conscious of him or herself as a body, as a perceiving subject, in isolation from an audience. This reverses the usual loss of "self" that occurs when a spectator looks at a conventional work of art, where the "self" is mentally projected onto and therefore identified with the subject of the art. My sculpture/pavilions call attention to the look of the spectator, who becomes the subject of the work. A two-way mirror and steel structure is an analogue of the surrounding city. The two-way mirror has "cinematic" special effects.

My sculpture/pavilions allude to modern office buildings. The 1980s corporate office building's two-way mirror glass facades are one-way reflective on the outside (reflecting the sky and other building facades) and do not allow visual penetration by the spectator of the interior, but give the interior viewer a transparent view of the exterior. My pavilions subject this one-way relation to a serious transformation, being equally transparent and reflective both inside and outside. The changes in overhead sunlight affected by altering cloud cover continuously alter the relation between reflectivity and transparency of each other.

The Dia roof plan alludes to the solar lighted atriums extending 1980s corporate office building lobbies with a video/coffee lounge developed from an existing roof storage space. The central area is raised to give a better view of the Hudson River and the surrounding city skyline above the obtrusive existing skylight domed top.

My work requires a large, socially self-aware public audience, in contradiction to Dia's 1970s and 80s meditative interior, with its artificially well-lighted, perfect viewing conditions.

Programmatically, I also intended my "installation" to modify Dia's function, in order to initiate its transition into a 90s merging of 70s alternative space—like its geographically adjacent neighbor, The Kitchen, which features work by a large variety of artists working in video, performance, and music—

with 80s corporate atrium "museum" spaces like the IBM Atrium or the Wintergarden in the New Financial Center in Battery Park City, which also incorporate park-like settings and coffee and pastry bar concessions. To facilitate the historical links to video, music and performance works featured in spaces such as The Kitchen, I organized a program at Dia which purchases and screens an archive of videos selected by guest curators, focusing on music, performance, animation and architecture.

My original plans for the design (for the coffee/video lounge) of indoor inflatable two-way mirror furniture, giving a soft, intersubjective body feeling which complements the "hard" effects of the two-way mirror glass surfaces, has proved temporarily unrealizable, but is still being researched.

Note

This text was written in 1991. It is previously unpublished.

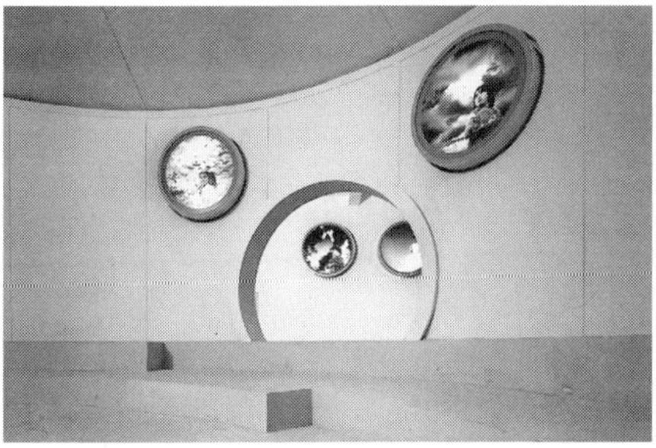

37
Jeff Wall and Dan Graham
The Children's Pavilion, 1989

A Guide to *The Children's Pavilion,* a Collaborative Project by Jeff Wall and Dan Graham

The Children's Pavilion (1989) is a public building located at the periphery of a playground. It is built into, and enclosed by, a landscaped hill. The structural shell of the hill-form is engineered in concrete. It includes a network of stairways, leading to a walkway around the summit. Large areas of the exterior surface are planted with lawn. The structure is entered through a portal in the form of a three-quarter circle. The interior floor, made of concrete, is composed of three descending concentric rings with a system of steps leading from level to level. The central circle is a water basin.

The interior walls form a drum, which supports a low dome, at the apex of which is an oculus. In the oculus is installed a one-quarter sphere of two-way mirror glass, its convex surface facing the interior.

Visitors inside the pavilion can look out through the oculus, and those on the walkway at the summit can look into the building seeing the sky continu-

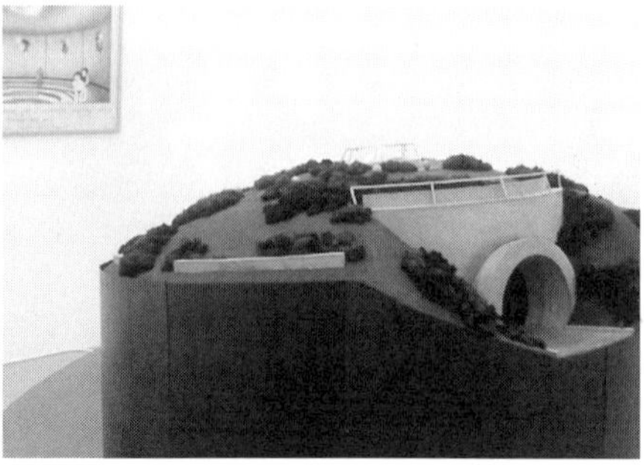

38
Jeff Wall and Dan Graham
The Children's Pavilion, 1989

ously altering, as it alters the relations between their reflected image of themselves and the sky and the transparent view through the lens of people inside looking up, and the wall-mounted circular photos of children against various photographic skies. The diameter of the water basin is the same as that of the portraits. The diameter of the quarter-sphere in the oculus is twice that of the portraits.

Architectural Typology

Playgrounds are the special domain of children, but the children who inhabit them are usually attended and observed by adults—parents or guardians. Playgrounds are therefore also for adults, who are given the opportunity to witness their children's experience of childhood. In this setting, however, the children behave less as members of individuated nuclear families than as part of a horde of youngsters who mingle there in commotion.

The playground customarily features one or more symbolic mountain or hill forms. These are archetypes of complex experiences because they permit penetration underground through various openings, a primal exploration of the earth, and, at the same time, an occasion for ascent and conquest, for the attainment of a privileged overview as "king of the mountain." In this process, one child becomes a big shot by gaining the special place at the summit. At the same time, others are burrowing below, lurking in dark hiding places, and springing back into the light. These might then go up to the top, while the one on top tumbles or races back down, girls and boys chasing each other, round and round.

The inside of the hill is, of course, like a cave or a grotto. Grottoes are usually watery, and are associated with lunar goddesses, nymphs, prophecy, birth, and a passage through subterranean realms to rebirth. They suggest also the invisible, but often audible, flowing of water inside the earth, and the sudden, surprising appearance of springs.

Both grottoes and the damp, but less watery caves are sites of primeval image-making. Prehistoric adults took shelter in caves from animals, and there created icons and pictures celebrating both their fear of these animals and their triumph over them in the organized hunt. The totemic image is a powerful element in tribal self-identification as well as a symbol of the maturation of the hunter. The skill in depicting the animal is a mark of maturity and mastery, and parallels the skill in hunting it: these skills are those of the provider, the magician, the leader.

Another typological element for the *Children's Pavilion* is the Pantheon, which is a public temple and mausoleum, dedicated to the memory of the gods and heroes, to patriarchs and to the state. The great Pantheon in Rome features an open oculus which permits a focused beam of direct sunlight to move around the interior in the course of the day. Depending on seasonal conditions, the light from the oculus sweeps across an arc which may coincide with particular features of the interior, such as the tomb of Raphael, giving it a natural spotlight. The Pantheon has had an immense influence on the forms of modern state temples, notably Les Invalides in Paris and the U.S. Capitol building in Washington.

Follies and pavilions in landscaped gardens have a direct relationship with the *Children's Pavilion*, as the name indicates. These structures often replicate, on a reduced scale, ancient monuments with literary or mythological references, such as the tombs of Abelard and Heloise, which are found in English gardens in France. Patriotic and heroic memorials, as well as shelters for retreat and meditation, are also included in this type. These pavilions are places which combine the provision of temporary shelter with an inducement to participate in specific acts of memory, contemplation, and philosophical speculation. They are related to the process of creating literary and philosophical works, which may take as their subjects the nature of the environment in which the pavilion is itself sited. They often suggest utopian alternatives to present civilization. Another aspect of this typology is provided by the observatory and the planetarium. Both derive from older things, structures like Stonehenge, for example, which was apparently used by the Druids for sighting positions of the planets. But they establish their genetic identity in the modern, scientific epoch, the period of rationalism and world navigation. The planetarium belongs specifically to the era of democratically inspired dissemination and production of knowledge, in which the study of the heavens was made available to all citizens, not just an esoteric caste, like the Egyptian priests who controlled the ancient calendars.

The observatory is a structure devoted to optical study of the sky. It has no interest in studying the earth, and never looks at it. It is most curious about the farthest reaches of the visible universe. It treats the earth only as an Archimedean point from which it can calculate how far it can see. It does this by means of curvatures of glass or other materials which focus energy, whether in the form of light, radio signals or other things. It is a photographic or cinematographic apparatus, a solar eye. It scans the universe for signs of other life forms and for data necessary for developing cosmological theories.

The planetarium is, on the other hand, a cinema. It reproduces, stages, and projects cosmological narratives as entertainment and education. The darkened dome of the planetarium evokes the primitive world when early man first contemplated the stars and attributed totemic power to constellations, for example the Great Bear. The modern totemism of the planetarium is, however, attached to telescopic power and cinematographic projection itself.

The spherical form of the planetarium is reiterated elsewhere. In recent world's fairs, for example, spherical structures present the cosmos and our earth as one world. These are emblems of a promised future, to be achieved through scientific progress, which would unite us into one global community, one "family of man." The mirror-clad "La Géode" in Parc de La Villette in Paris is the most recent and striking example.

The final element to be noted is something which is not, strictly speaking, architectural. This is the space capsule or flying saucer, which is round, cylindrical, disc-like, spherical or hemispherical. These are mostly seen in films, often films aimed at children, but are also featured as rides at amusement parks and science museums (which often resemble each other). The spaceship promises an adventure, a journey to other worlds, a voyage into a hypothetical future. It is often a toy played with in the process of constructing adventure narratives of this kind, adventures in which past and future are intermingled, in which archaic forms appear futuristic and futuristic forms can be ruins.

Photographs of Children

The group of nine "rondels" or "tondi" includes portraits of children of different racial and ethnic backgrounds. The organization of the portrait group is related to the concept of the nation–state and of its gathering of all its children into systems of universal public education, health, recreation, culture, and citizenship. The concept of the nation includes in its substance the outcome of the great immigration patterns of modernity in which a variety of peoples with different customs have confronted each other within the terms of a common body of law. The group of children can signify the nation, and specifically the nation's future, in a Pantheon-like assembly.

At the same time, the group's multiracial composition implies the plurality of nations and, therefore, forms an image of world culture. One classic manifestation of this idea is the photographic exhibition and book, *The Family of Man,* organized by Edward Steichen in 1955. In his essay "The Traffic in Photographs" (1981), Allan Sekula wrote, *The Family of Man* "moves from the celebration of patriarchal authority—which finds its highest embodiment in the United Nations—to the final construction of an imaginary utopia that resembles nothing so much as a protracted state of infantile, pre-Oedipal bliss."[1]

The universal/national children of the portraits appear in circular frames. The tondo form is associated with ceremonial and decorative portraits and figure groups often featuring women, children, and angels; but it is also related to coins, on which the heads of rulers are minted. The circular form also relates to the sphere, and therefore to the symbol of the cosmos, but also to a rubber ball flying through the air above a playground. Balls, bubbles, lollipops and other shiny, happy forms are part of the world of toys—roller skates, Frisbees and the like—which are vehicles in adventure fantasies.

Each of the children is viewed against a background of the sky. Each sky is unique, representing different times of day, different weather conditions, different seasons. The individuation of the children is expressed in the unique relation to the cosmos signified by the association of one specific child with one moment in time. Each child has a unique place, a special trajectory into the future, signified in part by the mood of the sky. The celestial void is the home of angels or "putti," infant beings without family, who emanate directly from God in infinite numbers at every second of endless time. They exist briefly, before vanishing again.

Oculus and Spectator

The oculus, as its name suggests, functions as the eye of the pavilion. The whole interior is gathered and reflected on the convex surface of the quarter-sphere of mirror glass. At the same time the transparent character of the glass allows the spectators inside the building to see the actual sky outside, and to see as well anyone looking in. Furthermore, anamorphic, distorted reflections of people looking down through the oculus from the outside, created by the concave form, give the children a giant view of themselves looking down on the gazes of adults and other children, as well as the images of the Cibachrome transparencies inside. The entire play of gazes and reflections generated by the architecture and the photographs is condensed onto the outer and inner surface of the glass. The optical dynamics are connected with the pavilion's relationship to observatories and planetaria, forms dedicated to intensive searching, gazing, and observation. Science and fatherhood are implied here, and this implication is augmented by the structure's references to national temples. At the same time, the oculus is set into the form of a hill or mountain, which suggests a more maternal enclosure, a cave or grotto, but one which includes an optical ordering principle. Thus, traditional symbols of both parents are present in the architecture and organize the forms of interaction between adults and children in and around the building. All users of the *Children's Pavilion*—children, parents, and other adults—can be observers of the behavior of others, from a variety of positions. And all can be contemplated in comparison with the giant transparencies of children.

For safety, the exterior of the oculus at the summit is provided with a protective railing.

Note

1. See Allan Sekula, "The Traffic in Photographs" (1981), in *Photography against the Grain: Essays and Photo Works 1973–1983,* ed. Benjamin H. D. Buchloh (Halifax: The Press of the Nova Scotia College of Art and Design, 1984), p. 77.

This text, co-written by Dan Graham and Jeff Wall in 1989, supplemented their collaborative project, The Children's Pavilion, *1989. The text was originally published in* Dan Graham and Jeff Wall: Children's Pavilion *(Lyons: FRAC, 1989), n.p. It has been expanded for this publication.*

Heart Pavilion

Contemporary art museums function as locations for romantic rendezvous, just as 18th-century landscape gardens encouraged purposeful strolling, punctuated by pauses at pavilions and arbors. The form of this sculpture comes from a popular symbol for Valentine's Day. It is a romantic abstraction of an anthropometric form which can serve as a meeting point. Here the two-way mirror glass pavilion is in a lobby or corridor space which generally is a dead space for art, but is related to the look of recent atria in corporate buildings or hotels, with their plants, reflective surfaces, and curved columns, in which an illusory space, neither inside nor outside, is constructed.

All my glass pavilions are made in relation to architectural forms as well as to the sculptural (haptic) and visual (optic) senses. In its siting, this pavilion is deliberately positioned between the glass entrance doors of the museum and a reflective silver painting, Andy Warhol's *Elvis Eleven Times,* mounted on a dark granite surface opposite. Its aggressive American subject contrasts with the function of the pavilion.

Looking at the hemispherical reflections on one side of the triangular pavilion, the viewer on the inside sees a distorted double image of him or herself.

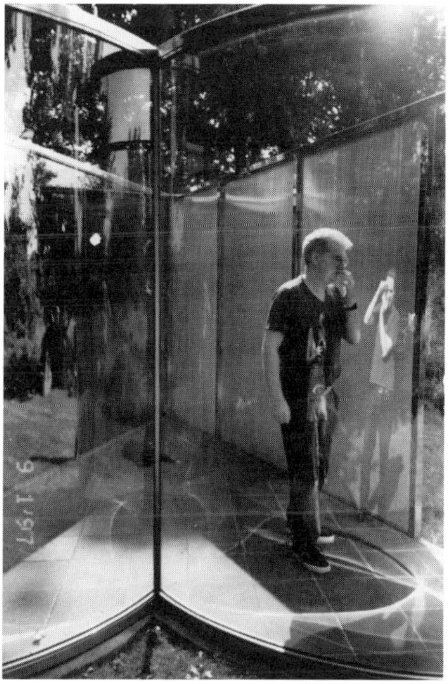

39
Dan Graham
Heart Pavilion, 1991

From the outside the viewer sees two convex images, squeezed together like the effects of a fish-eye lens. Where the two curved mirror glass sheets meet a strange illusion occurs—another mirrored column appears. At the corner of the triangle are prismatic reflections and secondary reflections of the anamorphic reflections. Both inside and outside spaces are in constant flux according to the changing light conditions and the position of the sun, which affects the reflection and transparency of the glass.

Rectangular and cylindrical forms repeatedly occur in the work. This piece relates to my early film *Body Press* (1970–1972), in which two cameras form rectangular framing elements and human figures circle around each other within a cylinder. In all my work—whether in the fields of video, film, and performance or in the sculptural/architectural pavilions—geometric forms are inhabited and activated by the presence of the viewer, and a sense of uneasiness and psychological alienation is produced by a constant play between feelings of inclusion and exclusion.

Note

This text was written in 1991 following the installation of the Heart Pavilion at the Carnegie Art Institute in Pittsburgh. It is previously unpublished.

Two-Way Mirror Power

In Western culture the pavilion placed in a park setting began with the Renaissance garden, where it was often used for Disney-like special effects. In the 19th century it grew in size into the Crystal Palace of the 1851 World's Exposition in London. It now encompasses the quasi-utilitarian modern "non-place" bus shelter and telephone booth.

Two Adjacent Pavilions, first shown as a model in 1978, was realized at "Documenta 7" in 1981; it was my first outdoor two-way mirror pavilion. Each of the two square, enterable forms allows four to six people to stand or to lie prone inside. Each structure is the same size as the other. The four sides of each structure are made from two-way mirror glass of the same percentage reflectivity. The difference is that one pavilion has a transparent glass ceiling, while the other's ceiling is covered with a dark, non-light-admitting material.

The properties of the mirror-reflective glass used in the pavilions' sides cause one side to be either more reflective or more transparent than the other side at any given moment, depending on which side receives more light.

Two-way mirror used in office buildings is always totally reflective on the exterior, reflecting the sunlight and totally transparent for workers inside. Surveillance power is given to the corporate tower. In *Two Adjacent Pavilions* and other pavilions the inside and outside views are both quasi-reflective and quasi-transparent, and they superimpose intersubjective images of inside and outside viewers' bodies and gazes along with the landscape.

One of the two pavilions, the one whose ceiling is opaque, remains more reflective on the outside and transparent on the inside. The other pavilion is flooded with changing interior light, depending on the sun and clouds, shifting between being more reflective or more transparent.

40
Dan Graham
Two Adjacent Pavilions, 1978–1981

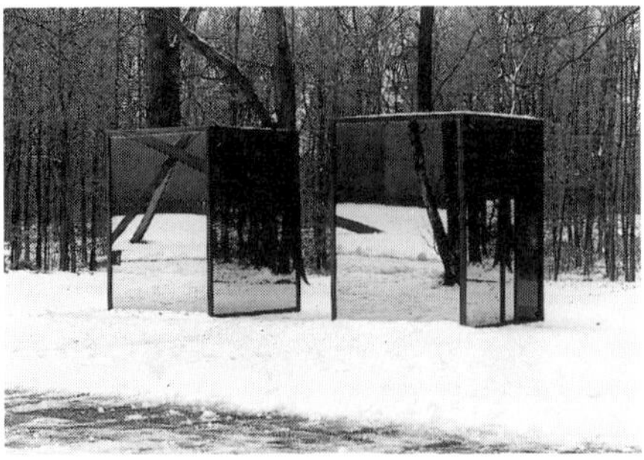

The work can be seen as a psychological, philosophical model; metaphorically, each pavilion may be seen as an "ego" which gets its identity in a continuous semi-reflection of another semi-reflective "ego."

Typologically, the work belongs to the park/garden's pleasure pavilion, which has been an antidote to the alienating qualities of the city as well as a utopian metaphor for a more plea-

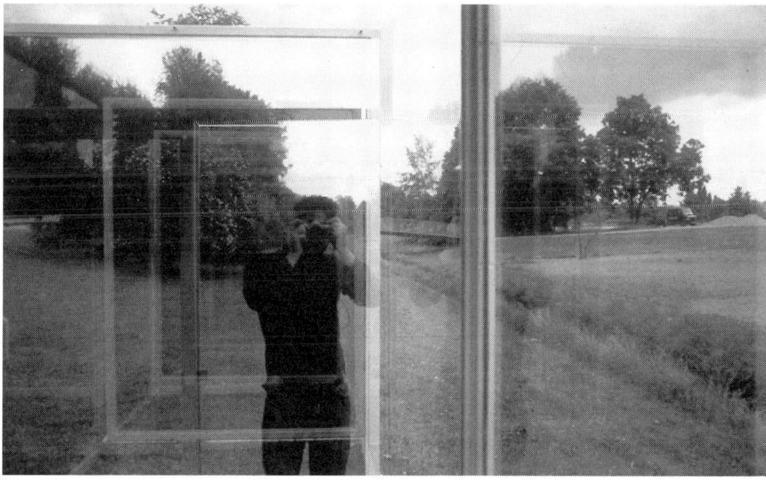

41
Dan Graham
Two Adjacent Pavilions, 1978–1981

surable city in the future. These pavilions are used for people at restful play—a fun-house for children and a romantic retreat for adults. They are both emblematic of the power of the corporate city and help to dissolve the city's alienation effects. They also relate to the 18th-century notion of the Arcadian "rustic hut." This type begins after the Enlightenment with the notion of the "elemental rustic hut" first proposed by Marc-Antoine Laugier. Laugier was a mid-18-century French urban planner and theorist. Like Jean-Jacques Rousseau, Laugier set up his model of the elemental "rustic hut" in relation to uncontaminated Nature. The "rustic hut" was supposed to be a reduction to man's and architecture's original nature, to its "own self-sufficiency," when there was no oppression of man by man: Architecture and Man were closest to "Nature."

Note

This text was written in 1996. It is previously unpublished.

Two-Way Mirror Bridge and Triangular Pavilion to Existing Mill House for Domaine de Kerguehennec

The Domaine de Kerguehennec is a sculpture park and nature preserve in Brittany, France. It is based around a central chateau and originally was landscaped as a French formal garden which was converted to an English picturesque garden. It was re-landscaped early in this century, with the planting of many species of forest-like trees and the enlargement of its main lake. Remnants of both the French geometrical garden and the English garden remain.

I have proposed for Kerguehennec that two sculptures be built to create a "modern" "allegorical" "narrative" form derived from the reflection of the oversized, triangular roof of the English garden mill. That reflection falls on the side of the lake near an existing "Chinese garden style" wooden bridge traversing a small stream which runs into a large lake. The bridge, in my plan, is to be replaced with a two-way mirror, covered bridge whose form is an equi-

42
Dan Graham
Two-Way Mirror Bridge and Triangular Pavilion to Existing Mill House for Domaine de Kerguehennec, 1987

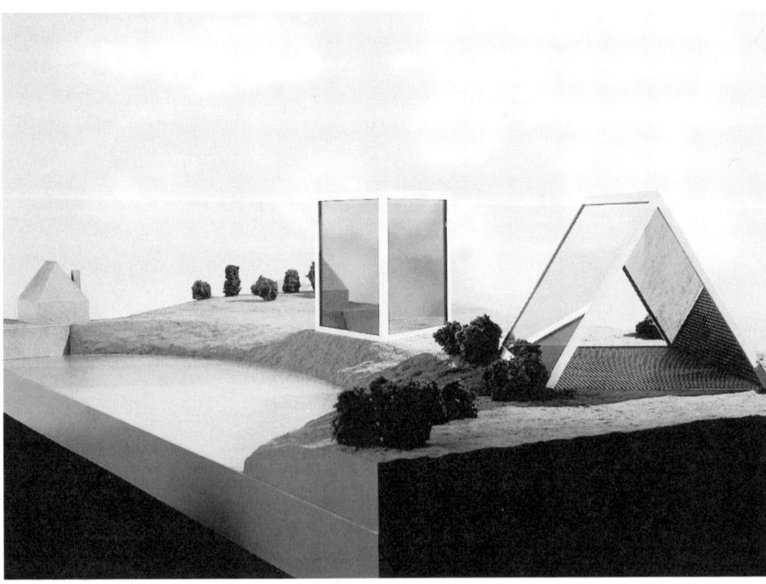

lateral triangular solid, enterable and usable by the public. The bottom of the triangle—the walkway surface—is steel grating with an open-square grid. It is the same surface used on Paris streets for air vents over sewers and the Metro. A spectator walking over the bridge could view reflections on the water's surface below the bridge's surface; the water would reflect the reflected image of the sky through the surfaces of the two-way mirror overhead, as well as views of the spectator's body and the surrounding landscape. The effect is to be prismatic.

In the distance from the bridge is an early 19th-century mill house (a survivor of the earlier English garden design of the park). Toward the mill house, closer to the edge of the lake and about twenty meters from the entrance/exit to the bridge, would be built a second pavilion in the form of an equilateral solid triangle. It would consist of two-way mirror glass on all sides, 2.5 meters square and 2.5 meters high. The roof would be clear glass. Its interior could be entered through a sliding door. Under most sun conditions a spectator inside the structure, with the door closed, could not be seen by an outside viewer. It would appear, at first, as closed as the mill house to penetration. The reflection of the mill house could be seen several feet from the mirrored triangular pavilion reflected in the lake.

There is a relation between the pyramidal, triangular form of the large roof of the mill house and the two triangles of the covered bridge, and the triangular pavilion. A path alongside the lake connects the two objects, their optical/geometrical prospect and alignment varies as the spectator traverses this pathway. The intention is to construct a partial allegorical circuit along the lake, much like a park such as Stourhead, in England. That garden's series of pavilions in relation to a central lake was based on Virgil's *Aeneid.* In the English garden, pavilions were laid out to represent a text which had variously political, literary or moral meanings, activated as people moved through the landscape. In Stourhead, for instance, the spectator walks around an artificial lake down to a grotto metaphorically representing the underworld, then reemerges to walk to a replica of the Pantheon, symbolizing worldly greatness, then to the Temple of Apollo and to a Gothic cottage. The lake, viewed through various arches, reflects the sky and is the symbolic center around which the allegory takes place.

Note

This text was written in 1987 and first published in Dan Graham, Dan Graham-Pavilions, *exh. cat. (Munich: Kunstverein, 1988), p. 46.*

Three Linked Cubes/Interior Design for Space for Showing Videos

Three Linked Cubes (1986), a series of rectangular bays with one side open and with side panels of alternating two-way mirror or transparent glass, has a dual identity. Placed outside it is an open pavilion illuminated by the sun; placed indoors, it is transformed into *Interior Design for Space for Showing Videos* (1986). Here various video monitors and speakers are placed to allow three separate programs for audiences subdivided into six groups. The effect of the changing illumination from the video images reflected on the glass panels creates the mirror "ghosts" of audience members seen in other enclosed bays on the divider. The work is both a functional exhibition design and an optical artwork displaying the video images as well as the spectators' reactions to the video viewing process in the social space of the video exhibition.

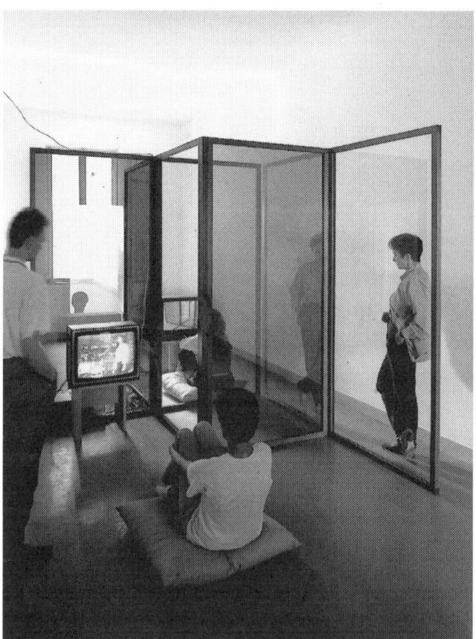

43
Dan Graham
Three Linked Cubes/Interior Design for Space for Showing Videos, 1986

Note

This text was written in 1986 and first published in Dan Graham, Dan Graham-Pavilions, *exh. cat. (Munich: Kunstverein, 1988), p. 46.*

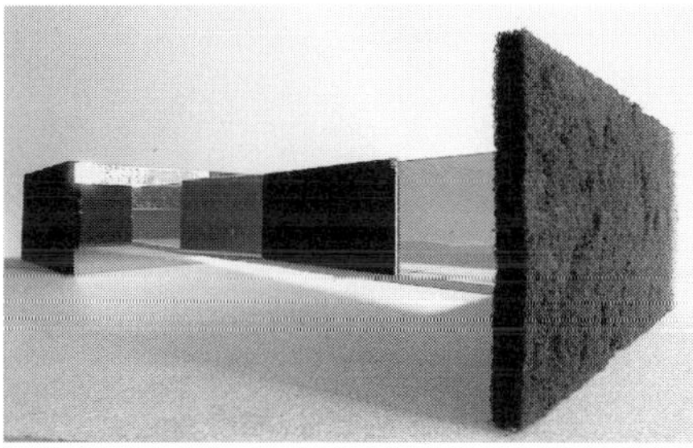

44
Dan Graham
Two-Way Mirror and Hedge Labyrinth,
1989–1991

Two-Way Mirror and Hedge Labyrinth

Sited as a resting place with one or two benches provided, this project was to be available to pedestrians crossing a large bridge traversing a major roadway and railway line. The work combines the traditional landscape or modern "suburban" landscape garden hedge boundary with both transparent and two-way mirror glass. The resulting hybrid creates a continuously shifting optical surface, emblematic of the modern urban corporate office building facade and the Baroque garden maze.

The effect of the changing sunlight illumination produces mirror "ghosts" of spectators on either side of the two-way mirror glass/conventional glass or hedge. The viewers see images of themselves gazing and other spectators gazing either at themselves or at them.

Note

This text dates from 1989–1991 and originally appeared in Dan Graham: Architecture *(London: Camden Arts Center and Architectural Association, 1997), p. 36.*

Skateboard Pavilion

Skateboard Pavilion, consisting of a large, concave cement dish for skateboarding and a canopy made of two-way mirror glass in the form of a four-sided pyramid, truncated at the top so that it is open, was first proposed in 1993 as a "stopping point" for the International Garden Year in Stuttgart, Germany. It was not accepted, perhaps because the notion of a recreational attraction intended primarily for teenagers was not thought to be a good idea.

It works optimally when the skateboarder approaches the lip or edge of the concave dish and looks up toward the sky/canopy and sees a combined kaleidoscopic reflection and transparent image of himself and the surrounding environment on the canopy form. The cutaway top produces a diamond-like

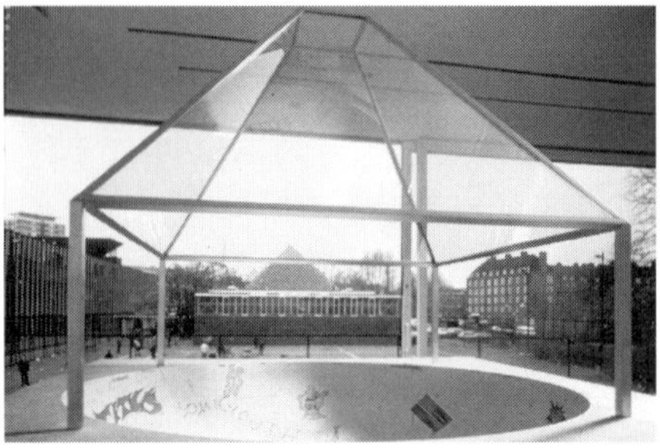

45
Dan Graham
Skateboard Pavilion, 1989

image also projected on the two-way mirror canopy.

The truncated two-way mirror pyramidal canopy alludes to the 19th-century wrought-iron canopy of the park music gazebo and, simultaneously, to the 1980s "Neoclassical" pyramid roof culminations on corporate office towers.

The experience also relates to amusement park mirror "fun houses" and, in general, to kaleidoscopes with their diamond-like patterns. The skateboarders see themselves reflected in the canopy against a kaleidoscopic pattern of themselves floating weightless merging with the sky.

Another aspect of the work is that it *encourages* graffiti on public "sculpture."

Note

This text was written in 1989 and first published in Dan Graham: Public/Private *(Philadelphia: Moore College of Art and Design, 1993), n.p.*

"Star of David" Glass Pavilion for Schloss Buchburg

This project, consisting of two superimposed equilateral triangular forms—one a basin of water, the other a 2.5-meter-high enclosed, two-way mirror glass pavilion—will be positioned to the side of and below the bridge leading to the castle's entrance. Originally this area was a moat; now it will be landscaped into a grassy, tree-shaded area ideal for picnics or quiet, restful leisure activity. The choice of water as an active element relates to a nearby river, which leads to an ecologically efficient electro-power dam designed by students of the curator of Schloss Buchburg. The Pavilion is intended for access and possible use by year-long residents of the local village as well as temporary use by visitors.

Each triangular form is four meters on each side. The enclosed pavilion is entered through sliding doors. Each of the exterior triangular water basins is

1.33 meters, as are the other stone-based outer triangular points. The interior area is filled with water (continuing the water of the triangular basin). The spectator can walk over the water on an overlying steel grid similar to the grids on urban sidewalks. On the ground level the three equilateral triangular water ponds are adjacent to the grass. The reflective glass pavilion can be entered through a sliding door on one of its triangular points, where the spectator first steps onto a stone floor.

The entire pavilion can be seen from above by looking through the overgrown ivy on the top of the wall at the side of the bridge traversing over the "moat-area" into the castle's entrance. From this vantage both water and two-way mirror become a complex of crystalline, multi-reflective surfaces in relation to the people in the pavilion and beside the "Star of David" form. The Jewish "Star of David" iconography of the configuration is very clearly apparent from above.

Note

This text was written in 1996. It was first published in Gloria Moure, Dan Graham, *exh. cat. (Santiago de Compostela: Centro Galego de Arte Contemporànea, 1997), p. 168.*

46
Dan Graham
"Star of David" Glass Pavilion for Schloss Buchburg, 1988–1996

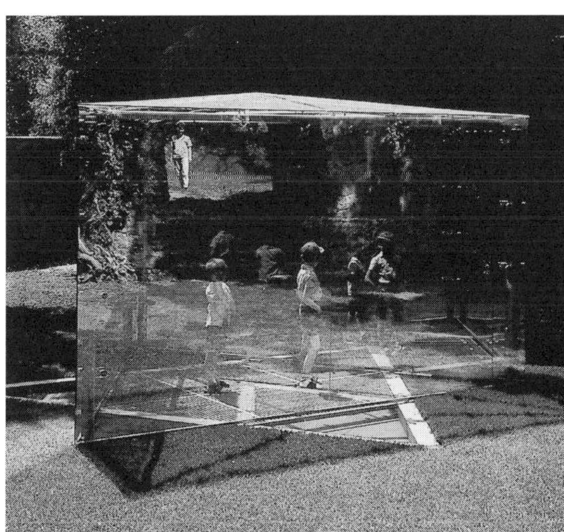

Dan Graham

Yin/Yang

This is a fairly large-sized building, sited as part of a landscaped hill, giving access underneath the water area to a space for a cafe and/or children's space. The yang part of the circle site, which is white raked sand or gravel, alludes to the classic Japanese "Zen garden" and parodies works that are "neo-60s" (i.e., 1990s) "lite" religion style.

The pavilion is situated on a slight incline. This allows the deeper water area to be adjacent to the sand area. The level of water diminishes as it approaches the rim above the underground space. There it is so shallow that it allows people in the space underneath the water to have a glimpse of the skyscape through the water.

The play of two-way-mirror anamorphic reflections, both concave and convex, the superimposition of people's bodies and gazes on each other inside and outside the form, the superimposition of people on the changing skyscape, and the reflections on the water are all in a constant flux of relative reflectiveness as against relative transparency as the overhead light conditions continually change.

Note

This text, written in 1998, is previously unpublished.

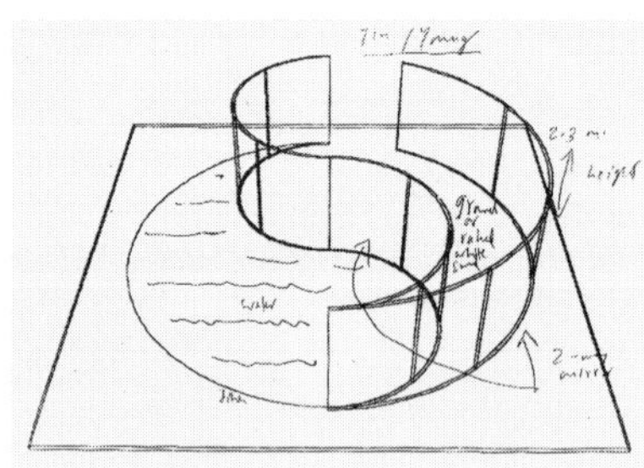

47
Dan Graham
Yin/Yang, 1997–1998

48
Dan Graham
Yin/Yang, 1997–1998

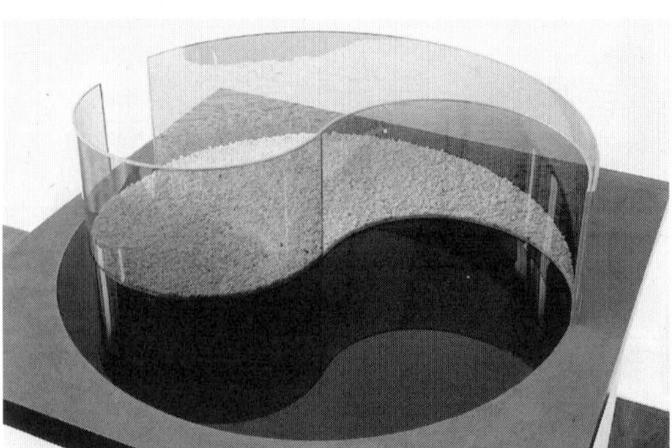

Dan Graham Interviewed by Mike Metz

Mike Metz

It's been almost thirty years since you first put together a battery of works that were projects specifically for various slick publications. What was on your mind then? They're so prophetic now.

Dan Graham

They were published because I had contacts through art magazine publishing. People who had been doing art magazines moved on to other magazines like *Harper's Bazaar.* I also did a series of advertisements in the *New York Review of Sex, National Tattler* . . . many of the advertisements were done gratis. The intention was to go for the slick magazine because that's what was on everybody's coffee table.

Metz

This move into such a radically altered context as a focal point of your art predated so much work in terms of artists who were finding gallery space constricting.

Graham

Well, it began with my being an accidental director of this short-lived gallery, the John Daniels Gallery. One thing I learned at the gallery was that the basis for getting attention was having reproductions of the work written about in magazines. I realized how dependent the art world was on publicity and information. It also was the golden period of artists like Lichtenstein and Warhol. Lichtenstein interested me because he was taking things out of magazines, blowing them up on canvases, and showing them in galleries, thus making a connection to the information system. I was also interested in the early works of Flavin, which were more Pop art than Minimal. He used fluorescent lighting from hardware stores to make temporary installations. The work was never deemed for sale, it would be dismantled and go back to the hardware store afterwards. But this idea of devaluing things so that they would be common currency and common decoration was being undermined because even these temporary installations were being bought by collectors. I thought it would be much more interesting to short-circuit all of these areas and put things directly into magazines. There was a period in Pop art when you began to realize that New York was basically about advertising, printed matter and design.

Metz

The critical difference in your work was the structure of information. What makes those early pieces seem prophetic is the fact that they are structures on which one sees the possibilities of specific information about the real world circumstances that was positive in intent.

Graham

Minimal art, which seemed to be abstract, took from suburban environments like hardware stores. The content was taken out, making things very abstract. In and around New York, you could see similar things as in a Godard film: housing projects, suburban life. Godard was also focusing on media as an information form. Mass circulation magazines. What I was trying to do with very minimal means was to simplify, reduce and to have work that could be done with no money. I saw information as a way of linking together criticism, philosophical issues, the films of Godard, and this installation art that was being done inside galleries. So it was a reduction of a kind of work that was tending toward reduction to begin with. People were attentive to information systems. It was vaguely in the air. Cybernetics was vaguely in the air.

Metz

The early work *Schema (March 1966)* identifies the number of nouns, adverbs, adjectives, the area occupied by the text, the typeface, and so on, in the magazine itself. The work is a media-generated text. *Schema* seems to be the first of many works that were meditations in that fashion.

Graham

Well, in the first pieces, each form usually illustrated a particular approach to media. In a material fashion, for instance, it was the name of the typeface, the type of the paper, the depression of the typeface into the surface of the page. *Schema* was also a very early computer piece, because a computer can generate many different possibilities for a hypothetical future that either existed or didn't exist. And there was a fictional element because even though the information was self-referring, it had to be interpreted. The idea was to build in as many different meanings as possible in a very simplified, available situation. While Lichtenstein and Flavin were big influences, I wanted to make a further reduction and make non-gallery art.

Metz

Sort of an influence in the reverse; you were heading in exactly the opposite direction.

Graham

Yes. As much as I admired the work, I saw contradictions in it. In the case of Pop art, instead of taking things out of the media, I decided to put them back into the media. Instead of having a show that had a photograph and a critical piece of writing about the show to validate its meaning, the idea was to stage the entire thing directly in a magazine. In a way, it was absolute and problematic because the work would never take on value. But they weren't Conceptual. They weren't for a hypothetical art "in the mind," they were about the "physicality" of printed matter—which would be equivalent to the physicality that you had in reproductions. In other words, the reproduction has its own kind of physicality as well as non-physicality. And then you have the idea of a reproduction of a reproduction. And then you have the fact that this physicality would only have a short life. It would fade away as the magazines were discarded, and go back into time and place. But they were geared to that present-time publication situation.

Metz

Homes for America moves into suburbia, with the diagramming and schematizing of specific social circumstances. At the same time the perspective shifts from yourself to that of the suburban spectator.

Graham

Homes for America was done intuitively, but I was also interested in the relationship between serial music and Minimal art. At the time, *Esquire* magazine was publishing sociological exposes like David Riesman's *The Lonely Crowd.* They used photographers in the school of Walker Evans, photographers who were showing vernacular workers' housing, suburban housing, but usually from a humanistic negative viewpoint. I wanted to keep all of those meanings but empty out the pejorative expressionistic meanings. On the other hand, I didn't want to go as far as Minimal. I wanted to show that Minimal was related to a real social situation that could be documented.

Metz

You referred to the Minimal pieces of the time. Those pieces were, if nothing else, hermetic. They were complete, in and of themselves. Whereas in *Homes for America*, or the article that appeared almost six months later called "Information," I took to be a code or description for how to look at *Homes for America*. This was the reverse of the Minimal tendencies at the time. Even though there are certain visual similarities in the structure.

Graham

If you put Pop art together with Minimal art together with Godard together with sociology together with serial music, you might come up with something like that. [Laughter] I was not working out of an art history, or even a philosophical tradition. I was working with what everyone had in front of them.

Metz

The *Income Outflow* piece—where was that placed? Did you ever actually run that anywhere, and did anyone ever buy any stock?[1]

Graham

My initial interest was the fact that to raise money and begin the process, you had to start with an advertisement. After a while, I realized that the main focus of my work was the artist buying an advertisement in a magazine. In other words, *Homes for America* was both an art essay by a critic and a work of art, in the sense that a Godard film was both an essay, a narrative, and a quasi-documentary. Sociological. That was a very late piece, it was 1969. After 1969 I did not do anything else for magazines.

Metz

Was your first use of architectonic elements *Body Press*, the two people inside a mirrored cylinder?

Graham

I thought it would be more interesting to make the piece optical and interior, and also to be about the skin of the performers. So I constructed a large mural-size cylinder, which was like a huge anamorphic lens surrounding two performers. The performers were a man and a woman, naked. And the cameras, instead of mapping out the surface of the area they walked outside, were actually mapping the surface of their bodies.

So the cameras were pressed against their bodies. You would be able to see the camera and the spectator by the reflection on the surrounding cylinder mirror. The camera's angle changed as it pressed against different parts of the body. You might see a lower part of the body on the anamorphic mirror, thus the camera would be filming itself and that part of the body that was next to it. Or it might be oriented somewhat upward, so you'd be seeing, reflected on the mirror, the eyes, the head of the camera person. The cameras were rotated, and, since they were more or less synchronous, when they were rotated each camera would be filming the other camera and the other spectator. Then they were handed between the two performers and the exchange continued onto the body of the person they were handed to.

Metz

It seems that here the two cameras in relation to the anamorphic mirrored cylinder, as lens, deflect meaning. The cylinder itself seems to be attacking the information. People see what's going on, yet the film doesn't seem to add up.

Graham

Here you see both the camera and the objects. Also, you have the fact that each of the performers is handling the cameras. So you become part of the camera, you identify with the camera that you can physically see. You also identify with the performers and their bodies. You can feel the body through the way in which the camera is pressed against it. You have a multiplicity of different viewpoints. Plus, you have two people and two different cameras at the same time. And I think the complexity comes with the two people.

Metz

Not to mention the fact that they're a man and a woman.

Graham

It sets up a relationship, whether you're identifying voyeuristically with yourself or with a sexualized, heterosexual image outside yourself. Or maybe putting the two on the same narcissistic optical level that Lacan's mirror stage begins with.

Metz

But there is that unequal footing of the nude female body and the nude male body and the difference between those gazes.

Graham

We have very conventionalized, cliched ideas of both.

Metz

Yes, exactly. And also the inability to truly read either due to the nature of the cylinder itself.

Graham

Well, I think the distortion varies. If you move very close to the image, extremely close, there's very little distortion.

Metz

Another type of distortion you have used is time distortions as recorded on video tape.

Graham

You can get delays from between five seconds and nine seconds so that the image you're seeing on the monitor from the playback machine is slightly delayed from the present time image. In other pieces, I used a delay of 24 hours. In *Yesterday/Today,* one space had a live camera with the monitor in a nearby space, where you heard a 24-hour continuous audio tape of what had happened in the space with the live camera that you're seeing on the monitor, 24 hours ago. All of this was a property of the very simple video technology available at that moment. All of it was in juxtaposition to the older film situation which showed past time, edited.

Metz

The objects of the technology seem to be a governing element. I'm thinking of the first pavilion pieces, where in effect you ended up with a formal architectural structure. What predicated this move?

Graham

It had a lot of stages. There were video projects which took place within showcase windows that were between two glass office buildings and displayed picture windows of houses. So you have all the possibilities using real urban and suburban architecture, consumer-oriented showcase window architecture, office buildings—all of the elements that actually I later used with pavilions because the pavilions are mediating between traditional park/garden historical references to references of the city and urbanism. The change, if anything, was a change from making pieces that were camera obscuras—which placed you almost inside the camera and were referring to the optical system per se—to showing the spectator, in terms of the perceptual process, as an audience, as a spectator, rather than as a work of art. The principles were the same, but these were the spectator in relation to materials commonly used in the city that had psychological and physiological properties.

Metz

Two-Way Mirror Cylinder Inside Cube and a Video Salon is your most visible piece here in New York. What did you see as the relationship between the two parts, the video salon and the two-way mirror?

Graham

Heiner Friedrich's original idea was to take one of the spaces downstairs and have a self-enclosed, discrete space, not framed by the city and outside distractions, and definitely a non-museum type of space. Something like a church. A meditational space for the ideal work of art. My idea, obviously, was the opposite. I needed a public social space, a space that would be quasi-functional. So one aspect of the piece is both a coffee bar and a video salon. Six curators were hired to buy a library archive of videos in the areas of cartoon animation, music, architecture, performance, and artist performance, which would be permanently installed as a library. The piece and the space around it were designed to be a kind of bar or lounge area, a space for openings and social gatherings, and a space for performances.

Metz

So you really mean for the piece to be used.

Graham

Well, it's part of the section of museums which are the most interesting architecturally: the bookshop, the coffee bar, social lounge area, romantic rendezvous area. It's all to be a part of that.

Metz

A great Friday night pick-up spot. I had heard that people were sleeping in *Two Adjacent Pavilions* during "Documenta."

Graham

My students would sleep inside the pavilions with their sleeping bags. I designed this pavilion to fit about five to ten people inside. So the dimensions are always human. In a park situation, people are often lying down, as well as standing up and looking around. There's always a reflection in my work between the work as an object in itself and the idea of people seeing themselves as perceiving and being perceived.

Metz

These pieces have the spectator at the center.

Graham

They're designed around the perception of the spectator and the idea of the public in relation to the private person. The relationship of the spectator to a private artwork in a museum or gallery as somehow the subject of the art, which was the case in Minimal and Conceptual art.

Metz

So it's moving the subject to the spectator and away from the object?

Graham

Well, my work became more involved with large public spaces, it shifted from one spectator to many spectators and not one public, but often two aspects of the same public.

Metz

Two-Way Mirror Cylinder Inside Cube and a Video Salon uses mirrored surface as a device to move the spectator away from the object. How long have you used this surface as a means of perception?

Graham

We were speaking about the *Body Press,* which was the last of the double projections. That was related specifically to the body. But there's also always a relationship in the double film pieces, between the outdoor surface of the body and the outdoor surface of the surrounding 360-degree environment: the two are mirroring each other. And the construction of the pieces has always involved a doubling or a mirror relationship. What was a structuralist procedure became first a physical device, and then performance. At that point, it seemed I could use video, including the video delay, in relationship to window glass and mirrors because video was a continuation of the Renaissance perspective that was built into the mirror and the window, but extended it in many ways.

Metz

With the window comes the notion of the "view in" and "view out." One individual at a time, one family at a time; it seemed to be separating the family unit, or separating the individual home.

Graham

You're referring to one piece, *Alteration of a Suburban House,* where I'm extending the picture window, I'm making it larger. So the view you get works less as a voyeuristic piece and more as a piece where people on the outside see themselves in a so-called public space outside the so-called private space. It's revealing the outside environment around the inside. What happens inside isn't that important because it's only the livingroom. It's often covered up, so it's really a trap for people on the outside to reveal their own situation.

Metz

What kind of a house did you grow up in?

Graham

Until age thirteen, a public, government housing project in a rural area on the edge of a New Jersey suburb—basically, army barracks. Most of the people were upper-lower class, but we were surrounded by the growth of middle-class and upper-middle class suburbs. When I was thirteen, my family moved only a few miles away to a very upper-middle-class suburb.

Metz

Do you always envision a picture window in a suburban house?

Graham

A picture window, that was definitely the name of the game. Two styles were rampant. We had a Cape Cod, but the other style was a ranch house.

I guess picture windows were important in Holland and American suburbs after the war. So I was simply extending that convention. It's also, in terms of architecture, related to Philip Johnson's glass house, which derived from the Farnsworth house. On the other hand, the composition of many of the Venturi houses derived from the composition of the adjacent house or the one across the street. So, the facade of the house has been destroyed, but what you see in the mirror are people outside, people on the inside, and the houses across the street. I'm doing the same thing, I'm imploding it all onto one surface. The surface of the mirror behind and also the semi-surface of the glass window in front.

Metz

In a curious way, the two-way mirror is quite aggressive. What led to this?

Graham

They come out of work that came before. The first time I used two-way mirror glass was in a very simple video installation, and it attracted itself to me because this material had been used in psychological laboratories and was also used for surveillance. It was replacing, in many of the urban contexts, let's say Toronto or Los Angeles, the sheer glass of the International Style office building. The illusion of openness that the International Style glass office building wanted to maintain was falling apart. The inner core of the city was becoming more dangerous, people were moving out of the city. The two-way mirror glass gave a certain amount of security, in that people couldn't look in during the day, but people could look out. And the opposite at night. Plus, it was ecologically efficient, and it was definitely the new cliche of mediated social space on the inside of the city. For "Documenta 7," I came up with the idea of doing an outdoor piece, but I wanted it to relate to the city, the suburbs, as well as the traditional park situation. It was to be used the way garden architecture and garden pavilions function in a normal large park. So I was picking up all those things at the same time.

Metz

How do you see the difference in function between the pavilions and the pergolas? The pergolas seem to be much more relative to a planned garden environment.

Graham

You haven't seen pavilions in the United States. In fact, they were just as garden oriented. The one from Münster had a wooden roof, and a wood pole . . . it was in relation to an octagon, an 18th-century palace. The layout for the grounds around the palace were octagonal. I was trying to coalesce different time periods.

Metz

This pavilion was made with mirrored glass.

Graham

Mirrored glass made it into a photo opportunity. And the idea of an amusement park, a fun-house situation creating kaleidoscopic space. And also a kind of fun division between parents and kids on the inside, and photographing parents and kids on the outside. It was very similar to these half-open music pavilions of the late 19th century, where there would be a bandshell on the inside of a large estate gazebo.

Metz

Psychologically more playful, less aggressive.

Graham

But the shows are normally in the summer, and based on tourism, which means families traveling in their automobiles to specific locations where people go to see modern art in a country setting. And also they need to relax. And if they remain—let's say in Münster, most of the city is a large university city—so, these temporary buildings have to be used as young people would use them.

Metz

Speaking of young people, you've done two children's pavilions.

Graham

Well, let's see, the first was circumstantial and was part of this very large exhibition in Ghent called "Chambres d'Amis" which had as its theme artists using interior private spaces of people who lived in Ghent. People responded to advertisements to allow their spaces to be used. This included doctors, lawyers, architects, social workers, teachers. . . . People who were interested in the educational aspects of being temporary curators and guides; and also what would happen if their home and their private life became the subject of the artwork. I chose an architect because I liked the idea of doing work that was quasi-architecture for an architect. What turned out to be important was that I couldn't do a work in the large-scale size that I had normally worked in, because it would have dwarfed his own architecture. Secondly, the area we chose in the back was a very rough area used by his kids as a playground. There was also a playground across the street used by neighborhood children. I wanted to keep that relationship to the playground across the street and build that into the piece. So what was originally going to be a small botanical garden finally became something more of a dollhouse, a children's-size pavilion.

Metz

Was street traffic allowed through the property?

Graham

Well, sure, that was the idea. In other words, the property itself became part of the museum show or, let's say, it was related to these shows in public spaces inside the city. When I showed this video tape to Jeff Wall, he had the idea of designing a large-scale playground piece where he would do images of children very similar to the images of children he saw in the videotape. This became the *Children's Pavilion,* and it was a completely different proposal which came about, not because Jeff saw the original piece, but because he saw the television replication of the work. And, of course, psychologically, his identification with his children, his childhood. So I was operating from his interests and my own. At that time I was interested in underground architecture. For instance, one of the most salient playthings used by kids are these earth-mound mountains, that often have a hole in the top for kids to dive down into. The game has become a king of the mountain type thing except that they dive into space. So my children's pavilion was based around those conventions, and the conventions of the worship of children. The pantheon has an atrium hole in the top for the worship of the different gods whose images would be along the inside wall and illuminated by the sun overhead.

Metz

Virtually all your work deals with spectators becoming aware of their own consciousness, a mediated view of themselves. That particular children's pavilion is very much a media representation of how children are seen. It's the establishment of stereotypes of children.

Graham

In *Alteration of a Suburban House,* you're also dealing with the stereotyped idea of the suburban house after World War II as shown in magazines, the cliched prototype of a desirable, model house. The stereotype of a child probably comes from films; I think Jeff derived it from Spielberg films. We are both interested in Baroque paintings, the angels that appear on the ceilings in Baroque paintings. At the time I was doing *Rock My Religion,* where a teenager appears as an androgynous angel figure. The idea of children as angels comes from that sentimental idea of children that Jeff and I probably had concurrently. I also like the idea that on the outside, when you look down through the oculus you're looking through a concave mirror image of yourself vastly enlarged, against the sky, the real sky on the outside opposed to the idealized sky in the photograph. As the sky changes, your image of yourself is changing. With a two-way mirror you're seeing the idealized children below but you're also seeing real children with their parents looking up through the oculus.

Metz

In your reading, what kind of affinities do you have to any philosophical or religious outlook?

Graham

At the time of the *Children's Pavilion* it was a break with the anti-humanist liberalism of the Minimal period and a return to, if you want, the United Nations of Humanism. It was the beginning of the ecology period and I was looking for an underground, earth-oriented architecture.

Metz

I wanted to talk about those pieces that involve both indoors and outdoors. I'm thinking about *Altered Two-Way Revolving Door and Chamber with Sliding Door.*

Graham

Again, these are all projects that were given to me. I designed that for an inaugurating exhibition to celebrate the World Financial Center. It was on the outside of a large lobby of the office building. There was an L-shaped corner in the building which was itself made out of two-way mirror glass. I filled it in to make a triangle, which was a natural extension to the architecture which allowed for a viewing area for the people on the inside.

Metz

The general passerby coming across the door would have thought it was a doorway.

Graham

Well, I don't think after the opening of the exhibition people went there for the work. The work blended into other semi-functional, semi-landscape, semi-artistic things that were part of the exhibit.

Metz

The fact that it wasn't functional but looked like a doorway into the space . . .

Graham

But it did have a door that you could close and most people closed it. By closing the door you are creating a shelter for yourself. And you're implicated in all the relationships. I think as soon as you close it off, you're creating an architectural situation for yourself.

Metz

It's curious. I was over there a couple of times after it was set up. Anyone who went in closed the door and, after a few moments, would come out looking sheepish.

Graham

It was small enough that generally it was for one person, not a large group of people. And because it wasn't labeled as art you didn't have to look at it aesthetically.

Metz

More adventuresome but not intimidating.

Graham

You have to make a commitment in terms of taking time out. Most of the public/private pieces are to be walked past and not thought about. You're not really stopped in your tracks. They're really designed for semi-distracted observation.

Metz

You seem to be a move away from urban/corporate type works, with the use of the pergola, with its various plants, in a garden setting.

Graham

They're public/private spaces for people to stroll through. The large, two-way mirror hedge labyrinth piece has been built for a private collector as an extension of his garden and his hedge system. Another version of it was constructed for a gallery in London, in the center of Hyde Park. People stroll through it. You can see it if you're driving through Hyde Park. It functions as garden space, as Renaissance/Baroque theme park.[2]

Metz

Do you specify what plants are meant to go in those works? In other words, how much of a botanist are you?

Graham

Well, it depends on the actual situation. For example, when I was doing something in La Jolla, I was trying to match the plants they actually use as hedges. In fact, in La Jolla, I had to switch because there was a plant plague.

Metz

In La Jolla a lot of people have hedges made out of jasmine, which is fragrant and is associated with erotic gardens. Would you make a choice like that?

Graham

I was looking for something that was opaque when you looked at it from a distance but when you got close, had a lot of space between the flowers and the leaves. I wanted it to become more transparent as you got closer. Very similar to the mirror glass. There was a vacillation between it being opaque, translucent, and transparent.

Metz

As with your other work, you are looking for a certain degree of anonymity.

Graham

I was looking for a contextual match. In other words, it's related by context to a surrounding architecture or a plant. But it's a hybrid between it and something else. It's also emblematic of something that isn't there but allegorically is suggested.

Metz

You said a number of years ago that you really wanted your work to leave out both the artist and the notion of artistic vision.

Graham

Well, I don't know if there's been the elimination of the aesthetic vision. These pieces are inherently aesthetic. It's just that the aesthetic ideas are contained inside people's perception of the piece, not the environment and the architecture.

Notes

1. The work *Income Outflow* was proposed by Graham in 1969. It consisted of an advertisement for a public corporation that would allow buyers to partake of Graham's income as a dividend. The work was never realized.

2. Graham's *Two-Way Mirror Hedge Labyrinth* was initially made for the private collector Bob Orton, Jr., in La Jolla, California, 1989. A similar version was temporarily exhibited outside of the Serpentine Gallery in Hyde Park, London, in 1992.

This interview was conducted in 1994, and was first published in Bomb, *no. 46 (Winter 1994), pp. 24–29.*